'Like the rest of us fans, Billy can't quite believe what's possible when people plug in some cheap electronic equipment into a power socket and sing their story. His story is compelling because of his closeness with fans, not artists. I'm one of his biggest fans!'

— BONO, U2

'Good luck with *One Love, One Life*. I've known you for ages mate and you've always done me proud. I owe ya.'

— ROD STEWART

'His place is well and truly cemented in Scottish music history alongside Annie, Alex and Zal, Lonnie, Jim and Charlie, Gerry, Gallagher and Lyle and the plethora of artistes who have spread their talents globally over the years. Hold on tight . . . you're in for a fun ride!'

— MIDGE URE

'Billy has somehow kept his head in the clouds and his feet on the ground. *One Love, One Life* is a reminder of how music can make you feel, from a man who has seen it all up close.'

— PAUL BUCHANAN, THE BLUE NILE

'Everyone seems to be a legend these days, but Billy Sloan is the real thing. Haunting every sticky floored music venue in Glasgow since the 1970s.

He can lay claim to being there at the birth of every movement in Scottish rock music in the past five decades . . . and supporting them all unreservedly. But what comes across above all in this book, through all the ups and downs of his life as a rock journalist and DJ, is Billy's inspiring and heartfelt love of music.'

— PETER CAPALDI

'We've been chewing the cud with each other for over 40 years. Billy has the respect and the ear of many great artistes. He writes from the heart – like a real fan – and broadcasts with a true and obvious love of the music and those who make it. He is a rare breed.'

— STEVE HARLEY, COCKNEY REBEL

'From the seventies till now, if there have been any seminal moments in music, Billy was there. If songs are bookmarks in our lives . . . this is the book.'

— FRAN HEALY, TRAVIS

'When you've been in this business a long time there's people that you've never met before and they want to interview you. And you go . . . are they going to ask the same old boring questions? But when somebody says: 'Billy Sloan wants to interview you' . . . I say: 'Oh fine,' because you are trusted. Anyone who's in the music business would be happy to be interviewed by you.'

— LULU

'Billy Sloan is as much a legend in the music world as any rock star you could ever meet. But I'd bet my life that he knows more about the world of music than any of them. This book is long overdue.'

— GARY NUMAN

'Billy Sloan is a central character to Scottish music.

Musicians all over Scotland are all grateful for Billy backing their music . . . and I know Deacon Blue would not still be in people's hearts had it not been for the support he gave the band.'

— RICKY ROSS, DEACON BLUE

'Billy is a great journalist and a real, passionate and incredibly knowledgeable music fan with a vast collection of tales of his encounters over the years.'

— CRAIG AND CHARLIE REID, THE PROCLAIMERS

ONE LOVE, ONE LIFE

ONE LOVE, ONE LIFE

STORIES FROM THE STARS

BILLY SLOAN

Black&White

Black&White

First published in the UK in 2023
This edition first published in 2024 by
Black & White Publishing Ltd
Nautical House, 104 Commercial Street, Edinburgh, EH6 6NF

A division of Bonnier Books UK
4th Floor, Victoria House, Bloomsbury Square, London, WC1B 4DA
Owned by Bonnier Books
Sveavägen 56, Stockholm, Sweden

A CIP catalogue record for this book is available from the British Library.

ISBN: 978 1 78530 630 3

1 3 5 7 9 10 8 6 4 2

Typeset by Data Connection
Printed and bound in Great Britain by Clays Ltd, Elcograf S.p.A.

www.blackandwhitepublishing.com

This book is dedicated to Janice . . . with all my love.

CONTENTS

Foreword

by Jim Kerr of Simple Minds

I SHOULD BEGIN MY warm-up act to this book by first offering the reader full disclosure.

Billy Sloan, author of this tome, is my pal. It's as simple as that. He is a good friend, mate, confidante, chum, comrade, and accomplice. I'm sure you get the picture. But that's not all.

It also has to be said that in moments of peril and real-life family drama, on a number of occasions – typical of Billy – he has dropped everything in order to help out in any which way necessary. Much in the manner one might hope and expect from a genuine blood brother.

And how did this friendship come to be?

Well, rare as it is, it just so happens that you can indeed meet someone for the first time, and within minutes feel you have known them all your life.

The chances of that occurring are, of course, slightly less rare when you are both part of the same generation and share almost exactly the same social backgrounds.

In the case of Billy and I – raised in resoundingly working-class households and therefore cut from the same cloth – we were born in the 1950s. Which was coincidentally the very thing that became the backbone of both our existences . . . I'm talking about glorious rock and roll music itself.

Fate also saw to it that we had our respective umbilical cords cut in the same maternity hospital, situated a mere stone's throw from the gothic arches of Glasgow Cathedral. Perhaps the cut was made with the same set of scissors, for all we know. Albeit that Billy, not ever known to be a slouch, characteristically got out of the traps earlier by making his earthly stage entrance four years before yours truly. Born in a period of post-war optimism then – timing his birth perfectly – particularly given what he would go on to do in life.

Who's to say it was not written in the stars for Sloan?

The very year he was born, princely crooners such as Frank Sinatra, Perry Como, Nat King Cole and Tony Bennett were paving the way in the popular charts for the new kings of music. I, of course, refer to Elvis Presley, Chuck Berry, Little Richard and Buddy Holly. At the same time, an entirely embryonic culture was about to take over the planet as radio and television excitingly emerged.

In any case, fast forward two decades to when Billy and I came face to face on opposite sides of a microphone. And again, just for the sake of it, let's explore the phenomenon that occurs on first meeting when we instantly recognise someone we identify as a kindred spirit.

What exactly is it that makes it possible to pick up on those subtle cues that our conscious mind may not be aware of? From where does the intuition arrive that leads us to trust an emerging gut feeling about someone erstwhile unknown?

Whilst all of that might be decent stuff to mull over, as I am doing, it doesn't mean you should look to me for the answer. Patently, it's all a bit of a mystery. One of many that happen of their own accord, and we all know that life consists of plenty of those.

Forgive me if I say it again then. Some things are written in the stars.

Luckier for me still, it so happens that I have a handful of best pals including Billy. That I love them dearly but have so far never told them is probably as you would expect. Such is the way with Glaswegian males of my generation. Made of rock and rain, or so we were told, we still tend to hold on too much to the 'granite' we would like to believe lies at our emotional core.

However, there is one humongous thing that genuinely makes Billy unique among the coterie of friends I cherish. Fact is, sometimes it's hard to get a bloody word in during any conversation. Not

because he likes the sound of his voice more than anyone else's –
although he is certainly a natural raconteur and quite brilliant
with it. More because of the life he has led and, as a result of the
experiences his work has given – as you are no doubt about to
discover – Billy continually arrives with a never-ending amount of
fascinating and entertaining tales and anecdotes to tell.

Hence this book. One that in my opinion is both overdue and not
to be missed out on by anyone who, just like me, relishes 'ringside
commentary' on all manner of popular culture.

It's delivered in a style both heartfelt and powerfully enthusiastic,
written by someone who to this day cannot quite believe his luck in
regards to the cards that life has dealt.

Jim Kerr
Taormina, Sicily

Preface

I SAT DOWN TO write this book after spending forty-five successful years as a journalist and broadcaster. But I've been a music fan a lot longer. My chosen profession is an extension of my biggest passion. It never seemed like work.

Over those years, I got lucky. I've interviewed some of the biggest names in rock history and for the most part it's been an absolute pleasure. I've met three Beatles, five Stones, four Beach Boys, a Kink, Ol' Blue Eyes plus a Led Zep here and a Jon Bon there.

Not to mention a string of pop icons – Bowie, Bruce, Kylie, Bono, Cher, Rod, Cliff, Alice, Elton, Dusty, Tina, Ozzy and Smokey – people so famous they can get by on just one name.

At the age of fifteen I went to my first-ever gig, The Who at Green's Playhouse in Glasgow in 1971. I queued out overnight in freezing conditions to buy my ticket, priced 85p. Seeing Roger Daltrey, Pete Townshend, John Entwistle and Keith Moon on stage was a life-changing moment.

Fast forward ten years from that memorable concert and I'm sitting in a hotel room interviewing Daltrey and Townshend. For someone whose life had been consumed by rock music, it was the things that dreams are made of.

Pardon me for such unashamed name-dropping. But don't tell me you wouldn't go for a little bit of that. I remain a music fan, first and foremost and am proud to be so.

I've had some amazing adventures, and hopefully there are still a few more to come. But I'll admit, there have been times when I've had to pinch myself to make sure the events were real.

One Love, One Life – Stories from the Stars should definitely be listed as non-fiction. Believe it or not . . . every word is true.

Introduction

I WAS THE LEAD singer of Coldplay for a twenty-four-hour period. You will not find this nugget of information in any pop history book. I'm willing to bet Chris Martin still has no idea he'd been temporarily replaced.

Jim Kerr of Simple Minds once invited me to share a mic with him in front of 15,000 fans in a stadium in Rio de Janeiro. I'm sure they thought they were seeing a surprise guest spot by Robert Smith of The Cure ... as we do share a similar dishevelled appearance and body shape. The audience's disappointment was reflected in the rather muted applause when I walked out on stage.

I am also one of the few people to play drums with the legendary Spinal Tap and not die later in a mysterious gardening accident or from spontaneous combustion (at time of writing).

Each occasion was as close as I ever got to living my dream of becoming a bare-chested, swivel-hipped rock god. Roger Daltrey and Robert Plant were not looking over their shoulders.

But my disappointment was counterbalanced when I decided on an alternative route into the music industry. Being only too aware of the limitations of any genuine musical talent, I decided to pick up a pen instead of a plectrum. It was the correct decision. For the last forty-five years, I have made a successful career as a music journalist and broadcaster.

Someone said you should never meet your heroes as they wouldn't live up to your expectations. I don't go along with that. Over those years, I've met most of mine. My strike rate is high with ninety-five per cent of the stars more than living up to their exalted celebrity status.

Try to imagine what it's like to sit in a room with Paul McCartney or Mick Jagger or David Bowie – have their sole attention – and ask them about their career and lifestyle. All three were guys whose pictures I'd pinned up on my bedroom wall.

I've also been lucky to attend some of the greatest gigs in music history including Live Aid, Live 8, The Freddie Mercury Tribute, the Nelson Mandela 70th Birthday concert, The Sex Pistols on Christmas Day in 1977 and the Rock and Roll Hall of Fame 25th anniversary . . . plus the reunion shows by Led Zeppelin and Cream.

Music has taken me around the world. Before I got into journalism I didn't even have a passport. Where was I going? I certainly wasn't lacking ambition . . . but I had no grand plans.

To date, it's been a thrilling, rollercoaster ride through many different musical genres and ever-changing periods of pop culture. But, perhaps inevitably, there remains that 'what if' yearning where you wonder how better life would be centre stage, bathed in a white spotlight. Even for just a brief moment. And, it's okay to dream.

In my teenage years, I'd laid down a £6 deposit on an Eko Ranger acoustic guitar at McCormack's Music Shop in the centre of Glasgow. It seemed the logical progression from pulling shapes with my tennis racket in front of the wardrobe mirror. The store was a mecca for local musicians, with gleaming instruments and drum kits displayed over three floors. Scottish artistes such as Alex Harvey, Billy Connolly, Nazareth, Jack Bruce, Stone the Crows and Gerry Rafferty were among their more high-profile customers. It was time to add my name to that distinguished list. I'd learn to play guitar, strut my stuff and see my name go up in lights. What could be simpler?

My plan was thwarted when the credit firm – hired by McCormack's accounts department – dispatched an inspector to check up on me. It was his job to ensure the name, address and personal information supplied on the hire purchase form, which guaranteed the weekly payments on the balance of the £25 guitar, were one hundred per cent accurate.

When he arrived on the doorstep, he immediately viewed me with suspicion. His customer-relations technique was akin to the interrogation methods employed by the Stasi, the ruthless East German secret police. Surely Jimmy Page had never endured such humiliation? The ordeal left me so incensed that I marched straight into McCormack's the following day and cancelled my order. I took the £6 deposit refund and went around the corner to Jackson the Tailor, where I used it as a down payment on a made-to-measure suit.

In hindsight, he probably did me a favour. I was never going to make it as a pop star. But it didn't stop me from occasionally dipping my toe into the water in later years.

In the mid-nineties, I sat in on a rehearsal by my close friends GUN at Park Lane Studios in Glasgow. The Scots group have enjoyed a successful – and ongoing – career with a run of eight Top 40 hit singles, an MTV award and support slots with The Rolling Stones, Bon Jovi, Iron Maiden and Lynyrd Skynyrd.

In a break between songs, I proffered the jocular suggestion they could attain even greater success if they had a smouldering natural talent like me fronting the band. Lead singer Mark Rankin looked at me quizzically before handing over the mic and saying: 'Why not show us what you can do then?'

The mood changed. I froze. The only times I'd ever sung in public was belting out 'Onward Christian Soldiers' at my Sunday School class or taking part in chants at football matches. But GUN meant business. I'd thrown down the gauntlet and they were calling me out.

'What's your first song?' said guitarist Jools Gizzi. I chose 'Substitute' by The Who.

Seconds later, the band launched into Pete Townshend's classic 1966 composition. My body was rigid with fear. . . hands seemingly welded to the microphone stand.

I heard my voice boom out from their PA system and bounce off the walls. I somehow got to the end of the song without hyperventilating. I think I was in tune – at least. But the stern looks on their faces were no indication if I'd passed the audition or not.

GUN's second guitarist, Stephen 'Baby' Stafford, was a Rolling Stones' obsessive who idolised Keith Richards. I asked if he knew the Stones' version of 'Love In Vain', written by US blues legend Robert Johnson in 1939. Of course he did . . . and he could play it note perfect.

I felt confident enough for the band to tape the track. Taking my obvious musical limitations into account, the end result – enhanced by some reverb and echo on an Akai 8-track recorder – was impressive. It sounded BIG . . . like a delta blues song being performed in an empty, cavernous Wembley Arena.

I had made my first 'record'. It was time to introduce it to a wider public.

The following week, I played this new version of 'Love In Vain' on my late-night, alternative music show on Radio Clyde 261.

Claiming a UK exclusive, I told listeners it was the hot new single by U2, which I'd bought on import as it had only been released as a limited edition in Canada and North America. I said it featured The Edge on lead vocals, explaining that as Bono felt the guitarist's voice was more suited to the song he was happy to step aside for this one-off studio departure.

The reaction from the public was encouraging.

One letter said: 'I have been a U2 fan for years but at times I think the band get stuck in a bit of a musical rut. But this new approach takes the group in a refreshing, different direction. Let's hope The Edge does more of this.'

A well-known Scottish musician sidled up before a gig at King Tut's and told me: 'That Edge guy is some singer. I think his voice is better than Bono's.'

I played the recording again on the show before coming clean on air and confessing it was all a ruse. Let's just say the subsequent comments were more abusive and personal in nature. I later told U2 of my on-air deception. They pissed themselves laughing.

Several years on, a Make-A-Record booth was opened in the unlikely location of the departure lounge at Glasgow Airport. Pop star wannabes were invited to choose a selection from a list of several hundred hit songs. An engineer stood you in a glass-fronted booth and played the backing track of your choice . . . as you sang along. Once completed, he handed you a cassette tape with vocals and music beautifully mixed together. All for the princely sum of £9.99.

There was a catch, however, as the audio was relayed via speakers for the dubious entertainment of passengers on the way to catch their flights. The experience could be very uncomfortable for those of a more questionable musical talent. The sheer humiliation pre-dated the ordeal of a 'Pop Idol' or 'X-Factor' audition in front of Simon Cowell, by more than a decade.

I invited a number of Scots celebrities to record a track as a feature for my column in the *Daily Record*, then the biggest selling newspaper in the country. Among those who agreed to take part were actress Elaine C. Smith, Radio Clyde DJs 'Tiger' Tim Stevens and Paul Coia, model Elaine Wynn and footballer John Colquhoun, who'd played for top clubs such as Celtic, Heart of Midlothian, Sunderland and Millwall FC. I also decided to record a song. But I had some inside information, which had not been shared with my fellow participants.

I contacted Mickie Most, a giant in the UK music industry who – as a producer and founder of RAK Records – helped launch the careers of acts like The Animals, Jeff Beck, Herman's Hermits, Hot Chocolate and Suzi Quatro. In the sixties, he'd also steered Donovan with 'Sunshine Superman' and Lulu with 'To Sir With Love' to No. 1 in the US charts. Maybe Mickie would see me as the next Scot to be successful on his star-studded roster? It was worth a punt.

I sent him a cassette tape of the six songs – carefully omitting the name of each 'contestant' – and asked him to offer his valued professional opinion. Not surprisingly, Elaine C. Smith – who is an accomplished singer – rated a score of 8/10 for a great rendition of 'Killing Me Softly With His Song', the 1973 hit by Roberta Flack. But I was stunned when he chose me as runner-up for what I'd term a highly individual version of 'Let's Dance' by David Bowie. He awarded me a very respectable 6/10 and said: 'There's something in this guy's voice . . . there's definitely some potential there.' I was cock-a-fucking-hoop. This was the big break I'd been waiting for.

I never heard another word from Mickie Most. The silence was deafening. I don't bear a grudge. He probably did me a favour too.

SIDE 1
CAREER OPPORTUNITIES

Chapter 1
Got a Feeling Inside . . .
I Can't Explain

ON THE NIGHT OF 21 October 2021, I retraced my steps down a narrow lane in Glasgow city centre, carefully avoiding the broken glass and potholes. I came to a stop near the end of the block and turned to face a bare brick wall . . . completely lost in my thoughts. In that instant, the late-night din of taxis screeching to a halt to pick up fares and drunken revellers making their way from pubs to clubs was silenced. I'd shut out the cacophonous city noise. As I stared at the wall, my life began to rewind and stopped on exactly the same date some fifty years previously. Now, I was hearing something very different. If my calculations were correct, this was the location of what had once been the stage door of Green's Playhouse.

The modern building, which stands like a giant monolith on the site today, houses an Australian theme bar and multi-screen cinema complex. It is hideous, with none of the character – or history – of the crumbling 3,500-capacity theatre that defied the odds to become one of the greatest pop concert venues in the world before it closed its doors in 1985. As I stood alone in the darkness I began to have a surreal, almost out-of-body experience. At that moment, my fifteen-year-old self was back in seat C32 of the front stalls of Green's . . . overcome with excitement.

The ticket for my first-ever gig had cost 85p, paid for with the wages from a weekend job in the Barras market. Some months previously, I'd had to beg my father to allow me to join my mates, and hundreds of other music fans, to queue outside overnight on

Sauchiehall Street – which was still a busy thoroughfare and open to traffic – to buy tickets for the concert. Green's did not have its own dedicated box office as it operated more as a picture hall showing the latest films.

But when the venue staged gigs, for some bizarre reason, tickets for these events were sold from House of Clydesdale, an electrical store that stocked washing machines, fridges, vacuum cleaners and other household goods. In the back room of the shop, two ladies sat at a trestle table dispensing them – on a first come, first served basis – with a limit of four per person.

The feeling when I got to the front of the queue and bought my ticket to see The Who live on stage on 21 October 1971 was in itself thrilling. I took it home, carefully placed it in an envelope and hid it between two T-shirts in a drawer in my bedroom for safe keeping.

As I counted the days to the gig, I'd check it was still there . . . a bit like a child continually asking how many sleeps they had until Santa Claus came down the chimney at Christmas. That 85p admission fee would prove the single most significant financial investment of my life.

Alone – facing the wall – I was back in Green's. Once again, I could hear the roar of the audience as the lights went down. It was deafening. The Who were about to take the stage. Suddenly, Roger Daltrey, Pete Townshend, John Entwistle and Keith Moon stood before me . . . bathed in white spotlights.

The impact of seeing each musician within easy reach – both physically and emotionally – was overwhelming. Before that moment The Who had simply been pictures, cut out from the pages of *New Musical Express* or *Melody Maker*, to be pinned up on my bedroom wall.

All these years on, I could vividly see Townshend strapping on his Gibson SG guitar and hitting the chords of the opening song, powered by the ultimate rhythm section of Entwistle on bass and Moon behind his sprawling drum kit. Daltrey was once more swinging the microphone lead manically around his head, before catching it expertly, at exactly the right moment, to deliver the opening lines of lyrics.

All around me, more seasoned fans were leaping up and down, headbanging or playing air guitar. Was this the protocol for a rock concert? Was I expected to take part in what was, for me, an alien ritual . . . something I'd obviously never done before? Instead, I stood motionless, totally absorbed in what was happening on that infamous 15ft-high stage which raked down perilously towards the audience.

I think I was in shock . . . initially not able to come to terms with the fact that Roger, Pete, John and Keith were in front of me. The first two songs they played were 'I Can't Explain' and 'Substitute'. It was my dream start and felt like those two great songs had laid down a real marker for my future musical experiences.

The band were showcasing their new album, *Who's Next*, with tracks such as 'Baba O'Riley', 'Bargain', 'My Wife' and 'Behind Blue Eyes'. The seventeen-song set also featured an excerpt from their landmark 1969 rock opera, *Tommy*, with stunning versions of 'Amazing Journey', 'Pinball Wizard' and 'See Me, Feel Me'. Laser beams shot above the heads of the crowd during 'Won't Get Fooled Again' – then, their current single – as Daltrey marched on the spot before delivering the ear-piercing scream that came at the end of the number.

I'd never seen anything like it. At the climax of the show I felt an exhilaration I'd never experienced before. The emotional impact of their performance was profound. It sounds dramatic, but in that moment I thought . . . I want more of this. I NEED to be involved in music. I just didn't know what road I should take.

If you had told me then that ten years later I'd be sitting in a room as a music journalist, interviewing Daltrey or Townshend, I'd have said you were insane.

I'd wanted to commemorate the fiftieth anniversary of that pivotal first-ever gig and had contemplated going to see another band play on that date. But looking down the concert listings, nothing captured my attention or imagination.

So instead, I found myself standing conspicuously in a dark alley in Glasgow staring at a brick wall, my thoughts racing back to a night I can only describe as life changing. If any passers-by spotted me, they must have thought the local lunatic asylum was a man down in the final head count before lights out.

Three weeks after that monumental first gig, I saw The Who perform for a second time when they returned to play a hastily organised extra show at Green's to satisfy the enormous demand from fans.

From then on, I had an insatiable appetite for live music and snapped up tickets for whatever my meagre budget would allow. In the months that followed I saw Free – billed as 'The Free' on tickets priced at a mere 40p – plus a seminal gig by The Faces, just as Rod Stewart was making the transformation from singer to superstar.

Another early highlight was a Sunday afternoon benefit concert to raise funds for striking workers staging a sit-in at Upper Clyde Shipbuilders, which starred Donovan and Gallagher & Lyle, with aspiring local comedian Billy Connolly acting as compere.

More great memories came flooding back.

For the next thirty minutes, I walked slowly around the building, visualising what Green's had looked like. I stopped at the frontage of the new structure – opposite the surviving Pavilion Theatre – that now stands on what was formerly listed as 126 Renfield Street, Glasgow.

In 1971, Green's – which had opened forty-four years previously – was falling apart and in a state of disrepair. Two years on it would be leased by entertainment entrepreneurs Frank Lynch and Max Langdown of Unicorn Leisure, who relaunched the old cinema as a designated concert venue and renamed it the Apollo.

When I later became friends with Frank, he confided he'd only chosen the name 'Apollo' because at a cost of £250 for each individual neon letter it was the shortest, and most economical one he could think of.

Now I wasn't seeing the garish Australian theme pub, Walka-bout. I could visualise entering the double glass doors of Green's for the first time and having my ticket checked by a bouncer in a black suit and bow tie.

While you could walk the full length of the lane in approximately thirty seconds it seemed to take an eternity to actually get to your seat. The venue had an aura of the Tardis, Dr Who's famous time-travelling police box. The interior was cavernous. Stairs led down into the bowels of the building and its vast stalls, with a maroon custom-made carpet that had the owners' famous slogan 'It's good . . . It's Green's' woven into it. Between them was a staircase leading up to the balcony with its golden divan seats so favoured by courting couples on a romantic night out at the cinema. On either side, were twin rows of boxes, regarded as the real posh area with the most expensively priced tickets.

Kiosks sold sweets and soft drinks but there was no alcohol. The adjacent Lauder's Bar, on the opposite corner, was the recognised pre-gig rendezvous for concert-goers.

To the left of the main entrance was West-End Misfits, a tailoring firm that specialised in suit hire for weddings and formal occasions. In later years, to the right was Mr Chips, a fish and chip shop whose menu of deep-fried fare was a crucial post-concert pit stop.

I walked round into Renfrew Street to the location of what had been the entrance to the ballroom above the main theatre. It had played host to dance bands led by greats like Duke Ellington, Joe Loss, Ronnie Scott and Oscar Rabin. It too was rebranded several times, first as Clouds discotheque and then Satellite City and The Penthouse. I'd seen acts such as Elvis Costello, The Rich Kids, Magazine, The Skids and Shakin' Stevens and the Sunsets perform there – and attended the debut gig by Simple Minds in 1978.

Further along the street, the main entrance to Cineworld, also sparked another vivid memory. On that spot in 1972, I'd helped a bunch of ticketless fans force open an emergency exit door to skip in to see Alice Cooper perform one of his earliest gigs on UK soil. The US rocker had so outraged the British establishment that MPs petitioned Home Secretary, Reginald Maudling, to refuse him entry into the country, while morals campaigner Mary Whitehouse, demanded that his shock stage act should be banned. The furore only made me more determined to see him live.

It's now impossible for me to go see a movie at Cineworld without thinking back to when I'd sneaked in without paying. And it wasn't the only time I'd gained free admission to Green's.

I got word the people who ran the venue were recruiting volunteers to work as security staff at future concerts. I enrolled as a member of the balcony team led by a great guy called John Fallon who marshalled his 'troops' with the stern discipline of a military commander. Before each concert he would bark out orders – carefully tailored to suit the requirements of the act performing that night – and woe betide anyone who questioned his authority.

When John assigned you to a location in the vast theatre, he handed out an armband with the word 'Steward' boldly printed on it in white letters.

Bingo . . . this was your Willy Wonka golden ticket to the biggest stars in rock. You didn't get paid for doing the job, but who needs money when this coveted armband was an access-all-areas pass to every gig staged there? It meant you could go anywhere in the venue including – most crucially – backstage.

Over the next few months I was given a real baptism of fire, rubbing shoulders with Elton John, Genesis, Chuck Berry, Status Quo, Hawkwind, Rory Gallagher, Mott The Hoople and Slade. Watching Paul McCartney soundcheck with his new, post-Beatles band Wings was a rare treat. And seeing Eno play his first – and only – headline UK tour as a member of Roxy Music was also very special.

But one magic moment stands out.

On 18 May 1973, John instructed me to take up a position at the stage door to await the arrival of an artist whose popularity was soaring so dramatically he'd agreed to play two shows . . . a matinee and an evening gig. When his limo pulled up in the lane, a phalanx of real bouncers battled with hysterical fans to clear a path inside. The star jumped out of his vehicle, burst through the door and literally landed in my arms. David Bowie looked like an alien from outer space with his flame-red Ziggy Stardust hairstyle.

I escorted him to the dressing room . . . a dark, cramped cellar beneath the stage. But as soon as I stepped inside, it was like going into another world. His array of colourful Ziggy costumes, created by top Japanese fashion designer Kansai Yamamoto, were laid out ready to be fitted.

Bowie quizzed me about the notoriously tough Glasgow audience that awaited him. He seemed genuinely worried how he was going to make his escape after the concerts.

Within weeks, he would shock fans by killing off his most famous pop alter ego telling the audience at Hammersmith Odeon: 'Of all the shows on this tour, this particular show will remain with us the longest. Because not only is it the last show of the tour . . . but it's the last show that we'll ever do.'

Little did I know that ten years later, I'd meet Bowie again when I interviewed him backstage at Murrayfield Stadium in Edinburgh during his record-breaking 'Serious Moonlight' Tour.

My decision to mark the fiftieth anniversary of my first gig in such a personal way proved to be the correct one. All of my subsequent musical adventures were borne from that memorable night. So, my unique – if rather offbeat – solitary journey back to the alley where it had all begun was validated.

On the long walk home, even more memories came flooding back. Another was so surreal it raised a smile. I'd once received a call from a member of the marketing team at Epic Records to arrange an interview with Ozzy Osbourne for my weekly slot on *Scotland Today*, the highly rated daily news programme on Scottish Television.

'He wants to do the chat at Green's Playhouse,' said the promo guy.

I explained that the cinema – which had morphed into the Apollo – had closed its doors in 1985 and the building was demolished two years later.

'Oh, I'm not sure if Ozzy is aware of that,' was his reply.

The following day, he was back on the phone saying the singer was adamant . . . he wanted to do the interview at the location of what had been his all-time favourite concert venue.

The self-styled Prince of Darkness had played Green's for the first time with Black Sabbath on 5 June 1970. In the years that followed, he performed a string of gigs with the band at the venue plus three sell-out solo shows. Both the audience and the building had a profound effect on him.

On the day of the interview, a TV cameraman and I waited on the pavement next to where the Apollo had once proudly stood. It was now a massive gap site strewn with rubble and fenced off to the public for safety. Bang on time a black limousine drew up and out jumped Ozzy with his record plugger and a security man.

Halfway down the lane a section of the wooden fence had come loose, leaving just enough space for us to climb inside and scramble down into the basin of the demolished building. And then, Ozzy was off. He retraced his steps – just as I had done – and came to a halt where he thought the old Apollo stage would have been.

'Right, this is roughly where my vocal mic would be placed . . . we'll do the interview here,' he told me.

For the next twenty minutes, I interviewed the flamboyant singer on the very spot where he'd first looked out into the stalls, golden divans and boxes all those years ago. Any passengers on the upper decks of the buses pulled up in West Nile Street must have thought they were seeing things.

'The Apollo is a very special place for me because after leaving Black Sabbath, on this very spot here – where I'm standing – was the first official Ozzy Osbourne solo tour gig,' he said. 'You can imagine how many shows I've done, but I can remember how I felt before I went on stage . . . saying will they like me, will I go down okay, will they accept me and my music? But the Glasgow crowd were amazing. They just set me off.'

It was important to Ozzy to revisit the exact location that had so many memories. He still felt a real emotional attachment to the place.

He told me: 'The atmosphere in the building was electrifying. If I was standing on the stage, here now, in my mind's eye, I can see that balcony – and it wouldn't just shake – it would bend up and down by a foot each way.

'Many a time I'd think, one day that thing is gonna snap. The crowd, the atmosphere and the whole vibe of this place was so wonderful.

'I will forever – until the day I die – remember the Apollo.'

As we packed up the camera gear, I shared my experience of that concert by The Who a little more than a year after he'd performed there with Sabbath.

'You never forget the first time . . . it's always special,' said Ozzy.

In 2017, The Who returned to Glasgow to play a sell-out show at the SSE Hydro. They again opened a thrilling two-hour-long set with 'I Can't Explain'. I met Pete Townshend backstage and told him about my first-ever gig at Green's and how the experience had changed my life.

'That's good to hear . . . and thanks for staying with us over the years,' he said.

Chapter 2
Blackwood and Moody

I DON'T THINK I could have been more ill-prepared to embark on a career as a music journalist. What were the qualifications for the job? Was there a manual you could consult with a helpful list of instructions? Where did you start?

I didn't have a clue where to begin. So, I thought I'd utilise the tried and tested route of seeking the advice of my careers master at Albert Secondary in Springburn, Glasgow. His professional expertise would surely prove invaluable.

'Forget journalism,' he said, grimly. 'In ten years' time newspapers will be on the way out. Choose something else.'

That was the full extent of his careers guidance. Even if it were true, he should have been encouraging – not discouraging – me. I left his room feeling completely deflated but determined to prove him wrong.

Among my wide circle of friends I didn't know anyone who'd ever attempted to write a song or whose big brother was planning to form a rock band. I had nobody to turn to for advice. There was one thing I was certain about however . . . I had a real passion for the job. I knew I could do it if given the opportunity.

Up to that point, my music education had been fairly mainstream. But fate surely played a hand in my professional destiny. When I was born on 21 December 1955, the omens couldn't have been more favourable. I arrived within weeks of some of the most seismic events at the birth of rock and roll. Bill Haley and His Comets had just topped the charts on both sides of the Atlantic with 'Rock Around The Clock', the theme song of the movie,

Blackboard Jungle. Chuck Berry scored his first major hit with the single, 'Maybellene' on Chess Records in Chicago. And, after protracted negotiations, Colonel Tom Parker finally signed his protégé, Elvis Presley, to a major contract with RCA Victor. The label immediately put their new artist into the studio to record 'Heartbreak Hotel'.

A few months later, Little Richard unleashed 'Tutti Frutti', an aural explosion that changed the face of music in just two minutes and twenty-three seconds. His 'A-wop-bop-a-loo-mop-a-lop-bam-boom' vocal interpretation of the song's drum pattern became a rebellious rallying cry that swept the planet.

Here at home, Lonnie Donegan – a fellow Glaswegian – released a cover of an old American folk song first recorded by the inmates of Arkansas Cummins State Prison in 1934. His version of 'Rock Island Line' reached No.1 and triggered a nationwide skiffle craze that captured the imagination of aspiring performers like John Lennon, Paul McCartney, David Gilmour and Jimmy Page who all began their careers playing that style of music. It seemed I couldn't have come along at a more opportune moment.

My earliest childhood memory also had a strong musical link. I vividly remember the day – in late November 1958 – when my mother, Peggy, and father, Bill, proudly brought my new baby sister Ann home from Rottenrow Hospital. Even as a two-year-old, I realised she was an important addition to our family. It felt special. In the days that followed, relatives and friends helped my mum get back on her feet and adjust to everyday life again.

One night, in the run up to Christmas, she told me to watch a guy on television who she described as 'the greatest entertainer in the world'. What I saw was compelling. His carefully manicured bouffant hairdo gave him a real larger-than-life appearance. He wore a gold lamé suit and played a glittering grand piano that made him positively shimmer . . . even from a tiny black-and-white TV set with a fuzzy picture. A beaming smile – interspersed with nods and knowing winks directly to the camera – gave the illusion he was playing solely for you. Seeing Liberace for the first time was astonishing. His flamboyant persona, complemented by that famous effeminate drawl – leapt out of the screen. It was the first time real music of any kind punctuated my life.

Now, when I see photographs of the superstar who died in 1987 or watch the uncanny portrayal of him by actor Michael Douglas in the award-winning movie, *Behind the Candelabra*, it takes me straight back to that time in my childhood.

My brother Alan arrived three years later to complete our family. In those early days, I barely saw my dad. He'd go off to work as a crane driver at King George V Dock on the River Clyde before we woke up, and not return – after doing much-needed overtime – until well after our bedtime. He also drove the giant cantilever Finnieston Crane, which remains one of the city's most famous landmarks. So I only really got to spend quality time with him at weekends.

Our home – a rundown tenement flat at No. 30 Martyr Street in Townhead – would now be classed as slum housing. We were crammed into two rooms that lacked the most basic amenities, and we shared a toilet on the common stair landing with two other families. It was primitive. What I did have, though, was an abundance of love. I didn't feel forced to navigate a path through any kind of genuine hardship or poverty. Wasn't everyone living in the same way?

My mother was a keen listener to the wireless, as radio was then more commonly known. She did her daily chores tuned in to the BBC *Light Programme* and her favourite shows included *Workers' Playtime*, broadcast at lunchtime from the canteen of a factory somewhere in Britain. She was also a regular listener to *The Billy Cotton Band Show*, *Two Way Family Favourites* and *Woman's Hour*.

The songs that really stick with me from that era were ever-green classics like 'Volare' by Dean Martin, 'Rags to Riches' by Tony Bennett, 'Just In Time' by Judy Garland and 'Green Door' by Frankie Vaughan. They seemed to get played in what we'd now call 'heavy rotation'. But while those songs were great, it was music for grown-ups.

That changed when The Beatles burst on to the scene in 1962. The impact of those four loveable mop-tops can never be underestimated. Their music seemed to impregnate every aspect of day-to-day life. My childhood unfolded to a soundtrack of the songs of Lennon and

McCartney, with The Rolling Stones, Jimi Hendrix, The Monkees, Cilla Black, The Small Faces, The Beach Boys, Dusty Springfield and The Kinks, to name but a few.

I saved up my pocket money to buy a 'Beatle wig' from Woolworths. It proved a vital accessory when me and my mates would play at being The Fab Four. Using a brush pole as a microphone, the metal shovel from the fireside companion set as a guitar and an upturned leather pouffe footstool as a drum, we'd perform our spirited versions of 'She Loves You' or 'I Want To Hold Your Hand'.

In November 1963, when The Beatles appeared at the Royal Command Performance – attended by The Queen Mother and Princess Margaret – I was glued to the telly. The memorable moment John Lennon mischievously told the people in the cheap seats to clap their hands and the rest to just rattle their jewellery was a playful quip. But it was a message nonetheless to the British establishment that things were changing. They then tore through a blistering version of closing number 'Twist And Shout', as if to underline life would never quite be the same again.

When John, Paul, George and Ringo played the Odeon Cinema in Glasgow the following year I begged my dad to take me down to the venue, which was only a short walk from our house. I thought it would be great to catch a glimpse of the group being smuggled into the building amidst all the hysteria of Beatlemania. But he wouldn't hear of it.

'I'm no' going anywhere near all those screaming lassies,' he said, dismissively.

This new music explosion fuelled a rapidly evolving pop culture that was groundbreaking and will surely never be equalled.

Growing up in the era dubbed 'The Swinging Sixties' was fantastic. There was a definite spark of electricity in the air. You could feel something was going on. At that young age, of course, I didn't have a firm grasp of exactly what that 'something' was.

Leading figures such as Twiggy, Cathy McGowan, David Bailey, Vidal Sassoon and Mary Quant were splashed across the pages of the *Daily Record*, the *Evening Citizen* and the *News of the World*, the papers read by my parents. I didn't fully understand their importance, but I realised they were part of this fast-moving scene.

Carnaby Street and Kings Road became the centre of this new revolution with miniskirts, military style tunics and top hats de rigueur. The bank holiday seaside battles between gangs of Mods and Rockers – and even Bobby Moore lifting the World Cup for England at Wembley – brought a much-needed splash of colour into my rather monochrome life.

Every week, my mum bought *Reveille*, a popular tabloid newspaper that carried photo-led feature stories about movie stars, pop singers and TV personalities. Their glamorous world of champagne receptions and glitzy showbiz parties was alluring and strangely seductive. I read it from cover to cover.

On the morning of 24 February 1964, I went with her to our local dairy to help carry the groceries. She met a couple of friends in the queue waiting to be served and they quickly became involved in a loud, animated conversation about some news event happening the following day.

'I hope big Sonny punches that stupid grin right off his face and shuts him up,' shrieked one lady, to the full agreement of everyone in the shop.

I had no idea who they were talking about until twenty-four hours later when Cassius Clay won the World Heavyweight title from the fearsome Sonny Liston, despite being a seven-to-one underdog.

'I shook up the world. I'm so pretty. I won the title and I'm only twenty-two. I shook up the world,' the fighter dubbed 'Cass the Gas' screamed at the ringside media.

I was captivated. Who was this guy?

Within days, every TV impressionist had added the fast-talkin' Clay to their comic routines. Now he was a household name – even more so when he changed it to Muhammad Ali – and would remain that way for the rest of his life.

It would be fifteen years before I got to interview the man known as 'The Greatest', who became one of the most important sporting and political cultural figures in history.

Our tenement flat was perfectly situated. I lived just around the corner from two local cinemas, The Carlton and The Casino. Both provided a periodic escape from the real world. My parents were big film fans. A night out 'at the pictures' was a regular occurrence and I was taken to see movies such as *Goldfinger*, *The Alamo*, *One Million Years B.C.* and *Our Man Flint*.

The first music film I remember was *Your Cheatin' Heart*, the biopic of Hank Williams, with George Hamilton in the leading role. It sparked off a lifelong love of the songs of the troubled US country and western pioneer.

Help! was my earliest opportunity to see The Beatles on a big screen in full colour . . . after their black-and-white adventures in *A Hard Day's Night* the previous year. With such a diversity of music, movies, television, news and sport it felt like I was viewing the sixties through a kaleidoscope. It was thrilling.

In late 1965, our lives changed when my mum and dad chalked up enough points with Glasgow Corporation Housing Department to qualify for a move. They were offered a brand-new maisonette in Springburn, a working-class area renowned worldwide for its railway manufacturing sites centred on the Caledonian St Rollox Works . . . nicknamed 'The Caley'.

Maisonette! What was a maisonette? I'd never even heard the word before. We were going up in the world. In our new home, my parents and my sister, brother and I each had a bedroom with fitted wardrobes. The living room and separate dining kitchen were huge by comparison with our previous house, the latter coming complete with a fridge, washing machine and hot-water boiler. For the first time we had a bathroom; a toilet and bath with a shower fitting. The whole place was kept warm as toast by a central heating storage system. And, just when you thought things couldn't get any better . . . we had a veranda. On the few days of the year when the weather was actually warm enough, you could sit out in the fresh air with a cup of tea and read the paper.

Directly across the street was Springburn Park where I could go to play football on grass – instead of in a filthy back-court strewn with broken bottles – or enjoy a round of putting on the eighteen-hole green. It was like moving to Beverly Hills. Suddenly, we were living like Littlewoods Pools winners.

After eighteen months, I prepared to go to high school. This was crucial to my musical development. I was enrolled in Albert Secondary . . . or 'Big Albert' as it was widely known being the next step up from the local primary of the same name. Throughout my school years, I had scored good grades with sufficient high marks to be placed first or second in class. So there was a real prestige attached to qualifying for a place in such a respected senior secondary.

And overnight, the landscape changed.

As part of the new decor for our maisonette, my mum spent arguably the best £46 of her life when she ordered a radiogram from top city department store, Arnott & Simpson. When it got delivered, I stood in awe at the sheer beauty of this polished wooden sideboard that combined a record player and a radio. If you lifted the lid on the left-hand side there was a black turntable that played discs at 33, 45 or 78 rpm. On the right was a cabinet in which to store your singles and albums. Only problem was I didn't own any.

My mates in class talked about music all the time and swapped records. It was like they were speaking in a foreign tongue. I felt excluded. I had no immediate reference point when they discussed the merits of *The Yes Album*, *Split* by The Groundhogs and *Five Bridges*, the debut LP by The Nice that included keyboard player Keith Emerson's radical nine-minute-long reimagining of 'Intermezzo: Karelia Suite' by Finnish classical composer, Jean Sibelius. They'd play that track over and over again.

All that changed in the summer of 1971 when I went with the 200th Boys' Brigade Company to our annual camp located that year in Rhyl, Wales. It was my first real holiday away from my parents. The Who had just released their fifth studio album, *Who's Next*, led by the single 'Won't Get Fooled Again', which was a Top 10 chart hit. I knew the group only from their previous singles such as 'My Generation', 'I Can See For Miles' and 'The Seeker'. During the trip, I spent a large chunk of my camp money buying my first-ever records . . . 'Won't Get Fooled Again' and the album, *Live* At *Leeds*, which had been recommended by a mate, from Woolworths in the seaside town. The rest of the holiday was spent waiting patiently for the moment when I could get home to play them.

I'd also become friends with two guys who would accelerate and influence my musical education. Bill Blackwood and Lex Moody were one year older and in the form above me at school. They were a formidable pairing and almost looked like rock stars themselves. Blackwood – with his red hair styled in a loose feather cut – wore skintight blue jeans which left nothing to the imagination. Moody had long, straight hair that flowed down into the small of his back and he always dressed to impress.

But it wasn't what they were wearing, more what they were carrying. They were the very first guys I saw who'd walk up to school with an LP under their arm. The album selected was a statement of their identity. It said exactly who they were.

One day, it could be *Get Yer Ya-Ya's Out!* by The Rolling Stones and *Every Picture Tells A Story* by Rod Stewart. The next *Déjà Vu* by Crosby, Stills, Nash & Young, and *Fire And Water* by Free. I don't remember ever seeing them showcasing an LP that I didn't later regard as an all-time classic.

And their choice of bands was also a definite statement with which to impress girls. The walk to and from school became an essential part of my day. I'd pump each of them for information about new bands or records.

Blackwood and Moody were also the first guys I knew who'd actually gone to a live gig. They'd seen a string of acts in venues like Green's Playhouse and the Kelvin Hall. That September, the pair caused a sensation when they bunked off school to hitch-hike down to London to see The Who play at The Oval cricket ground. No tickets. No pre-booked accommodation. No local contacts. Nothing. It took them almost forty-eight hours to reach the capital. Their parents were apoplectic. But, somehow, they managed to blag their way into what became one of UK rock's earliest all-star charity concerts in aid of famine victims in Bangladesh.

The music paper, *Melody Maker*, carried a front-page report on the show – which also starred Rod Stewart and The Faces, Mott the Hoople, Lindisfarne and Quintessence. That simply validated the endeavour of their actions and, on their return, the pair were treated like all-conquering heroes, and almost carried shoulder high in the playground.

We became good mates and had a similar taste in music, frequently swapping albums or attending the same gigs. In hindsight, I'd probably still have got there without the valuable assistance of Blackwood and Moody. It would just have taken a little longer. But they were so generous with their knowledge and opinions it was a speedy apprenticeship. Thanks to them, I was fast-tracked into an exciting new world. The influence they had was immeasurable. They recognised I was every bit as passionate about music as they were. I owe them big time.

In later years when I'd meet Bill our lengthy conversation would inevitably focus on music. What records have you been listening to? Got any good gigs coming up? He was still recommending new bands to check out. Sadly, he passed away several years ago.

Lex is still around but I've not seen him in a long time. Not for any particular reason . . . our paths just haven't crossed. I know he's out there. It would be good to catch up. I can guarantee he'll still have an album collection I'll want to devour.

Chapter 3
Record Store Day

THE DELIVERY VAN WAS running late, but that simply increased the expectation levels for what was to come. When the driver eventually pulled up outside Listen Records in Cambridge Street in Glasgow, I followed him inside as he dumped a large box on the counter.

The boss of the shop wasted no time in slicing open the sealing tape and pulled out the first copy of *Aladdin Sane* by David Bowie. He held the album up in the air displaying it to customers with the pride of a midwife showing off a newborn baby. I stood open-mouthed. And I wasn't alone.

The shot of Bowie – flame hair, eyes closed and with a red and blue lightning bolt dissecting his face – was stunning. The impact of the 1973 album sleeve, conceived by photographer Brian Duffy, was monumental. It became his most enduring visual image and confirmed suspicions that maybe Bowie WAS other-worldly and not of this planet after all.

I bought a copy immediately.

When I got home – bursting with excitement – I placed the needle on the opening song, 'Watch That Man', and what I heard over the next forty-one minutes pinned me to the chair. While I'd fully expected the record that followed *The Rise And Fall Of Ziggy Stardust And The Spiders From Mars* to be a bold, forward step . . . this was a revelation. From Mike Garson's improvised jazz piano solo on the title track to the controversial line in 'Time', where 'he flexes like a whore/falls wanking to the floor' it was clear Bowie had upped the ante musically and lyrically. I made a mental note not to play that one when my parents were in the vicinity. 'Drive-In Saturday' and 'The Jean Genie' were challenging and ambitious and eclipsed most other singles in the UK chart during that fertile 'glam rock' period. The epic, closing ballad 'Lady Grinning Soul', was a thing of genuine beauty. As I played the album over and over, I clutched the sleeve to my breast in a firm embrace . . . almost like I was tenderly caressing a lover. It helped bring me closer to the art. Didn't everyone do that?

I've always enjoyed music as a tactile experience. It's got to be more than just listening to a song. Discovering a new album is all-consuming. A great record should be something you are able to feel and taste or be thrilled by and become emotionally involved in. And for me that is best enjoyed with a vinyl disc, packaged in a stylish sleeve with a lyric sheet and full list of songwriting credits and studio personnel. It's something I've experienced on countless occasions and the excitement has never diminished.

I bought the first five Roxy Music albums without hearing a single note of music. They looked so fucking cool. I HAD to have them. The shot of Bryan Ferry – dressed as a chauffeur – observing his then girlfriend, Amanda Lear, walk a black panther on a leash on the sleeve of *For Your Pleasure* is now described as being just as famous as the songs on the album itself.

The same can be said of the image of *Playboy* model Marilyn Cole – a former Playmate of the Year – lying provocatively in the jungle for the cover of *Stranded*. Or Jerry Hall – to whom Ferry was also romantically linked – crawling across the rocks on a beach in Anglesey on the front of *Siren*. Both were styled by leading fashion designer, Antony Price, and perfectly captured Roxy's unique brand of pop retro-futurism.

Some of the cornerstones of my early collection – such as *Kimono My House* by Sparks, *Next* by The Sensational Alex Harvey Band and *The Psychomodo* by Cockney Rebel – were all bought solely for their aesthetic value alone. How ironic then that my first album was the total antithesis to that.

The Who's *Live At Leeds* is packaged in a plain cardboard sleeve stapled together, with the title crudely stamped on the front. It looked more like a bootleg. But to open that sleeve was to enter a world previously unseen. A collection of inserts – including handwritten Pete Townshend lyrics, a rejection letter from EMI Records and a cancellation notice for the Locarno in Swindon on the grounds that 'The Who are not the type of group that would go down well in the ballroom' – gave an insight into the turmoil and excitement being created simultaneously by their music. The contract to appear at Woodstock for a fee of $12,500 plus the famous poster for their Tuesday night Maximum R&B residency at the Marquee in London somehow brought you closer to the six songs on the record.

Back then, music was our social media and those extraordinary designs – laid out on that definitive 12-inch square canvas – connected us in a way that short-circuited the conventions of the time. My daily walks to school with Bill Blackwood and Lex Moody had proven to be invaluable. But with eyes now wide open – in music terms – I soon discovered pockets of like-minded people also struggling to find their identity. I lost count of the number of times I'd look up and see another previously unremarkable kid cross the playground. There would be a splash of colour against his black school blazer and I'd suddenly recognise *Ogdens' Nut Gone Flake* by The Small Faces tucked under his arm. I knew I'd found a fellow traveller.

Or you'd sit four desks away from somebody in the maths class for a year without a word passing between you. And then, one day, the same kid would walk down the corridor carrying *There's A Riot Goin' On* by Sly And The Family Stone. Instantly, they were transformed into somebody you now desperately needed to know.

I frequented local record shops like Listen, Bruce's, 23rd Precinct, Hades, Gloria's and Graffiti. In Virgin in Argyle Street – one of the first branches to be opened by Richard Branson outside London – you could sit on giant cushions on the floor and listen to albums. The shop discreetly sold bootlegs by the likes of Bob Dylan, The Beatles or Neil Young. It felt so daring, like real forbidden fruit.

I'd also go on day trips to Edinburgh, trawling around Bruce's, Avalanche, Hot Licks and Ezy Ryder. Each record shop had an almost mystical quality. I was enthralled by their window displays that would change weekly to accommodate new releases.

When you stepped over the threshold of Listen you were hit by a unique aroma, similar to the distinctive smell in an old second-hand book or comic store. The racks of vinyl records were carefully laid out with an almost feng shui precision, an accidental variation on the ancient Chinese tradition of arranging items to harness energy forces and create balance with the natural world.

Even if I didn't buy anything I'd spend hours flicking through albums stacked in alphabetical order or by musical genre to a soundtrack of new and classic tracks being played by the staff. These shops cultivated a real sense of community among fellow record buyers who would recommend an album or compare notes on a particular artist. It was so much more than just walking in, handing over your money and leaving. In an era before twenty-four-hour television, world news conveniently packaged in bite-sized chunks and streaming services, music was our lingua franca.

As a teenager, money was still in very short supply . . . I simply couldn't afford to buy too many records. So, to meet someone who was into the same kind of music and might have a couple of LPs I coveted was important in a way that doesn't quite translate in today's world. But it went much, much further than simply swapping albums. To connect Bob Dylan or The Beatles or The Rolling Stones or Stevie Wonder or MC5 was to plug into a vibrant counterculture that was truly revolutionary.

There is a famous photograph by William E. Sauro of *The New York Times* taken just before Christmas in 1969. It shows a massive billboard at the intersection of Times Square and Seventh Avenue. He captured passers-by staring at a message that was as profound as it was disarmingly simple. In huge block capitals it proclaimed: 'WAR IS OVER' with a challenge printed underneath saying: 'If you want it'.

The dramatic power of those seven words on one of the world's busiest street corners was overwhelming. At a time when American soldiers were fighting in Vietnam it was a controversial statement to make. The smallest print on the billboard told us who we had to thank for this beautifully concise piece of agitprop. It read: 'Merry Christmas from John & Yoko'. And it was erected just yards from a recruiting office for the US Marines at 42nd Street.

But music was reflecting the mood – and anger – of the times. Whether it was James Brown's 'Say It Loud – I'm Black And I'm Proud' or Crosby, Stills, Nash & Young's 'Ohio', musicians were plugged into and influenced by current events. There were no focus groups or PR advisers telling them not to speak out. As a result, we got a series of undiluted perspectives on world news, which you probably wouldn't have read about in the papers.

It wasn't just current affairs either. The album widened our horizons too. Whether it was poring over the sleeve of *Sgt. Pepper's Lonely Hearts Club Band* trying to figure out who everybody was or decoding the lyrics of 'Lucy In The Sky With Diamonds' to determine if it really was all about taking LSD.

In later years, Storm Thorgerson, Roger Dean, Guy Peellaert, Peter Saville, Malcolm Garrett, Jean-Paul Goude, Jamie Reid and Barney Bubbles became huge names in their own right thanks to important and powerful art presented on an album sleeve roughly the size of a ceiling tile.

There were no videos for most songs. With the exception of the film clips which accompanied 'Strawberry Fields Forever' and 'Penny Lane' in 1967, I don't think I really saw a proper music promo until Queen released their iconic video for 'Bohemian Rhapsody' eight years later. So albums – words, music, art, information – were a valuable conduit and vital to emerging pop culture.

Today, a new generation of fans source music in a simpler, more convenient way. Their experience is very different. Now, you are just a few mouse clicks away from sourcing the most obscure tracks imaginable. The advantages of being able to store thousands of songs on a smartphone or tablet are self-explanatory. Musicians can reach a global audience in a matter of seconds by posting a new song online.

The streaming numbers are phenomenal. Lewis Capaldi recently set a benchmark when it was revealed his 2018 single, 'Someone You Loved', had been listened to on Spotify more than 2.6 billion times. The Scottish singer-songwriter would never have achieved anything like that with a disc. Even so, I still prefer to discover – and be seduced by – a great album in a more natural, organic way.

During a lecture to college students on a music industry course, I once tried to describe the sheer adrenalin rush of hearing a landmark record for the first time on vinyl as opposed to downloading it on a faceless computer file. I said it was like the difference between masturbation and sex. My claim was that in the right circumstances, the former – described by US movie director Woody Allen as being 'sex with someone I love' – would suffice. But, I argued, it just didn't reach the true orgasmic heights of full-blown sex. The class looked at me as if I was mad, then went back to skimming through messages on their mobile phones.

In 2021, Noel Gallagher was named as an Official Ambassador for Record Store Day. His albums with the High Flying Birds are released on every digital format plus CD and vinyl to maximise the reach to fans around the world. But the former Oasis guitarist and songwriter is old school. Like me, he still values the more traditional album concept.

'These things were the poor man's art collection,' he said, in a video clip to launch Record Store Day.

'When you'd go to someone's house and they had loads of records I'd flick through them.

'To young kids now it's all about the phone and all that. But to have an album in your hand – it's real – it means something.'

Noel is right. It means everything.

Chapter 4
Building Sites and Bay City Rollers

'SPELL THE WORD MANOEUVRE.' The request came from the guy on the other side of the desk. He sat back in his chair awaiting my reply.

Shit! He'd caught me on the wrong foot. I'd not seen this coming. Up until that point I thought the interview had been going quite well.

I'd applied for a job as a junior reporter on an agricultural magazine, popular with farmers and people living in more rural areas across Scotland. The position had been advertised in the employment section of the *Glasgow Herald*. These small ads for journalists were few and far between, so I thought it was worth throwing my hat into the ring. It could be a while before I got another opportunity. In the mid-1970s, it was almost impossible to break into the print industry. Most newspapers insisted that their writing staff were members of the NUJ – the National Union of Journalists – but it was difficult to join that organisation unless you had a firm offer of a job. It was a real catch-22 situation. I reckoned if I could find a publication that operated in a less stringent manner, I could maybe work my way in through the back door.

Spell manoeuvre. I gulped and said: 'm – a – n', clearly on a roll, before stumbling to a halt. It was the 'o-e-u-v-r-e' bit that proved to be my undoing. I did manage to nail it, at the second attempt. I've never had a problem with the word since that day although I can't ever recall having occasion to actually use it in any verbal or written conversation.

But such dubious spelling ability – coupled with the fact it was crystal clear I knew nothing whatsoever about the world of live-stock, combine harvesters and crop rotation – sealed my fate. A polite rejection letter dropped through the letter box the following week saying, 'thanks, but no thanks'.

It was back to the day job.

I worked as a builder's labourer for the maintenance department of Glasgow Corporation, the city council. We were based in a yard which is now home to the Tron Theatre. I have a real problem every time I go to see a new play there.

The main auditorium was once the plumber's store and no matter which riveting drama production is being performed on the stage, I can still visualise the place stacked ceiling high with toilet bowls, sink units, enamel bathtubs and lengths of copper piping.

We'd report every morning to the gaffer to be given our assign-ments for the day. The job could be dirty and it was heavy manual work at times but I absolutely loved it. I was given a permanent placement at a new tower block called McIver House, joining a seventy-strong squad of bricklayers, joiners, electricians and plumb-ers whose job it was to turn the empty shell into offices and meeting rooms. The craic was hilarious and non-stop. I've never laughed so much in my life.

McIver House was adjacent to two locations vital to the local music scene . . . Radio Clyde 261 and The Albany Hotel.

Clyde's HQ was just a two-minute walk away. Launched in 1973, it was the first commercial ILR or Independent Local Radio station outside of London to challenge the dominance of the BBC. When they were recruiting staff, a local DJ, Tim Stevens – who had learned his trade on the city's tough nightclub circuit – turned up for a job interview. He was dressed in a fur tiger-striped suit complete with tail, wore a Roman centurion helmet on his head and brandished a huge plastic sword. Clyde founder and managing director, Jimmy Gordon, didn't ask him a single question. He took one look at the colourful figure who had invaded his office and hired him on the spot. So the legendary 'Tiger' Tim was born. He's still THE most recognisable name to ever broadcast on Clyde's 261 medium waves.

On the site, we'd hear hordes of girls scream as he was smuggled into the building for his anarchic 'Aff Its Heid' show. Week in, week out, music's biggest stars would visit Clyde to promote their latest albums or tours. It was bizarre to see them being led into the main reception located next door to McOnomy, an electrical discount store which was a forerunner of Comet and Currys.

I remember ducking off the job to get an autograph from Neil Sedaka as he stepped out of his limousine. It was odd meeting the US music legend – who'd learned his craft as a staff songwriter at the Brill Building in New York City – as he slipped up the fire escape stairwell unnoticed. When I got to interview Sedaka many years later he entertained me with stories of the now legendary publishing house at 1619 Broadway, in the heart of America's Tin Pan Alley. He reminisced about his early days as a fledgling writer when he'd rubbed shoulders with other rising talents such as Burt Bacharach and Hal David, Neil Diamond, Paul Simon and Carole King and Gerry Goffin. They composed some of the most popular songs in music and Sedaka recalled that in one particular week in the early sixties, ten of the Top 20 singles on the Billboard Charts had been penned by the creative assembly line in the Brill Building.

Little did I know that just a few years later I'd become part of Clyde's team of DJ's, hosting my own late night alternative music show.

Across the concrete walkway stood The Albany Hotel where touring bands would check in before appearing at Green's Playhouse, later to become the Apollo.

In 1971, I camped out with my mates in the foyer – suited and booted – to try to catch a glimpse of The Who before attending their gig later that night. I discovered that guitarist Pete Townshend was booked into a room on the first floor . . . as far away as possible from the group's madcap drummer, Keith Moon, who was holding court in the tenth-floor penthouse suite.

Me and a mate sneaked past security and ran up one flight of stairs, then we moved furtively along the corridor knocking on every door in sequence. As it was mid-afternoon, most rooms were unoccupied until finally we hit the jackpot . . . a door opened and there stood an understandably startled looking Townshend. We couldn't believe it. Our hero was right in front of us.

The nerves kicked in as we blurted out that we were big fans of the band, delivered in a machine gun-style staccato. From his bemused look, I'd hazard a guess he didn't understand a single word we said. We then presented him with a gift we'd bought earlier . . . a HAGGIS wrapped in silver tinfoil.

What the fuck was one of the greatest guitar players in rock history meant to do with a haggis, while holed up in a five-star hotel on tour with his group? I'll come clean – it was a question that had never occurred to either of us.

Townshend viewed this little keepsake of his visit to Scotland with suspicion, like we'd handed him some Semtex explosives. But – and it's to his eternal credit – he seemed to appreciate the sentiment behind this rather bizarre gesture. Whilst you'd have maybe expected him to throttle us for disturbing his pre-gig nap, I think he was more taken aback by our ingenuity.

He autographed my copy of the band's 1965 debut album, *My Generation* – on the original Brunswick label – with good grace and posed for a photo.

A few months later, the Faces set up base camp in the Albany bar prior to their gig at Green's. We staked them out too.

With Rod Stewart and Ronnie 'Plonk' Lane taking on the self-appointed roles of mine hosts, the party was in full swing and continued throughout the day. The numbers swelled as everyone was welcome to join the festivities.

'We'd still be there boozing at nine o'clock that night . . . having the time of our lives,' Rod once told me, 'then Woody would say: 'Haven't we got a gig to do?'

'We'd roll out of the Albany, into the limos and head for the venue completely shit-faced. We DID like a little drink. But it didn't affect the show. We could always play great . . . drunk or sober.'

Fast-forward four years, and I'm unloading building material from a lorry outside McIver House when the city calm is shattered by ear-piercing screams. The Albany was under siege round the clock by hundreds of prepubescent girls dressed from head to toe in tartan. The date was 11 September 1976, and Scottish pop supergroup, The Bay City Rollers were playing a sell-out gig at the Apollo.

I'd turned down the chance to work overtime that night because I was going to the concert. When word spread around the site that I'd paid £2 for a ticket to see the Rollers on stage and I got absolute pelters. Every tradesman on the job demanded to know: 'What are you going to see those five nancy boys for?'

Although it wasn't put quite so politely as that. I couldn't go anywhere on the job without the lads bursting into a spontaneous chorus of 'Shang-A-Lang'. I got roasted alive.

But I had good reason to want to see the band perform. I was a little too young to really appreciate the hysteria created by The Beatles. So I was keen to experience 'Rollermania' – the biggest pop phenomenon since then – firsthand.

The hotel was surrounded by hordes of girls, many crying tears of frustration because they couldn't reach their idols. Every time a van arrived at the service entrance to deliver food supplies or fresh laundry, the hapless driver was besieged. You could hear their screams for miles. The girls thought the Rollers were being smuggled into their rooms. Truth was, they were nowhere near the place. The group's security team had hidden them away in a secret location on the outskirts of their native Edinburgh, forty-five-minutes' drive along the M8 motorway.

At the gig, I saw exactly why the Rollers had captured the imagination of female fans in the UK, Europe, America, Australia and Japan. Aside from the band and the bouncers, I was one of the few males in the venue that night.

The lights dimmed and an intro tape – appropriately a NASA Apollo countdown – was played over the PA system.

'Five-four-three-two-one . . . ignition, we have lift off.'

They launched into a set that featured hits including 'Money Honey', 'Rock N' Roll Love Letter' and 'Bye Bye Baby'. It was bedlam. You virtually couldn't hear a note they were playing because of the sustained screams of the audience.

A team of technicians from Glasgow University had once conducted an experiment that found that the balcony bounced fully eighteen inches up and down during the most volatile concerts. I feared that this was the night the theory would be put to the test. I thought it was going to snap in the middle under the sheer weight of the audience leaping around.

What I saw made the fan hysteria created later by acts like New Kids On The Block, Take That and One Direction appear lukewarm by comparison.

I'm still a huge fan of the group. I make no bones about it. And I continue to unashamedly fly the flag for The Bay City Rollers. It's a bold tartan one, of course.

My time as a builder's labourer also had other built-in advantages. I was as fit as a fiddle and earning a take-home pay of around £70 a week – considerably more than what my mates were on – thanks to plenty of overtime and weekend shifts. Such a steady and well-paid job certainly made life a little easier, particularly where having the finances to buy records and go to concerts was concerned.

There were occasions when I did have some cash-flow problems, however. I once was forced to borrow the 20p bus fare to get to work on payday, to pick up my weekly wages. I was totally broke having spent all my money on up-and-coming gigs. In a bedroom drawer was £40 worth of tickets to see a string of acts including Cockney Rebel, The Kinks, Slade, Wings, Roxy Music, Sparks and The Sensational Alex Harvey Band. In an era when the average price of a concert ticket was around £1.50, it was a significant investment. I didn't drink or smoke, so what else was I going to spend my hard-earned cash on?

But I still had ambitions to make a career as a journalist. That was my real goal. In my final year of school, I'd taken secretarial studies as an additional subject. My sexuality came under scrutiny when mates discovered I'd be doing periods of typing and office practice three times a week. I still shudder at some of their barbed comments.

There was real method in my madness. I was the only guy in a class full of thirty pretty girls . . . it eased the pain ever so slightly.

It paid off. I managed to gain an O-level and my typing speed was superior to many of my classmates. I bought a portable typewriter to use at home so I didn't get rusty. I also enrolled in a shorthand course at college that I attended after work on the site. But that was much less successful. I'd been away from a classroom setting for several years and it felt too much like going back to school again. I couldn't hack it.

At lunchtimes in McIver House, I'd sit in the canteen – when most of the lads had disappeared off to the pub or the bookies – with the *New Musical Express* or *Melody Maker* spread out in front of me. I desperately wanted to be part of that world. But I still wasn't sure how to go about it.

Over the years, some of my most successful endeavours have simply been down to being in the right place at the right time. It's often said you make your own luck. I decided to try to shape my own destiny. It was a roll of the dice . . . and could go either way.

Chapter 5
The Write Stuff

NINA YOUNG TOOK A chance on me. I'm forever in her debt. Did she spot my potential? I don't know. In the many years we've remained friends it's a question I've somehow never gotten around to asking her.

I'd decided it was time to grab the bull by the horns in an effort to break into journalism. I wrote a letter to the editor of my local newspapers, the *Bishopbriggs Times* and the *Springburn Times*, saying I noticed they didn't have a music column. I volunteered to write one for free, with the simple proviso that they printed 'by Billy Sloan' on any articles published.

My plan was to build up a cuttings file of bylined stories to stick under the nose of any future employers. Maybe if they saw examples of my work, it might enhance my prospects of landing a job.

I was called into the *Times* office for an 'informal chat'. There was nothing informal about Nina. She was a formidable character. Flowing red hair. Smart suit. Larger than life. Great sense of humour. And she talked in rapid-fire bursts. It was impossible not to be swept along by her enthusiasm. I liked her instantly, and the feeling appeared to be mutual. We hit it off.

I made my pitch about launching a music column which could perhaps attract a younger readership. It would also bring a bit of much needed 'glam' to both papers.

But she had other ideas. Nina led a staff of five people who each week produced the *Bishopbriggs Times* – on a shoestring budget – from a tiny office in the town just north of Glasgow. The Springburn version was a slip-edition of the main paper with a few pages of more localised news.

She was looking to hire a reporter specifically to cover the Spring-burn area – that was only a mile down the road – in a bid to increase circulation. Was this a job I'd consider?

Young MUST have seen something in me, for this offer was dropped into my lap after a mere forty-five-minute conversation. She had never read any articles I'd written . . . there were none. Instead, she handed me a reporter's notepad and a pen and immediately sent me out to find some 'news briefs' for that week's edition.

'You came back an hour later with a number of items including one from a church minister and another about a forthcoming flower show,' she recalled recently. 'It wasn't big stuff, but it was the kind of material which was the lifeblood of any local paper. You were also very irreverent and chatty and I liked that too.

'I remember you telling me that you worked on a building site. It was very honest of you to admit that. You didn't have any experience at all. But I could see how badly you wanted it. I thought . . . what have I got to lose?'

What I grew to like most about Nina was that she was a real straight talker. She was also compulsive and very instinctual and most of her snap decisions paid off. She always put her cards on the table too. There were no grey areas.

This was no exception. Nina explained that, as she operated on a prohibitive budget, the wages were £19 a week, and I'd be permitted to take £1.50 from the petty cash to cover any bus fares to and from jobs. My heart sank. I'd thrown a 'sickie' from labouring on a building site – to attend the meeting – with a guaranteed wage of at least £70. How could I survive on less than a third of that? I was also married and had my first child – a baby daughter, Melanie – so for the first time in my life I had real responsibilities.

I tried to conceal my disappointment and asked if she could give me forty-eight hours to think it over. I'd been painted into a corner. It was my big break . . . finally. I desperately wanted the job. But the terms were financially challenging, to say the least.

Luckily, I had savings. Not a fortune but a sufficient amount to provide some kind of safety net, however temporary. After much soul searching, I called her two days later and accepted her offer.

To say my starting day as a reporter in 1976 was a baptism of fire is an understatement. There was NO formal training. It was assumed you could write a story – and do it to deadline. I read the 'big' papers and knew what made good copy. I had total confidence I could do it.

My first assignment was a real taste of what was to come. I don't think my arse had even touched the seat when I was given the name and address of a local man who'd won £1,000 in a spot-the-ball competition in a national newspaper. Twenty minutes later a photographer and I were on his doorstep asking how he planned to splash the cash. It was like being kicked off the top of a diving board. You could either sink or swim.

My next few months were hectic, spent covering a diary full of council meetings, Girl-Guide displays, football matches, feature interviews and local jumble sales. I thrived on it.

At Christmas, I rode with the driver of a Post Office van as he delivered festive parcels in the area. I was dressed as Santa Claus – padded tum, full white beard, 'yo-ho-ho's, the lot. The reaction of little kids when they opened the door and saw Santa himself pull out a package from his Christmas sack was priceless. It made for a great centre-page photo spread.

I was nothing, if not versatile.

Nina's number two was a subeditor named Andy Pattison, who was an old school newspaper man. I learned so much just by looking over his shoulder. But the office was a total dump. There were no toilets. The three female staff used the facilities in the hairdresser's downstairs, while Andy, another reporter and I went to the gents public convenience at Bishopbriggs Cross. And it closed at 6 p.m.

Before I was hired, burglars had gained access to the building and burst in through the ceiling with the intention of ransacking the place. But after a quick look around they realised there was not a single thing worth stealing . . . and climbed back out again. The gaping hole in the plaster was never repaired, so I'd sit at my desk as pigeons 'coo coo-ed' in the gap above my head. It was difficult to be creative with feathers floating down onto the keys of my typewriter. The office must have contravened every environmental health-and-safety rule in the statute books.

Readers would arrive at the door to hand in small ads and say: 'Is this the *Bishopbriggs Times* office? I thought it was a derelict building'. But Nina was skilled in keeping up morale and making work fun. She was the key to our continued success.

The difference between Bishopbriggs and nearby Springburn could not have been more pronounced. The former was an affluent, largely middle-class area . . . Tory voting, privately owned houses, car in the driveway, beautifully manicured lawns and two foreign holidays a year. As a result, there was an apathy that wasn't conducive to producing a hard-hitting or dynamic newspaper. It was not unusual to arrive in the office on a Tuesday morning – deadline day – and not have an eye-catching splash to put on page one because 'nothing was happening'. Luckily, we always managed to cobble something together.

But Springburn was the opposite side of the coin . . . a tough, fiercely working-class neighbourhood where the inhabitants used their local paper as a cudgel to go into battle against authority. I'd get phone calls from community councils or residents' associations saying: 'They're getting rid of the lollipop man at the primary school down the road. What are YOU going to do about it?' The paper was then expected to take up the fight. Which we did.

Every Saturday morning, I'd hoof it around the local surgeries to meet Labour councillors trying to solve the problems of their constituents. If we carried a story of how they'd sorted some long-running dispute, it provided valuable column inches.

They loved seeing their picture appear in the paper and wallowed in such positive publicity, so it was a two-way street.

A close ally was Michael Martin, who quickly rose up through the ranks of the Labour Party to become the Member of Parliament for Springburn. He was a gentleman and took an encouraging interest in how my career was progressing. Michael would tip me the wink if there was anything he thought I should know about.

In 2000, he became Speaker of the House of Commons, and held that prestigious role for nine years, later becoming Baron Martin of Springburn and taking a seat in the House of Lords.

Both papers would soon benefit from my passion for music. In a quiet news week, we'd be scratching around looking for stories. On several occasions we'd find ourselves with a gash half page 'near the back of the book' with nothing substantial to fill it. So Nina would ask me to write a pop column that would not only quickly solve the problem but also add a bit of additional colour to the edition.

It was a real labour of love. I'd come up with news items about album releases, gossip stories and gig information on bands playing in Glasgow or Edinburgh in the coming months.

At long last, it felt great to see articles about some of my favourite bands with 'by Billy Sloan' attached to them. A real sense of achievement, even in a small way.

These sporadic music pages also brought a positive response from younger readers. I got a call from a local musician, Graham Scott, a singer/guitarist who was inspired by the punk rock explosion in London to form his own band. Would I like to interview them?

The Exile had released their impressive debut EP, *Don't Tax Me* on the self-financed Boring Records label in August 1977. The yellow gatefold sleeve – designed by A. Moron – had a picture of the group doing their best to look mean and moody. They pressed up 1,000 copies and distributed them around record shops.

The EP came within weeks of 'God Save The Queen' by The Sex Pistols being banned by the BBC and every other major radio station across the country. The music biz 'establishment' conspired to deliberately keep the single off the No.1 spot in the charts in Jubilee week, to save Her Majesty any unnecessary embarrassment as she celebrated twenty-five years on the throne.

I met Scott, with band mates, Stan Workman, Robert Kirk and Dougie Burns, and fortunately they turned out to be nowhere near as scary as they appeared on the cover of the record. I was wet behind the ears. So were they. It was completely new territory for both of us. We were learning on the job.

The interview went well and the following week we got a great reaction to what was the band's first sizeable piece of publicity in a more mainstream publication. But they were there on merit. I thought the four-song EP was great.

One track, 'Fascist DJ', was an attack on local DJ, Tom Ferrie, of Radio Clyde, who'd dismissed punk rock and refused to play it on his show.

The Exile had really put down a marker with their disc. Scott later told *Kingdom Come* fanzine: 'We recorded the EP in just three hours. In the first, we rehearsed the three songs newly written, in the second we recorded the whole thing, and in the final hour we mixed the tracks. One fanzine in Japan devoted three full pages to us. I don't know what the fuck it said though.'

Across Scotland more like-minded bands had also chosen a similar path. The Drive, a Dundee band fronted by singer Gus McFarlane, released 'Jerkin' on their own NRG label in early 1977. It is regarded as the first-ever Scottish punk rock single.

In Edinburgh, The Rezillos exploded onto the music scene with the brilliant 'Can't Stand My Baby'. And, also in the capital, The Valves put out a great debut single, 'Robot Love/For Adolf's Only', on record shop owner Bruce Findlay's innovative Zoom label.

While along the M8 in Glasgow, PVC 2 – fronted by Midge Ure who'd quit chart-topping teen act Slik – unveiled 'Put You In The Picture', also on Zoom.

Across the city, Johnny & the Self Abusers saw 'Saints & Sinners' come out on seminal London indie-label, Chiswick. It proved to be their first – and only – release, for the band split up on the very day it hit the shops. A few weeks later, two of the main members, singer Jim Kerr and guitarist Charlie Burchill, formed Simple Minds.

In twelve brief minutes The Exile had made a powerful punk rock statement, and all from a house at 23 Dalkeith Avenue in the rather posh locale of Bishopbriggs. It seemed a far cry from The Clash roaming the dark alleys of urban decay beneath The Westway in London, 450 miles further south. But geography was not a factor. In its own way, the music The Exile made was equally as powerful and potent.

Another visitor to the office was Joe McKenna, an aspiring singer who was destined for stardom. How did I know this? He told me.

Joe lived in Kirkintilloch, a town four miles up the road. From the second he walked in the door, he hit me with a checklist of ambitious goals as both a musician and actor. I liked him instantly. His enthusiasm was so infectious you'd have been a fool to bet against him.

Joe turned out to be the real deal too. Later that year, he landed the role of Peter Barlow in *Coronation Street*, and starred on the famous Weatherfield cobbles for the next twelve months. He stayed in touch and kept me up to date on what he was up to career-wise.

In 1982, Joe enjoyed some success with the Euro-dance single, 'A Cha Cha At The Opera' on Island Records, which was popular in the clubs.

Four years later, he was cast in the movie, *Absolute Beginners*, adapted from the Colin MacInnes novel based in London's Soho in the late 1950s. Director Julien Temple's big screen musical-drama starred Eddie O'Connell, Patsy Kensit, James Fox, Steven Berkoff and David Bowie, who had a smash hit with the film's theme song.

And there was no stopping Joe. He moved into the world of fashion and became an influential stylist working for designers such as Giorgio Armani, Yves Saint Laurent, Gianni Versace, Prada and Calvin Klein. His work as a fashion editor appeared in *Vogue*, *The Face*, the *New York Times' T* magazine and *I-D*. Amazing to think that one of his earliest bits of publicity was when I had interviewed him in his local paper.

A regular feature of my music column was a competition that proved popular with readers. I did a deal with Tom Russell, a DJ who had opened his first record shop at Bishopbriggs Cross. Each week, he gifted two singles as a prize in return for a bit of free publicity.

It's confession time. On a few occasions, I deliberately made the question so difficult or obscure that we got no correct entries. I'd print a bogus name as a winner and pick up their choice of singles from Tom, to pass on to our non-existent, 'lucky reader'.

'No One Is Innocent' by The Sex Pistols and 'Complete Control' by The Clash are two memorable punk singles that remain in my collection ... obtained under those larcenous circumstances. All these years on, I send Tom my heartfelt apologies. I hang my head in shame.

And if any members of the Serious Crime Squad are reading this ... I plead Not Guilty on the grounds of diminished responsibility.

My two-and-a-half-year period on the papers turned out to be some of the happiest times of my working life. Not to mention a valuable apprenticeship. But all good things must come to an end.

In 1979 Nina had another of her 'informal chats' ... this time with the boss of Collins Publishers, who had a massive office complex and distribution centre in the area, employing hundreds of local people. He was seeking advice on how to revamp *Collins News*, the company's in-house magazine and asked her to take a look at it. Nina told him what she thought was needed.

He too was impressed by her straight-talking and enthusiastic approach and he invited her to become editor of *Collins News* and also run their public relations team. It was an offer she couldn't refuse.

A few months later, Andy was also headhunted, becoming editor of the *Kirkintilloch Herald*, our main rivals. I found myself running both papers by sheer virtue of the fact I was the last man standing.

The ownership of the titles also changed hands. It was time to make a move.

I was approached by a team who were planning an ambitious new magazine being launched by Radio Clyde. The weekly entertainment tabloid – *Clyde Guide* – was almost like a version of the *Radio Times*, showcasing the output and activities of the hit Glasgow station. Its pages would be full of music features and celebrity interviews and focus on the exploits of their dream team of DJs which included Richard Park, Steve Jones, Dougie Donnelly, Dave Marshall, Bill Smith and of course, the now legendary 'Tiger' Tim Stevens.

It was the perfect job for me. I was in the right place at the right time, again.

Chapter 6
The Bear Necessities

THERE WAS NO SUCH thing as a typical day in *Clyde Guide*. A case in point was the moment a total stranger marched into reception, glared at me across the office and said: 'Get your jacket . . . and come with me.' His brusque tone suggested he wasn't taking no for an answer. I reckoned he was punting some new band.

I had nothing much on, so I followed him. What's the worst that could happen? If I was lucky, I might get a free coffee in the cafe on the corner. My hunch proved to be correct.

Ged Malone had a car waiting in Royal Exchange Square and beckoned me to get into the back seat. He jumped in beside the driver.

'Where are we heading?' I inquired. There was a stony silence. Neither said a word . . . not even to each other. Was I being abducted?

It was reminiscent of the terrifying closing scene in the 1980 gangster movie *The Long Good Friday*, where Harold Shand – played by Bob Hoskins – is seized outside The Savoy Hotel in London, by two IRA assassins.

We drove through an area of Glasgow I wasn't familiar with. Finally, after twenty-five minutes, we reached our destination. A large metal sign at the gate said: *St Vincent's Primary School, Carnwadric.*

They led me straight to the school gymnasium where a young five-piece guitar band – on a stage at the far end of the hall – launched into the first of four songs. There was no dialogue, friendly or otherwise, between numbers. They were good. I was impressed, but it was important not to show it. They then went into an adjoining classroom and I was told to follow.

As soon as I walked in, motormouth drummer Martin Hanlin kick-started a verbal barrage: 'Why don't you write about us in your fucking paper . . . instead of all those shit bands you've been wasting your time on?'

Singer Owen McGee chimed in: 'We're the best new band in Scotland. Nobody has got songs as good as ours. You just heard them.'

I was in a room with a bunch of guys I'd never seen before . . . outnumbered seven-to-one. My best form of defence was attack. I let rip.

Who were they? What had they done? Best unsigned band in Scotland? Every new group says that. It was time to get real.

I fought my corner. I don't think they were expecting that.

This was my introduction to Venigmas.

We talked on and thankfully the meeting ended on a more amicable note. A few weeks later, I interviewed the band to help promote their debut single, 'Turn The Lights Out', released on the indie label Graduate, in 1979.

It was played by DJ Peter Powell on BBC Radio 1, who raved about the band on his show.

Graduate – based in the West Midlands – hit pay dirt a few months later with *Signing Off*, the first album by UB40, which reached No.2 in the UK chart and went on to sell 500,000 copies.

Things didn't go quite so well for Venigmas though. Despite building a strong local following over the next two years, and releasing a second single, 'Strangelove', the group went their separate ways. But their passion and determination had not deserted them. The main players managed to make their mark individually.

Drummer Hanlin and bass player Joe Donnelly formed The Silencers and made two albums with the band. They toured with U2, David Bowie, Simple Minds, The Pretenders and Squeeze.

Singer McGee adopted the name Owen Paul and scored a 1986 summer hit with 'My Favourite Waste Of Time', a cover of the song by Marshall Crenshaw.

Malone relocated to the US and married Jane Wiedlin, guitarist and co-founder of all-girl group The Go-Go's. He was involved in guiding her successful solo career.

Such encounters were typical at *Clyde Guide*. The magazine became a magnet for local bands, who would send me their latest demo tapes or drop off self-financed singles, in a bid to get coverage for their music.

In 1978, most daily newspapers refused to print programme listings for ILR stations. The *Radio Times* – which had a huge circulation – was a UK publishing institution that carried previews and details of all BBC television and radio shows. *TV Times* – a more glossy variation – did a similar job for all of ITV's regional channels. Several attempts were made to persuade *TV Times* to include Radio Clyde's programmes in its Scottish edition, but to no avail.

So, station boss, Jimmy Gordon, decided to launch a tabloid magazine to showcase the talent of their crack team of presenters and highlight the diversity of their weekly output.

I wrote a piece on Debbie Harry and Blondie which was the cover feature of *Clyde Guide*, issue number one, that hit newsagents on 28 September 1978 . . . coincidentally fifty-five years to the day since the first edition of *Radio Times* went on sale. The magazine was heavily promoted on air and was an immediate hit with listeners.

I'd hang out in Clyde's chaotic H.Q. and be given access to stars visiting to promote their latest records or books. Two of the most memorable were Hollywood legend, Lauren Bacall, and Italian screen actress, Sophia Loren, who brought a bit of razzmatazz to the station.

The Clyde presenters proved a non-stop source of material for the magazine. Madcap DJ 'Tiger' Tim – whose exploits often defied belief – could always be relied on to deliver a great story or two. His colleagues – big hitters such as Paul Coia, Jim Waugh and Frank Skerrett – all wrote columns popular with readers.

There was never a dull moment. In those heady days, record labels and publishing firms had budgets to take their artists on radio tours. In any given week it was the norm to come face-to-face with a string of huge stars who were only too happy to chat and pose for pictures if it garnered publicity for what they were promoting. Over the next few months, I interviewed acts such as Iggy Pop, The Bay City Rollers, Alex Harvey, The Three Degrees, David Essex, Boney M and Midge

Ure. I was also out most nights reviewing gigs by The Kinks, Roxy Music, Darts, The Jacksons, Billy Connolly and Showaddywaddy.

There was always something going on.

When The Stranglers came to the city to headline Glasgow Apollo on 30 September 1978 they agreed to talk to me. Landing an act of that stature was a real scoop . . . they were choosy about who they spoke to.

The band had a formidable reputation and were known to take violent retribution against journalists who crossed them. I was so freaked out I took a couple of colleagues with me as backup. But when I chatted to singer Hugh Cornwell and drummer Jet Black they turned out to be cordial and very cooperative. I got a great interview and we did a photo session with them at the famous Paddy's Market, in amongst piles of old clothes, junk and bric-a-brac.

On 6 March 1979 I received a letter from publicist Brian Hogg – on formal Zoom Records headed notepaper – asking if I would be interested in talking to another new Scottish band. I'd been lucky enough to see their first gig the previous year but our paths had not crossed since then. He said: 'They have just completed their debut album and we are naturally excited about its forthcoming release. We are hopeful that a Scottish-based label can have success with a Scottish-based band . . . and we feel there may be an interesting story in that.' He also enclosed a biography and a bunch of press clippings to tempt me further. I didn't need much persuasion.

I met three members of the group in The Ingram Bar on Queen Street around the corner from the office. The singer did most of the talking . . . well, almost. He suffered from a nervous stammer that made being interviewed a real ordeal. But he was highly articulate and succeeded in putting his message across. His name was Jim Kerr and his group, Simple Minds, would become the most successful band in Scottish rock history.

They had played a Sunday night residency in the Mars Bar and took the unusual step of inviting London's top A&R (artist and repertoire) men to come up to Glasgow to see them play, rather than vice versa.

'It was really strange the way it happened. We seemed to do everything back to front,' explained Jim. 'Even now we're releasing our first album and we've not played a gig outside Scotland yet. The press has been very enthusiastic and anyone with any influence has really got behind us.

'But if the album comes out and it's anything less than brilliant, we're gonna get jumped on. Until now, we've had very good reviews but I know that in England there will be guys sitting waiting to give us a bad write-up. We want to break ourselves nationally.'

We shot them – Jim, keyboard player Mick MacNeil and drummer Brian McGee – standing self-consciously on the steps of Stirling's library, now the Gallery of Modern Art. It was one of their earliest photo sessions. Over the next twelve months, Jim grew in confidence, both personally and creatively. That first meeting was the beginning of a long and enduring friendship.

The seventeen-strong team at *Clyde Guide* – which included Russell Gilchrist, the former manager of Glasgow Apollo – consistently delivered a colourful product. The writers were led by news editor Loudon Temple, arguably the world's most enthusiastic man. He'd steer our weekly 'ideas meetings' that would produce copious amounts of potential features and stories. We never had any trouble filling the pages.

In early 1979, Loudon and I were dispatched to interview local nightclub owner, John Caulfield, who had an ambitious plan to launch Scotland's first-ever weekend music festival. As he laid out his proposal – which he was backing to the tune of £100,000 – we looked at each other in disbelief. It sounded amazing. But, could he pull it off? The answer was yes . . . and no.

Caulfield had gained permission to stage the Loch Lomond Rock Festival on a site at Cameron Wildlife Park in Balloch. We listened intently as he revealed how the inhabitants of two vast fields – a number of enormous brown grizzly bears – would be temporarily moved out over a weekend in May 1979 to transform the area into a concert arena.

The story leapt into the pages of *Clyde Guide*. We got on well with Caulfield and later got a call from him saying: 'I need two press officers to look after the media side of the event. Do you fancy it?'

We were paid the princely sum of £150, not exactly a fortune. But we weren't doing the job to get rich, more to benefit from the wealth of the experience. It was completely new territory for us. And so began two months of absolute madness. We loved every minute.

Caulfield had lined up The Stranglers, Dr Feelgood, The Skids, the UK Subs and several other acts to play on day one of the festival. He'd also booked the Average White Band, Buzzcocks, Fairport Convention and Rockpile featuring Nick Lowe to appear twenty-four hours later.

We organised a press launch on the banks of the loch, designed to create our first big splash of publicity. It was a photocall with a difference. Hugh Cornwell of The Stranglers, Lee Brilleaux of Dr Feelgood and Pete Shelley of Buzzcocks travelled to Balloch to pose for a picture to help kick-start ticket sales. But all three nearly died when they saw who we'd also invited to take part . . . Hercules the Bear.

The huge brown grizzly, who tipped the scales at nearly thirty stone, arrived in the back of a van with his owner, former champion Scottish wrestler, Andy Robin. He'd bought him as a cub born in captivity in a Scottish wildlife park for £50. When attempts to rehome the animal failed, Robin stepped in to save him from being put down.

Hercules became a celebrity in his own right, appearing with him at wrestling matches around the country and later landing a part in the James Bond movie, *Octopussy*, starring alongside Roger Moore.

The photo of a stunned Cornwell, Brilleaux and Shelley – trying to carefully keep a safe distance from big Herc – is a classic. It was splashed across newspapers the following morning.

The stunt went so well we followed it up a few weeks later. Caulfield hosted a more formal press conference in The Albany Hotel, and promised disbelieving journalists that Hercules would make a surprise appearance. Loudon and I were dispatched to greet Robin when he drove his van into the loading bay. He opened the back doors and out jumped this massive bear who towered over us when he stood up on his hind legs. Robin calmly led Hercules into the hotel like he was walking his dog.

One of the highlights of my career – albeit terrifying – was going up to the penthouse in the goods lift as he placated Hercules with a saucepan full of frozen prawns. The press guys couldn't believe it when they arrived in the suite.

Ticket sales for the festival, while steady, were not flying out of the box office with the desired effect. So Caulfield pulled out all the stops. He burst his budget to sign The Boomtown Rats who'd scored a huge chart hit the previous year with their second album, *A Tonic For The Troops*. The Irish new-wave band had just put the finishing touches to the follow-up, *The Fine Art Of Surfacing*. They were poised to release the lead single from it, so the timing was perfect for the festival. Led by outspoken singer, Bob Geldof, they leapfrogged the Average White Band to go top of the bill.

When the Rats walked out on stage at Balloch the crowd were stunned by their opening song . . . a then unknown ballad inspired by a school shooting in San Diego, USA, a few months previously. Geldof spat the lyrics out – accompanied by Johnnie Fingers on piano – and the crowd were transfixed. So was I . . . it was a very powerful moment.

He had read a news report about the arrest of sixteen-year-old Brenda Ann Spencer who'd fired a gun indiscriminately into a playground, killing two teachers and seriously injuring eight pupils and a policeman. When arrested she was asked why she'd carried out such a heinous crime, and she allegedly replied: 'I don't like Mondays.'

The audience were among the first music fans in the UK to hear the classic single that shot to No.1 two months later and won a pair of coveted Ivor Novello Awards for songwriting.

The festival attracted a weekend audience estimated at 35,000 and was a success, though maybe not financially. Caulfield staged another the following summer starring The Jam, Stiff Little Fingers, The Tourists, Wishbone Ash, Saxon and Ian Gillan. Both proved that music fans did have an appetite for such events and were a forerunner for T in the Park, which was still fifteen years further up the road.

But *Clyde Guide* wasn't faring so well. After the initial novelty value of the new product had worn off, circulation took a real hit.

The magazine was of little interest to anyone outside the station's broadcast catchment area and we were operating in a highly competitive marketplace. As a result, advertising revenue, the lifeblood of any publication, suffered badly. It was given an overhaul and a decision was made to publish fortnightly in a bid to stop the slide. We soldiered on, but eventually – and regrettably – the plug was pulled.

The last of forty-two issues were delivered to newsagents on 28 September 1979 ... exactly one year after Debbie Harry had been the cover star of *Clyde Guide* number one. It had been a real roller coaster ride, and a highly enjoyable one at that. But the shock of losing my job was cushioned when I got another lucky break.

Two months earlier I'd been approached by Noel Young – the then husband of Nina – who was Deputy Editor of the *Sunday Mail*, the biggest selling newspaper in Scotland. He knew how passionate I was about music and what it meant to me. The *Mail*'s pop music column had become tired and jaded. Every week, a couple of London stringers would supply stories and gossip items to be knocked into shape by a middle-aged staff member in their HQ at Anderston Quay. Most of them didn't know the difference between snarling punk rocker Johnny Rotten and kilted Scots comic Johnny Beattie. And it showed.

Noel wanted to relaunch the page. Make it a bit more in-your-face and colourful, to reflect what was really happening on the fast growing Scottish pop scene. He was looking for a writer – a young gun – who actively bought albums, hung around city record shops and went to gigs on a regular basis. What was the inside track on the hot new releases? Who were the new Scottish bands breaking through? What was all the backstage gossip when the stars came to town?

It was time to rebrand the column and give it a much-needed makeover. Noel laid out his plans one afternoon.

Was I interested?

Chapter 7
Billy the Kid

MY HEART SANK. I staggered back and bounced off the wall. It took all my strength not to collapse in a heap on the pavement. I'm sure people thought I was pissed. Traumatised, more like.

I'd just bought a copy of the streets edition of the *Sunday Mail* from a vendor outside Central Station to read my first-ever music column. It should have been an exciting moment, one of the proudest of my fledgling career as a journalist. But I couldn't believe my eyes.

'Pop Gossip by The Disco Kid' screamed the banner headline at the top of the page. The Disco fucking Kid! Was I seeing things? Who the fuck was that? I suddenly realised . . . ME.

It was 2 a.m. I was tired. Maybe I was hallucinating. I read it again. No, it was for real.

My mate tried to appease me saying: 'Be positive . . . more than a million people will read what you've written in the morning. You're now working for the biggest paper in the country. Everybody buys the *Sunday Mail*.'

It only made me feel worse. The Disco Kid was born. Why did I want to smother him at birth?

The previous day – 1 September 1979 – I'd gone to the Edinburgh Rock Festival, at the Royal Highland Showground on the outskirts of the capital, organised by Pete Irvine and Barry Wright. As concert promoters they changed the face of live gigs north of the border with their innovative company, Regular Music.

The festival starred Van Morrison, and its stellar bill also featured Talking Heads, The Chieftains, Steel Pulse, Squeeze and The Undertones, plus several local acts. In the week leading up to the show I'd been preoccupied gathering material for my first column. I wanted to make a real splash. It was a great opportunity. I submitted my copy to Noel Young and he was delighted with the results. It was a special moment when I watched one of the top layout artists design the page.

Early on Saturday morning, a problem arose. What should they call the column? I'd assumed they'd stick my name on it, similar to other columnists, such as showbiz editor, Scott Robinson or football writer, Allan Herron. But Noel felt it would have greater impact if the page was fronted by a 'character' of some kind.

He called me at home to see what my thoughts were. By this time, I was heading for a muddy field adjacent to Edinburgh Airport with 25,000 fellow music fans. In this pre-mobile-phone era, he had no way of reaching me, so a snap decision was made, no doubt by some middle-aged subeditor who clearly had a fixation with the Wild West.

I reached Noel later on Sunday to plead my case. He HAD to ditch The Disco Kid . . . it was cheesy, a terrible pun and just plain naff. How was the *Mail*'s music coverage ever to gain real credibility – at long last – if it was the work of somebody who sounded like they'd come from the pages of a comic book?

But the paper had launched The Disco Kid with a real flourish . . . they couldn't kill him off after just seven days. My only saving grace was that at least I could hide behind a cloak of anonymity. If only.

I walked into my local pub on Monday night to meet my mates and the place erupted. I was hit with comments like: 'Reach for your gun, Disco' and 'I hope you've not tied your horse up outside the saloon on a double yellow line'. When I walked through the bar to go for a piss, they whistled the theme tune of *A Fistful of Dollars*. You had to laugh.

Over the next few months, I transformed the *Mail*'s music coverage with star interviews, insider gossip and hot gig news about bands who were heading for Scotland. Being quick off the mark with the big stories was vital. Every Sunday I'd write: 'I can exclusively reveal . . .' followed by some piece of information I claimed was still hush-hush in the industry. The term became an almost whimsical byword for the column.

In 2018, I popped down to see Roddy Frame of Aztec Camera at the soundcheck before his concert at Kelvingrove Park Bandstand in Glasgow. I'd championed his band since their first singles, 'Just Like Gold' and 'Mattress of Wire', released by Alan Horne on seminal indie-label, Postcard Records in 1981.

During the show, Roddy mentioned we'd had a chat and reminisced about his early days as a musician when he read The Disco Kid religiously every Sunday. He got a laugh from the audience with his good-natured claim that if Jim Kerr of Simple Minds went down to the corner shop to buy a pint of milk . . . The Disco Kid would 'exclusively reveal' the news in the paper.

Unfortunately I couldn't go to the gig because I was at work, hosting my show on BBC Radio Scotland at exactly the same time he was on stage.

But my phone lit up with messages from mates texting to say Roddy had given me a playful namecheck. When I called him the following day he said: 'I hope you didn't mind me having a wee bit of fun.' Not in the least. I was quietly delighted he still had affection for The Disco Kid after almost forty years.

The column was well received by record companies and concert promoters. They could see that I had a real passion for what I was doing and would call to offer interviews with their acts. With such a huge readership, even a tiny mention on the page could result in a leap in album and ticket sales.

Chrysalis Records flew me out to Hamburg – all expenses paid – to interview Rory Gallagher, who was touring to promote his 1979 album, *Photo-Finish*. I'd never been abroad so had to apply for a passport.

Meeting the Irish guitar legend was a massive moment and one of my first face-to-face interviews with a major star. It was also a big deal when members of his band took me on a tour of the Reeperbahn, the city's infamous red-light quarter full of brothels, strip clubs and bars. The area, known as 'die sündigste meile' – 'the most sinful mile' – was where The Beatles learned their chops in the early sixties playing notorious venues like the Star-Club, The Kaiserkeller, Indra and the Top Ten.

John Lennon famously said: 'I might have been born in Liverpool . . . but I grew up in Hamburg.'

To say it was an eye-opener is an understatement, and a far cry from the nightclub scene back in Glasgow.

The column was flying but I faced a constant struggle with meddlesome – and middle-aged – members of the paper's editorial team. Week in, week out they'd lobby me to write about some duff pop act, simply because they were their kids' favourite group. I had to forcibly fight my corner to convince them that as they'd hired me because I knew my stuff, they had to trust my judgement. It didn't always work. They knew better. I would suffer that all through my career.

On one occasion, I'd secured an exclusive interview with Peter Gabriel, an artist who rarely talked to the tabloid media. As I made my pitch to the features editor, he just gave me a blank look and did not enthuse.

In sheer exasperation, I said: 'This guy is one of the biggest stars in the world. It will make a great piece for the paper, trust me. But you don't even know who he is.'

He shot back: 'Of course I do . . . he's the bloke with the tube in his mouth.'

That comment proved my point. My boss was confusing him with Peter Frampton, who pioneered the talk-box technique that made his guitar sound like he was 'speaking' to the audience.

There were two more stings in the tail to come.

After eighteen successful months the paper decided they wanted me to become a bit more opinionated. If there was a pop star or a band I didn't like, I was encouraged to line them up in the crosshairs and pull the trigger. I had no problem whatsoever in slating a new record if I thought it didn't live up to the hype or serving up a bad review if a gig was below par. It was also a good way to generate real interaction with readers who didn't waste time in firing off abusive letters if I'd dissed one of their music heroes. Even a bad reaction was preferable to no reaction at all.

But, just when you thought it couldn't get any worse, they changed the banner headline to 'Pop Gossip by The Disco Kid . . . with his cheeky chat.'

They printed that slogan on advertising bills that were posted out-side newsagents shops from John o' Groats to the Scottish Borders. My heart sank for a second time.

A few months later, the real coup de grâce was when they decided to unmask me. I feared the worst.

It turned out to be a blessing in disguise. My name – and photograph – at the top of the page suddenly gave the column a whole new identity. Readers could match the views and opinions to an actual person as opposed to somebody hiding behind a ridicu-lous, fictitious name.

The change was instant. Fans would approach me at gigs to share their views on the band or just chat about music. I also became the target for new local musicians who would send in their demos hop-ing for some free publicity.

My view was . . . the more, the merrier.

Of course, I did encounter the odd disgruntled reader who wanted to take me to task for spearing some awful heavy-metal band they rated more highly. Despite a few rather fraught exchanges, we'd usually find some common musical ground and part on favourable terms.

Now, being the recognised music correspondent for the *Sunday Mail* helped open doors. The next two I kicked my way through would be game changers.

Chapter 8
Radio Clyde 261 . . .
Altogether Now

THE ASSOCIATES HAD BEEN twiddling their thumbs in the Radio Clyde canteen for more than an hour. It was closed so they couldn't even get a cup of tea to help alleviate the tedium. The group had driven all the way down from Dundee to Glasgow – in a battered old van that was barely roadworthy – to record an interview to promote their 1980 debut album, *The Affectionate Punch*. But the DJ scheduled to talk to them had not bothered to show up. It was beginning to get embarrassing.

'I need your help. You know all the new bands. Go and talk to them. Try to smooth things over,' said Clyde programme producer, John MacCalman in exasperation, as he burst into the record library where I was looking out LPs for my show.

Who were The Associates? I'd heard the name a few months earlier when they'd released their first single, 'Boys Keep Swinging', a cover of the David Bowie song from his thirteenth studio album, *Lodger*.

They caused controversy by having the gall to put it out within weeks of Bowie's own version reaching No. 7 in the UK charts. When asked by a music journalist why they'd made such a bizarre move, the band said defiantly: 'We were just seeking attention. Bowie was untouchable at the time and we were taking him on – or trying to – with his own song.'

Apart from that I knew nothing more about them.

When I walked into the canteen, guitarist Alan Rankine, bass player Michael Dempsey and drummer John Murphy looked well pissed off. And bored rigid. You couldn't blame them. But the singer was different. I'd fully expected to be hit by an angry mouthful after the way they'd been so shabbily treated. Any fears of being chewed out over my colleague's no-show evaporated when he bounded over and went straight into charm offensive.

His name was Billy Mackenzie.

I don't know exactly how you define charisma, but Billy had it. He positively glowed and exuded self-confidence. It was impossible not to warm to him. Billy gave me chapter and verse about *The Affectionate Punch* and promised to send me a copy.

When the LP arrived through the post the cover artwork was stunning. It showed Mackenzie and Rankine – dressed in vests, shorts and spikes – preparing to start a race on a wet running track. The shot had been taken on the sports ground of Wormwood Scrubs prison in London at 2 a.m. Mackenzie bore a striking resemblance to comic strip hero, Alf Tupper – *Tough Of The Track*, in *The Victor*. But I've never seen two less convincing-looking athletes.

When I listened to the album, their amazing songs – built on a foundation of Mackenzie's operatic-style vocals and Rankine's edgy, metallic guitar – were breathtaking. I played some tracks from it on my radio show and championed the group from that moment on. I would have more adventures with Mackenzie further down the line.

My brief tenure as music writer for *Clyde Guide* had paid dividends, the main one being it got me a foot in the door at the station which – until that point – had proven impregnable to the kind of music I was most passionate about.

Just prior to the magazine being binned, I got a phone call that changed everything. Dougie Donnelly – one of Clyde's star DJs – was taking some time off and they needed cover for the *Boozy Woogie Rock Show*, his excellent programme that aired every Friday. I was invited to host one of the shows. It was a real leap of faith by Clyde because I had no broadcasting experience.

Although I was a complete novice, I knew – or thought I knew – what would make a decent two-hour radio programme. I cherry-picked tracks from my own collection, being careful to keep within the musical parameters of the show, and introduced each song with a bit of information or anecdote about the band featured. Fuck knows what it sounded like. How I'd love to hear a tape of that show now . . . or maybe not.

I was gripped by nerves and feel sure I must have 'umm-ed' and 'ahh-ed' my way from midnight through to 2 a.m. But it felt new and was a pleasurable experience. I loved it. And so, it seemed, did Radio Clyde.

Station boss Andy Park was highly respected in the industry and not easily impressed. 'I enjoyed what you were doing. The music choices were great. I liked your style too . . . a bit of a sharpened claw in a velvet glove,' he told me.

Park, who was an accomplished musician, hosted an eclectic show called *Alternative Currents* every Thursday at midnight. He had such an encyclopaedic knowledge he could literally grab a bundle of albums at random in the library – jazz, rock, folk, pop, soul, opera and several other genres – and somehow come up with a narrative that seamlessly linked them all together.

Park's increasing workload meant he was forced to give up his show . . . would I like to take over the slot? What an opportunity. It was an offer I couldn't refuse.

For the first few weeks, I hosted programmes with a common theme. They were just a means to get me used to sitting in the studio hot seat and a trial run for what was to come.

Then it was time to really put my stamp on things. MacCalman – a founder member of Radio Clyde in 1973 – was another strong and valued ally. As music fans, our tastes were often at polar opposites but I think he saw in me a kindred spirit and was very supportive and encouraging.

Johnny Mac – as he was more affectionately known – was a good guy to have in your corner. We'd actually met in the very early days of the station when I was part of a team called The Communicators who entered Radio Clyde's first-ever pop quiz. We were so named because my two fellow members worked in Post Office telecommunications.

Despite tough competition, we won through to beat Strathclyde Police in the semi-finals, before going on to defeat Joanna's Disco in the final. The winner's trophy inscribed: 'Radio Clyde Pop Quiz 1974 – The Communicators' sits proudly on top of my office filing cabinet today. To my knowledge, the station has never staged another similar contest since then. So I'd argue that, technically, we're still the reigning champions almost fifty years later.

When I arrived in On Air 1 to host my new 'alternative music show' the heat was on. Luckily, Johnny Mac had scheduled himself as my T.O. (technical operator) so he drove the main desk, which to a beginner looked like something from Mission Control at NASA.

'What's your first record?' he asked.

I handed him a copy of *1969: The Velvet Underground Live*, a seminal album by the US rock band led by Lou Reed, now recognised as one of the most provocative and influential groups in music history.

'It's side one, track three . . . "What Goes On", recorded live at The Matrix in San Francisco,' I told him.

But when Johnny Mac read the label on the disc, the look on his face said: 'Houston, we have a problem.'

'What Goes On' has a duration of eight minutes, forty-seven seconds . . . most of which is a thrilling five-minute guitar thrash by Reed over some improvised organ lines by keyboard player Doug Yule.

'The song is a little long. It lasts nearly nine minutes. On Radio Clyde we don't really play records as long as this,' he said.

But I felt it was important for me to make my mark. In music terms, I was firmly planting my flag on the battlefield.

'I know it is,' I replied, 'but I'm trying to do something different. Is that not why you've got me here?'

I introduced the track, he pushed open the fader – no doubt against his better judgement – and for the next nine glorious minutes one of the most exciting live recordings of all time blasted out over Clyde's 261 meters on medium wave.

The following day, a mate called to say he'd been driving home along the M8 and switched on the radio. He was so stunned when he heard 'What Goes On' he claimed he almost swerved his car off the Kingston Bridge and down into the river below.

So the show got off to the perfect start and it looked like my timing was just right.

As the calendar moved from 1979 into the 1980s, there was a music explosion that laid the foundations for the most creative period in Scottish pop history. One of the groups leading the charge were The Skids from Dunfermline who'd been signed to Virgin Records by Richard Branson.

'A punk band from Fife! They'll be a bunch of farmers' boys. We're not having that,' said Jim Kerr of Simple Minds.

In early 1978, the Minds had set off on a fact-finding mission across the Kincardine Bridge to see The Skids play at the Kinema Ballroom simply to confirm their suspicions. But they were astounded by the raw power of the group led by singer Richard Jobson and guitar hero-in-waiting, Stuart Adamson.

'They were on fire. Absolutely incredible. We couldn't believe it,' Jim told me later. 'Nobody said a single word on the forty-mile journey back to Glasgow . . . there was total silence in the back of the van.'

In the three-year period that followed The Skids' debut gig at the Belleville Hotel in Dunfermline on 19 August 1977, the group toured non-stop and released three great albums, *Scared To Dance* and *Days in Europa* – both in 1979 – and *The Absolute Game* the next year. The hit singles, 'Into The Valley' and 'Masquerade', brought them nationwide attention when they appeared on *Top of the Pops*. They'd been given coveted support slots with The Clash, Buzzcocks and The Stranglers and somehow also found the time to record four John Peel sessions.

Through in Edinburgh, The Rezillos were also making their mark. In a frenetic twelve-month period, kick-started by the release of 'I Can't Stand My Baby' in 1977 – one of the first Scottish punk singles – the group, fronted by singers Eugene Reynolds and Fay Fife, brought a much-needed splash of colour to the music scene.

They were signed by Seymour Stein, owner of Sire Records, becoming label mates of Talking Heads, The Ramones and the Dead Boys. The band's first album, *Can't Stand The Rezillos* was recorded in the Power Station in New York and produced by Bob

Clearmountain, best known for his later work with Bruce Springsteen, The Rolling Stones, David Bowie and Paul McCartney, and
Tony Bongiovi, cousin of US superstar Jon Bon Jovi.

But after little more than a year in the limelight, they split.
I saw them play an emotional farewell gig at Glasgow Apollo on 23
December 1978. Sire agreed to release Reynolds and Fife from their
contract on the condition they didn't use the name The Rezillos. So
they relaunched – with new band members – and were soon back on
the road again as The Revillos.

Simple Minds were also emerging rapidly. The group, formed by
Kerr and guitarist Charlie Burchill, made their live debut at Satellite
City disco in Glasgow on 17 January 1978. Their landmark debut
album, *Life in a Day*, hit record shops in April 1979, followed by
Real to Real Cacophony later that same year.

Their musical forays into Europe exposed them to new political
and cultural landscapes that inspired Kerr's lyrics on *Empires and
Dance* in 1980.

Meanwhile, in a chaotic flat at 185 West Princes Street in Glasgow's West End, Alan Horne was staging a one-man revolution of
his own. He formed Postcard Records to launch Orange Juice, Josef
K and Aztec Camera under the banner, 'The Sound of Young Scotland'. The slogan was an appropriation of the advertising phrase
Berry Gordy had used at Hitsville U.S.A., the home of Motown
in Detroit, to present his stable of artists like Marvin Gaye, The
Supremes, Stevie Wonder and Smokey Robinson and the Miracles
to a wider world.

It's said Horne also wanted to sign Fire Engines, whose singer
Davy Henderson was a real star in the making. The group's debut
record, 'Get Up And Use Me' was voted Single of the Week by *New
Musical Express* and *Sounds* on release by Codex Communications,
a post-punk label set up by Angus Groovy. But they opted to go
with Bob Last and released two singles – 'Candyskin' and 'Big Gold
Dream' – plus a brilliant debut album, *Lubricate Your Living Room*,
on his Pop Aural label.

A co-headline show by Orange Juice and The Fire Engines – at
The Mayfair in Glasgow in 1980 – has taken on a near mythical

status. Bobby Gillespie of Primal Scream named it as one of his six all-time favourite gigs.

With just twelve inspirational homemade releases – eleven singles and one album, *The Only Fun In Town* by Josef K – Horne changed the face of UK indie pop forever and spawned a new wave of jangly guitar bands.

Records by all of those groups were the backbone of my show. My early playlists also featured albums such as *The Correct Use Of Soap* by Magazine, *Get Happy!!* by Elvis Costello And The Attractions, *Remain In Light* by Talking Heads and *Closer* by Joy Division.

Plus, *Scary Monsters (And Super Creeps)* by David Bowie, *Gentlemen Take Polaroids* by Japan, *Arc of a Diver* by Steve Winwood and *Warm Leatherette* by Grace Jones.

Apart from the occasional single which had burst through into the mainstream, all were artists whose new music seldom – if ever – got played on Radio Clyde.

The station now had a show that was an outlet for other more alternative acts like Siouxsie and the Banshees, The Damned, XTC, Ultravox and Stiff Little Fingers. The list was endless.

One afternoon, a plugger from CBS Records arrived at reception with singer Adam Ant and guitarist Marco Pirroni. They were on a UK radio tour to promote their debut album, *Kings Of The Wild Frontier*. None of the daytime presenters showed any interest in talking to them. But I interviewed both for my show and they were great guests.

A year later, as 'Ant-mania' swept the UK and Europe, the singer with the white stripe painted across his nose was the hottest star in pop. You couldn't get near him. But Adam always found time for me. He has never forgotten that early interview at Radio Clyde, when I helped give them a leg-up . . . when nobody else would. He still keeps in contact to this day.

On another occasion, Tony the Greek – the colourful promo guy for Island Records – lobbied DJs to feature a new Irish band he claimed were the next big thing. Again, there was zero interest. But I'd heard their first album, *Boy* and said I'd be delighted to have them on the show.

Fast forward two weeks – to Strathclyde University on 24 January 1981 – and you'd have found me sitting in a vacant gents toilet talking to Bono of U2. He told me – even then – that they were going to be world-beaters. Every word he said turned out to be true and that encounter led to a fruitful relationship. Bono, The Edge, Adam Clayton and Larry Mullen Jr. have all been my guests on numerous occasions over the years.

I had no grand plan for the show. Every Thursday night, I'd simply arrive at Clyde with a box of records I liked, play them and hope some of the people listening would maybe like them too. It was as straightforward as that. I'd cue up a classic opening track – by maybe David Bowie or The Clash – and fire it right after the midnight news and the greyhound racing results at 12.08 a.m.

I didn't have a script or running order . . . instead the musical thread of the show evolved much more organically. In the first twenty-five minutes, I'd got into such a rhythm the next song almost picked itself. That's how loose it was. I was VERY green so if my presentation technique was far from polished – compared to the other jocks on the station – I used to say: 'You're only one great record away from the next great record.' Music that was edgy, adventurous and innovative was the real currency.

I recently discovered Danny Baker had adopted a similar approach when he began his radio career presenting *Weekend Breakfast* on BBC Radio London in 1989. Talking to David Hepworth and Mark Ellen on their popular *A Word In Your Ear* podcast, he said:

'I'd never listened to radio – I'd never listened to Peel or Kenny Everett or anyone. *Two-Way Family Favourites* was always on in our house . . . otherwise you just played records.

'I thought you just went in with a big box of records and made a show up. And that was pretty much it. It don't work for everyone. I mean, I wish I could be more organised. Someone like Chris Evans had to know exactly what was coming next. Fortunately, I stumbled into that style where if a thought occurs then away you go.'

The reaction to my show from listeners and bands alike was overwhelming. Like other record buyers, I'd relied on music presenters such as John Peel, David Jensen or Johnny Walker to introduce me to cutting-edge new music.

But in Scotland there had never been a home-grown show like it before which put the focus on musical talent from the locale. So for a time, it was a real one-stop-shop for alternative bands.

Then the demos started flooding in.

There were some strict guidelines I was forced to adhere to, the main one being I couldn't play any song that wasn't released officially on disc. I was receiving twenty-five demo tapes a week from new groups tuning in from all over Scotland and beyond. They'd arrive in the mail or guys would physically hand them to me at gigs or in record shops. I was told in no uncertain terms that I was forbidden to play anything from a cassette as the quality wasn't considered good enough.

But most bands couldn't afford to finance the pressing of 1000 singles, particularly as they had no guarantee it would be played on radio and sell in sufficient numbers for them to recoup their cash.

I quietly overlooked that. Every Thursday, I'd arrive at the station and lock myself in a recording booth to dub off songs from cassette onto a cartridge that could be played in the studio. By the time the new song was heard on air, it was probably a fourth or fifth generation copy of the original track. One step up from a bootleg you'd buy in the Barras. But my theory was, if you can hear the singer AND the band, what else do you need to hear?

Most demos were often recorded on new TDK or Sony C60 and C90 cassettes, so at least the actual tape was of good quality. Some groups couldn't even afford to do that though. They would nick greatest-hits compilation cassettes from their parents' collections and stick adhesive tape on the tabs at the top to re-record their songs over the existing album.

Invariably, I'd hear three demo tracks, followed by a bit of 'hiss noise', then re-join the album midway through 'Cracklin' Rosie' by Neil Diamond or 'Bridge Over Troubled Water' by Simon and Garfunkel.

I played demo after demo and didn't receive one single complaint, official or otherwise. Bands loved hearing their songs receive their first bit of radio airplay, irrespective of what the quality sounded like.

One of the earliest demos to stand out was by Unity Express, a new band from Coatbridge formed by brothers Patrick and Gregory Kane. Their song, 'Love Is The Master' was very classy even in that primitive form. The most impressive thing about it was the obvious quality of the voice of lead singer, Patrick, whose lyrics were also a cut above the rest. I played it several times on the show.

Hammering 'Love Is The Master' on air gave them confidence to take things to the next level. They formed Hue and Cry eighteen months later and, with an impressive body of work built around fifteen albums, remain one of Scotland's best-loved bands.

The success of my radio show also got me a DJ gig at Night Moves, formerly The White Elephant disco, in Sauchiehall Street. I hosted alternative music nights with live acts such as Eurythmics – just as 'Sweet Dreams (Are Made Of This)' was cracking the UK singles chart – Orange Juice, Nico, Alex Harvey, Big Country and Aztec Camera.

Eurythmics had a now more familiar face in their ranks . . . a then unknown backing vocalist named Eddi Reader.

I was cornered in the DJ booth by a guy who didn't look like a Night Moves regular. Lloyd Cole was studying philosophy and English at Glasgow University while living with his parents who were club master and mistress of a posh golf course on the outskirts of the city.

'Can I give you my cassette?' said Lloyd in his pronounced Derbyshire accent, 'We're the best new band in Scotland.'

Yet another one.

But he was spot on. I was knocked out by 'The Power Of Love' by his group, The Casuals, crudely recorded as it was. I played it to death on the programme.

The reputation of the show had now gone nationwide. My playlist was monitored by A&R men from several record companies in London, all looking to sign 'the next big thing from Scotland'.

Lloyd began to get calls from a few major labels and turned to his mate, Derek MacKillop, to help him out.

'Well, the Falklands war had just happened and, daft as it sounds, there was talk of conscription,' recalled Derek in the sleeve notes for the *Collected Recordings 1983–1989* box set. 'So I went off on what you'd now call a 'gap year'. I was bumming around in Crete teaching English to bored Greek teenagers when, out of the blue, I got a telex message from Lloyd. Something like, "Billy Sloan's playing it on the radio . . . need manager . . . please come home" sort of thing.'

MacKillop took up the reins and The Casuals soon morphed into The Commotions. I also gave their self-financed single, 'Down At The Mission', on their own Welcome To Las Vegas label, its first spin on the show.

On the strength of the radio reaction, Polydor Records closed in and signed the group in February 1984. Two months later, they made their *Top of the Pops* debut with the single, 'Perfect Skin' that got to No. 26 in the charts. It was the lead track from *Rattlesnakes*, their album released in October, that stayed in the UK Top 100 for twelve months.

A few people had me marked down as some kind of mystical soothsayer who sat each week staring into my crystal ball, predicting which unknown band I would steer to stardom. If only. As previously said, if I liked a song, I'd play it. Hopefully you'd like it too. Job done. That's how basic it was.

I got demos from two brothers, Craig and Charlie Reid, from Auchtermuchty in Fife – with a hand-drawn caricature of the bespectacled twins on the cassette sleeve – and heard The Proclaimers for the first time.

A tape, from a local act called Woza, featured an aspiring songwriter, Ricky Ross, who'd quit his job as a schoolteacher to pursue a career in music. He formed Deacon Blue a short time later.

A few years on, another demo – from Shabby Road Studios in Kilmarnock – really stood out. The first thing that caught my eye was the name written in biro on the spine. I vividly remember thinking, I hope the songs are great because if they're not this is going to be a terrible waste of a BRILLIANT band name.

I played one track, 'Only Tongue Can Tell', repeatedly on the show. The song had a strong melody, inventive guitar playing and oh-so-clever lyrics. They blew me away.

The Trash Can Sinatras were born.

The floodgates had opened. A string of bands including Altered Images, The Cocteau Twins, Del Amitri, The Jesus and Mary Chain, The Cuban Heels, Goodbye Mr Mackenzie, The Scars, Wet Wet Wet, The Waterboys, H20, The Vaselines, The Big Dish, Hipsway and The Blue Nile led the vanguard of the Scottish pop explosion.

There was a period where it seemed that if anyone walked down Buchanan Street carrying a guitar case, some sharp-eyed A&R man would jump out of the shadows – chequebook in hand – and offer them a record deal on the spot.

In the office one day, a colleague and I began to compile a list of Scottish acts who'd released a record either on a self-financed, indie or major label. We passed the fifty mark, and gave up counting. Rock music was now a major Scottish export. Just like whisky and North Sea oil.

Chapter 9
Radio Clyde Welcomes

As YOU WALKED THROUGH the front door into the main foyer, the first thing that caught your eye was a black pegboard on the wall that said: 'Radio Clyde welcomes'. It was a key job of the receptionist every morning to sort through a box of white plastic letters which would spell out names of all the guests visiting the station that day. It was also the first thing that Boy George spotted when he arrived to be a guest on my show.

'When the fuck were they here?' said the singer of Culture Club, making no effort to disguise his disgust at the message on the pegboard that said: 'Radio Clyde welcomes . . . Haysi Fantayzee'.

Culture Club's name was spelled out underneath. The group, who spent three weeks at No.1 with 'Do You Really Want To Hurt Me', were second on the bill, according to eleven carefully spaced-out white plastic letters.

'They're in the studio now,' I replied. 'You're taking part in the same show as them.'

George – who looked resplendent in his tall black hat, dreads, ribbons and colourful flowing robes – went into an immediate confab with group drummer, Jon Moss.

It did not look good.

Unknown to me, there appeared to be some rivalry or bad blood between George and the band – Jeremy Healy, Kate Garner and Paul Caplin – who had cracked the charts with the novelty single, 'John Wayne Is Big Leggy'.

Both acts were my guests on *The Music Week*, a two-hour programme where visiting pop stars would review the latest singles.

The show's main host was Dougie Donnelly but I would frequently deputise if he took a holiday or had TV commitments. He chose the perfect week not to be around.

When I led George and Jon into the studio and introduced them to Haysi Fantayzee, to say the atmosphere was frosty would be an understatement. It was going to be a long night.

The fact that there was no small talk or attempts at friendly chat from either camp between songs was bad enough. But when I opened the mic to hear their views on singles by acts like Spandau Ballet and Duran Duran, things took on an almost illogical turn. If George praised the vocals on a track, Jeremy would be indifferent towards the singer's performance. Or if Kate enthused about another new release, Jon would be lukewarm about it. And so it went on for two painful hours. But I suppose I should be thankful, for at least I managed to elicit an opinion of some kind.

I was thrilled when Nico, the German chanteuse, actress and model – who had been a protégée of Andy Warhol in the 1960s – agreed to appear on the show. She'd taken lead vocals on three songs on *The Velvet Underground & Nico* – 'All Tomorrow's Parties', 'Femme Fatale' and 'I'll Be Your Mirror' – one of the most influential albums of all time. She was visiting UK radio stations promoting her latest album, *Camera Obscura*.

I was a huge fan and dying to meet her. But it was a disaster. The first record to be reviewed was 'Opportunities (Let's Make Lots Of Money)' by the Pet Shop Boys. When I asked for Nico's verdict of the single she said curtly: 'I do not like this song.' It sounded even more damning in her German accent.

When I asked why, her reply was: 'I don't know . . . I just do not like it.' That was her total review.

When we played the next single, her manager – who was fully aware it was a record review show – took me aside and said quietly: 'Please don't ask Nico to comment on somebody else's music.'

It was another long night.

I fared much better when reunited with Billy Mackenzie and Alan Rankine of The Associates. They'd kept in touch since that first awkward encounter in the Clyde canteen. Billy would send me letters about what the group were up to – scrawled in red biro – that looked more like ransom notes. He was rarely lost for words.

I played 'Fantastic Day' by Haircut 100 and asked if they rated the song. Billy's answer was priceless. He said: 'D'you remember when you were a wee laddie and your mother took you to the fairground, and as you were waiting to go on the Ghost Train you heard a record being played on The Waltzer? Well, that's what that record reminds me of.'

His take on 'Eye Of The Tiger' by Survivor – theme of the movie *Rocky III* – was equally as off-the-wall: 'You know that feeling you have when you eat six Cadbury's cream eggs in a row – then you eat a seventh one? That's how I feel having heard that song,' he told me.

Mental . . . but it made for GREAT radio!

I spent twenty-three very successful years at Radio Clyde, hired then fired on three separate occasions. Musically, I was the proverbial square peg in the round hole. This I regarded as a benefit and not a curse.

By focusing on up-and-coming new bands – whose records had little or no chance of being played on daytime shows – I ticked a major box where Clyde's commitment to supporting alternative and local talent was concerned.

I was fortunate to work with some consummate professionals during the station's real 'boom years'. You could not help but be impressed while watching real pros like Dougie Donnelly, Paul Coia, Jim Symon, Tom Ferrie or Jim Waugh sit down with a star guest and expertly tease anecdotes and information out of them. All were happy to share their knowledge and enthusiasm.

In the newsroom, Martin Frizell – now boss of ITV's *This Morning* – Paul Cooney, Bill Turnbull, Jackie Bird, Sheila Duffy and Alex Dickson – were accomplished journalists.

Paul was instrumental in tempting me back to Clyde in 2000 when he was programme boss. I had such a good relationship with him we did the deal on a handshake – no contracts or legal agreements – and I was there for fourteen years, my single longest stint on the station.

Ross King was another colleague. He rose spectacularly through the ranks from Saturday afternoon tea-boy to hosting his own show. Ross 'the Boss' is now one of the UK's most recognisable film and showbiz correspondents reporting each week from his home in Hollywood.

Another major figure at Clyde was Richard Park, who began his career as a pirate DJ on the offshore Radio Scotland in the 1960s to become, at one point, the most influential person in the UK broadcasting industry. He was also infamous for his scathing comments when he appeared as The Headmaster in BBC 1's talent show, *Fame Academy*, relishing being 'the man viewers love to hate'. Parky had a great ear for music and could spot a hit song a mile off. He wasn't scared to take chances too if he believed in a new artist.

In 1987, he spotted early potential in one new local band – formed just a short walk from the station in Clydebank – and pushed their music on air. Wet Wet Wet's drummer Tommy Cunningham remembers bursting with excitement when waiting in the queue at his local chippie and hearing the group's first single, 'Wishing I Was Lucky', being played by Clyde on a radio behind the fryer.

'I wanted to shout out to everyone in the shop . . . "Hey that's our record on the trannie." But I was too scared to open my mouth,' he told me.

And then, of course, there was 'the Tiger'.

James Gerard Dixon McGrory is the biggest legend in the history of Radio Clyde . . . and rightly so. No one else comes close. But it's a name that doesn't quite roll off the tongue, so he changed it to 'Tiger' Tim Stevens.

When the DJ described as a 'veritable nutter from a tough housing scheme in Easterhouse' was awarded an MBE by the Queen in 2006, nobody questioned what it was for . . . most just wondered why it had taken her so long to give it to him.

Tim, who is now seventy-one years old, is a man-child . . . a Peter Pan figure who never grew up. I love him like a brother. His exploits at Clyde are legendary. He had a mischievous party trick of baring his bum at the most inopportune moments.

Years before Jackie Bird became news anchor on *Reporting Scotland* on BBC TV, she learned her trade as rookie reporter Jackie MacPherson – her maiden name – on Clyde. She still comes out in a cold sweat whenever she recalls the day of her first-ever news bulletin: 'About five seconds before the mic went live, I looked round to see Tim's bare bum pressed hard up against the studio window. I'll never forget it. I was stunned. But nobody else in the newsroom was the least bit surprised. He did stuff like that all the time.'

The building directly opposite the DJ's office was the H.Q. for Glasgow's traffic wardens who patrolled the city centre. At lunchtime they'd sit in a rest room having lunch or relaxing between shifts. Tim had a captive audience. He bared his arse and stuck it out of the window in full sight of the wardens. They were so shocked that they submitted a formal complaint and the Tiger was carpeted by Clyde boss Jimmy Gordon and given a written warning.

But he was defiant. His arse didn't stay under wraps for too long. One night on *The Music Week* I had a guest list to die for . . . sitting with me around the studio table were Annie Lennox and Dave Stewart of Eurythmics plus Robert Plant of rock supergroup, Led Zeppelin. Just one of those artistes would have carried the show.

During an interview segment, I spotted something out of the corner of my eye, but was unable to have a proper look in case I went too far off mic. Tim had crawled into On Air 1 – trousers and pants at his ankles – with everything on show. As I was midway through a question, he grabbed my hand and shoved it up the cheeks of his arse. Dave Stewart and Robert Plant couldn't believe what they were seeing whilst Annie Lennox was absolutely horrified. I tried to placate my guests by explaining that this was nothing out of the ordinary and just a normal Thursday night on 'Radio Clyde 261'. They were speechless.

But there was never any malice in his crazy antics. If the 'Tiger' had thought for a minute that Annie was mortally offended he'd have been full of remorse.

I could fill this book with his exploits alone. One of his greatest was during a period spent as tannoy announcer for Celtic FC on matchdays at Parkhead in Glasgow. Before a UEFA cup-tie against crack Swiss side, BSC Young Boys in 1993, Tim announced that there would be a minute's silence before the game got underway.

'Is it for one of the players? Directors? A legendary club figure?' asked one puzzled fan.

There was no time to speculate as Tim went on to declare the silence was 'in memory of Rangers' European Cup campaign which was declared dead earlier today in Bulgaria'.

Celtic's main rivals had gone down to Levski Sofia 4-4 on aggregate – losing on the away goals rule.

'He got us hook, line and sinker. No one had seen it coming,' said the punter.

But the club took a dim view and didn't share in the joke. Tim was fired on the spot. He didn't even make it to half-time.

The main record companies – including A&M, CBS, EMI, Phonogram, Polydor, RCA, United Artists, Virgin and Warner Brothers – had offices or local reps in Glasgow and Edinburgh. Independent Local Radio stations like Clyde or Radio Forth in the capital were big targets. They all had a seemingly unlimited budget to promote their acts.

I welcomed Kate Bush to the station when she released *The Dreaming* in 1982. Interviewing the musical genius – and I do not use that term loosely – who'd exploded on to the scene four years previously with the No.1 single, 'Wuthering Heights', was a rare treat. I'd been fortunate to see her perform at the Usher Hall in Edinburgh on the 'Tour of Life' in 1979.

Before the gig, she met the media at a press conference in the Caledonian Hotel and posed for photographs outside – with Edinburgh Castle over her shoulder – stopping the traffic on Lothian Road. It was one of just twenty-four shows across the UK in what was her first – and only – concert tour.

Kate and I had a wide-ranging chat about all aspects of her career. She was fascinating and engrossing company but she saw her role as a musician as clearly defined.

'I don't know if I see myself as a pop star really. I can't relate to any of those labels at all,' Kate told me. 'I seem to just work and when I'm not trying to be the salesman I'm focusing on the creative side. I'm not on the promotional trail very often.

'When an album takes me a year or a show takes four to five months to prepare for, I'm operating on a very long timescale. But it's the only way I can do it to make sure it's right.'

It was when I pushed Kate to speculate on when we'd see her back on stage again that proved most prophetic. She said:

'Do I miss playing live? I do a bit, yeah. But I don't have a terrible craving for it. Maybe you'll see me sometime next year. But if the show is anywhere near as involved as the album, I'll probably be around eighty years old by the time I go back on the road.'

Her estimate was a little wide of the mark. Kate didn't perform in concert again until Before The Dawn, a twenty-two-night residency at Hammersmith Apollo in London in 2014 . . . her first live gigs following a thirty-five-year absence. All 100,000 tickets sold out in just fifteen minutes, but I was lucky enough to get one for the final show on 1 October. So, if Kate never plays again, I was there to witness her last-ever live performance.

As we said our goodbyes, she thanked me for my interest saying she'd enjoyed our chat and that it was her favourite interview of the entire radio tour. Knowing how committed she is about her music I don't think it's the kind of compliment she'd extend unless it was heartfelt. I was knocked out. Facing Kate Bush across a microphone was a career highlight.

There were a few occasions when guests got me into real hot water, however. In 1983, Malcolm McLaren joined me to promote his debut album, *Duck Rock*.

The self-styled Svengali figure behind The Sex Pistols was one of the most flamboyant and colourful stars on the music scene . . . and he never shut up. Not once. I struggled to get a single word in.

Malcolm arrived wearing a Buffalo Gals style hat designed by his partner, Vivienne Westwood, playing tracks from his album on a giant beat-box, with huge bullhorns attached, and sprayed with graffiti. During our interview, Malcolm said the word 'fucking' a couple of times . . . but not in a malicious way. He got a little over enthusiastic and the cuss words accidentally slipped out.

Normally, Clyde operated a six-second delay system that meant any inappropriate language or content could be dumped at the push of a button. But for some reason, it wasn't in operation that night. I got carpeted first thing the next morning and read the riot act.

Even worse was when singer Edwyn Collins of Orange Juice and Alan Horne, boss of Postcard Records, dropped in to talk about how they'd turned the UK indie music scene upside down. They sat and giggled their way through the interview, batting off any attempts to get them to give serious answers to my questions. They were childish and condescending, dismissing the merits of every band I chose to mention apart from The Velvet Underground who they described as the missing link between Hank Williams, The New York Dolls and Labi Siffre.

Even so, it was a bit of a coup to have them on the show.

'Orange Juice are a secret group. We've always been absent from the Glasgow scene,' revealed Edwyn, as Horne giggled in the background. 'We like to keep ourselves to ourselves and only ever speak to elves and a few gnomes.'

When I asked how he presented his songs to the other members of the group, guitarist James Kirk, bass player David McClymont and drummer Stephen Daly, he said: 'Could you ask me another question please?'

I didn't fare much better when I inquired what his process was for coming up with new material.

'I'm by no means prolific. Yesterday, for example, I was out pottering in the garden – I was growing these new dahlias my mum bought me – and this wonderful new song came to me,' he said. 'It was quite strange. It just came all of a sudden. What was it again? *I love Billy . . . Billy, Billy Sloan*'.

'We were also rehearsing new songs down The Hellfire Club today. One sounded like "You Better You Better You Bet" (by The Who) . . . and I'm afraid once again Stephen vomited over his new drum kit. I managed to remain upright.'

Things got worse when I brought Horne into the conversation asking why he'd scrapped an album by Josef K.

'Sometimes I like songs and sometimes I don't. And it's really all up to my whim. And when I have a whim . . . I have a whim,' he told me. 'I have some good songwriting and some bad songwriting on my label. Bad songwriting is mainly by Edinburgh groups. They don't really have the suss to write songs. It's because of the east-coast accent, I think.'

Robert Hodgens of The Bluebells later complimented me for somehow managing to keep the ship afloat, saying: 'I thought you

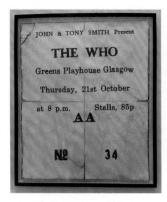

JOHN & TONY SMITH Present

THE WHO

Greens Playhouse Glasgow

Thursday, 21st October

at 8 p.m.   Stalls, 85p

A A

N⁰   34

A ticket from my first ever pop concert . . . the gig that kick-started an incredible musical adventure.

I meet my hero, Pete Townshend, at the Albany Hotel in Glasgow in 1971.

Face to face with Roger Daltrey in The Who's management office in London.

Backstage at Barrowland with The Bay City Rollers after they inducted me into the venue's Hall of Fame in 2015.

I give Hugh Cornwell and Jet Black of The Stranglers a guided tour
of the famous Paddy's Market in Glasgow.

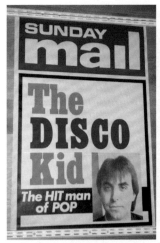

The Disco Kid unmasked
. . . here comes 'The HIT
man of POP'.

The much missed Alan Rankine and Billy
Mackenzie of The Associates guest on my
Radio Clyde show.

I'm a late arrival for the Kate Bush photocall before her 'Tour Of Life' gig at the Usher Hall in Edinburgh in 1979.

We meet again . . . when Kate drops in to Radio Clyde three years later to record an interview to promote her album, *The Dreaming*.

Brian Wilson . . . a man of few words. But it was still a huge thrill to meet the genius behind The Beach Boys.

This poster was outside newsagents' shops from John o' Groats to the Scottish Borders.

Above: Never mind the bans ... The Sex Pistols DID play. A rare ticket for their Xmas Day gig at Ivanhoe's in Huddersfield in 1977.

Right: A punk icon at the peak of his powers. Hanging out with Johnny Rotten before the show.

Alice Cooper gets me in a stranglehold. The King of Shock Rock has become a regular on my radio show.

Tea and cookies with the legendary Liza Minnelli at the Savoy in London.

My earliest encounter with Liam Gallagher and Bonehead of Oasis in Ayr in 1995.

On the tour bus with Noel Gallagher at the Fillmore State Theatre, Detroit in 2000.

Let me entertain you . . . Robbie Williams shares his pre-gig secrets as we head for the Main Stage at T in the Park.

Under the moonlight . . . the serious moonlight. I interview David Bowie
before his show at Murrayfield Stadium in 1983.

I'm given a sneak preview of
Bowie's 'Earthling' tour during
rehearsals at Brixton Academy
in London.

Bowie's final show in Scotland
was at the SECC in 2003. Ill
health forced him to cancel
an appearance at T in the Park
the following summer.

Man-on-the-run. Me and my dear friend Jimmy Kerr get the lowdown on the Great Train Robbery from fugitive Ronnie Biggs.

Don't you forget about me. I can only hope music fans are not still traumatised by my guest appearance with Simple Minds in Brazil.

I've interviewed Jim Kerr more than any other rock star. He always draws a huge global audience.

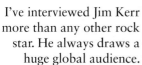

Brazil 3–2 Scotland (after extra time). The crack Simple Minds FC did the nation proud in the searing heat of Rio.

Bathtime with Grace Jones. This must count as THE most off-the-wall interview of my entire career.

I get close to 'The Killer'. With Jerry Lee Lewis – one of the founding fathers of rock 'n' roll – at the Clyde Auditorium.

Spinal Tap look less than impressed by my attempts to fill their drum stool. But at least I lived to tell the tale.

I hung around for six and a half hours to interview Bruce Springsteen … and 'The Boss' was well worth the wait.

One of my biggest scoops was when I revealed that The Proclaimers were a 'fraud'.

did really well holding it all together . . . we all did. I don't think Edwyn and Alan came across as well as they thought they did. If you had been at all annoyed – and reacted in that way – I think it could have been another Sex Pistols-Bill Grundy moment.

'But you didn't take offence. It wasn't aimed at you, that's just the way they were. You'd hear them talk like that every day in the Postcard Records flat.'

I got hauled in again and told – in no uncertain terms – that even if Orange Juice were No.1 in the UK and US charts simultaneously, they were never to darken Clyde's doorstep ever again.

I can't remember Horne ever having occasion to return, but after the dust settled, I managed to slip Edwyn back in under the radar.

You could always rely on him for a razor-sharp one-liner.

He told me:

'We were just merry pranksters and mischief makers. Without Postcard I don't think there would have been a Prince, possibly not a Bruce Springsteen and certainly not a U2.'

And what of Horne?

'He cloned himself and formed a group called The Proclaimers.'

Chapter 10
Scotland's No. 1
Pop Writer

THE INTERVIEW COULDN'T HAVE gone much better. But then Bernard Vickers dropped a depth charge.

'I want you to meet J.B.' he said, as he led me along the corridor to the office of one of his key executives. John Burrowes was the fearsome boss of the features desk at the *Daily Record* who had a reputation for chewing people up and spitting them back out again. I knew if I got the job that I'd have to cross paths with him, but this was all a little bit sudden.

'So you're Mr Rock 'n' Roll?' he said, peering at me suspiciously over the top of his glasses. 'It's Monday morning. If I told you to get an exclusive interview with Rod Stewart by tomorrow afternoon – words, pictures, the lot – could you pull it off?'

There was only one answer to such a question.

'Make it Wednesday . . . and you've got a deal,' I volleyed back.

I'd applied for a job as a features writer on Scotland's most influential national paper more in hope than expectation. After three years of successfully fronting the pop column in the *Sunday Mail* I was looking for something more secure. I didn't think I had a chance of being hired. The competition for such a coveted position was fierce.

I borrowed an ill-fitting suit from a mate to wear to the interview and arrived at the office of Vickers, editor of the *Record*, full of trepidation.

Bernie – a proud Mancunian – was an old-school journalist respected throughout the UK newspaper industry. He was dynamic, had a great personality and always backed his troops to the hilt . . . a rare quality, sadly not prevalent in a few of the editors I'd subsequently work for.

I thought I'd made an impression but still wasn't optimistic that I'd get the job. As the first of fifteen applicants, I felt sure he'd have forgotten all about me by the time he'd worked his way through the list to the final interview. But I got a boost from an unlikely source.

In recent months, the main tabloid newspapers in Fleet Street had woken up to the fact that pop music helped sell papers. In May 1982, *The Sun* launched 'Bizarre', a daily pop and showbiz column edited by John Blake. It was an instant success, carrying backstage gossip from the hottest gigs and trendiest parties. Blake was courted by all the top publicists and record companies eager to get coverage for their artistes.

The column is still going strong more than forty-one years on. Its past editors include Piers Morgan and Andy Coulson, the former Director of Communications for Prime Minister, David Cameron, who was imprisoned for his part in the *News of the World* phone-hacking scandal in 2014.

Soon Fleet Street would be choc-full of high-profile pop columnists including Rick Sky in the *Mirror*, Baz Bamigboye in the *Mail*, Geoff Baker in the *Star*, Lesley Ann Jones in the *Mail on Sunday* and the evergreen David Wigg in the *Express*. All the major papers ramped up their music coverage and, unwittingly, that was good news for me.

It was Bernie's original intention to recruit an all-purpose writer, but he changed his mind. His decision to appoint a journalist specifically to cover stories about 'guys with long hair who play the guitar' – for the first time in the *Record*'s history – raised a few eyebrows on the editorial floor. The paper had specialist writers for politics, football, boxing, education, health, motoring, television, industry and fashion. However, my field of expertise appeared to be exempt from inclusion.

When I took up my seat on the features desk on 14 February 1983 – St Valentine's Day – there wasn't too much love from some quarters. My appointment was viewed with suspicion by hard-nosed veteran reporters on the news desk and back bench. Even so, it felt like I had just signed for Real Madrid. I knew I had the ability to prove my worth and couldn't wait to get started.

The bustling office looked like the one in the movie, *All The President's Men*. It was a very intimidating environment. There was another similarity to the 1976 film that starred Robert Redford as Bob Woodward and Dustin Hoffman as Carl Bernstein,the *Washington Post* reporters whose investigation into the Watergate scandal led to the resignation of US President, Richard Nixon.

I sat adjacent to Stan Shivas, the Chief Features Writer. Big Stan oozed class. He looked like he'd just stepped off a movie set himself. He was widely regarded as one of the most accomplished writers of his generation who could weave his magic through any story. Stan cherry-picked his assignments and when he conducted an interview with a celebrity or political figure, didn't take notes or tape the conversation. Instead, the minute the interview ended, he would find a cafe nearby, order a cup of tea and scribble down all the key moments from the chat.

I'd see him sitting at his desk surrounded by scraps of paper, used matchbooks and airline boarding passes . . . with names, dates and titbits of information scrawled on them. It was identical to the scene in the Oscar-winning movie where Bernstein talked his way into the home of the bookkeeper who worked for Nixon. How he was able to recall screeds of quotes – and reproduce them with one hundred per cent accuracy – was nothing short of miraculous. When you read the finished article, Stan's words leapt off the page. He had a wonderful gift for painting colourful pictures no matter how mundane the subject matter.

All around me were some of the best journalists in the country including John Fairgrieve, Tom Brown, David Wastell, Jimmy Laing and Colin Dunne. On the sports desk, Alex 'Candid' Cameron, was the doyen of Scotland's football writers. With talent of such a high calibre it was a great environment in which to learn . . . and learn fast.

Bernie had admired my previous work for our sister paper, the *Sunday Mail*, so he expected me to really hit the ground running. On the *Mail*, I'd have a week to build up to a story. But with six editions of the *Record* the pace was relentless. I had to quickly adapt to producing music features at speed, often working on several simultaneously. It was the journalistic equivalent of perpetually spinning plates.

I was only as good as my last story.

John Burrowes ran a tight ship on the desk. I soon discovered that his brittle demeanour was all a front. He could spot a fake a mile off, but if you were prepared to put in a shift you had his respect. He was a good operator. He'd go on to write several best-selling books including *Benny*, the definitive biography of Scottish world champion boxer, Benny Lynch.

In my first few weeks in my new post, I interviewed Spandau Ballet, Annie Lennox, Ian Dury and Orange Juice and each article got a big projection in the paper.

Then came my first major press conference. I was dispatched to Claridge's, the luxury five-star hotel in London's Mayfair, to report on an important announcement by David Bowie. The superstar was launching his latest album *Let's Dance* and also revealing plans for the 'Serious Moonlight' Tour, his first live concert dates in five years.

The event was a real eye-opener. It was my earliest encounter with the hard-nosed press pack in London who behaved like rabid hyenas. It was every man, or woman, for themselves as they jostled to get pole position in the ornate banqueting suite where Bowie would face the media. I was taken aback by the ferocity of their actions.

Bowie had arrived in the UK following an arduous flight from Australia – bleached-blond hair, tan, smart suit – and looked a million dollars. Which was fitting, really, after reports he'd recently split from RCA and signed a new deal with EMI Records said to be worth £17 million.

Bowie announced concerts in London, Birmingham, Frankfurt, Berlin, Lyon and Fréjus as part of a massive world tour and then said to the scrum of reporters and photographers:

'Would anybody like to know anything?'

I managed to get the first question in when I asked him: 'Why are you not playing in Scotland?'

Bowie replied: 'It's something like a ninety-city tour so we're doing as much as we can in every country where there seems to be an audience for what I do.'

But I'd had a whisper there were plans to add more shows including one north of the border, which would be a huge story for us.

Initially, the singer's intention was to play 15,000-seater indoor arenas to showcase the songs on *Let's Dance*. Over the next few months, when the album proved to be his biggest commercial success, he was forced to switch to massive stadium venues to satisfy the demand for tickets. This was something he had not anticipated. In fact, he dismissed suggestions his increasing popularity would necessitate moving the tour up a gear.

Bowie said: 'I'd imagine the majority of most of my stuff would be indoors. I'm not much of a festival person. I'm not comfortable with it.'

It turned out to be one of those very rare occasions when Bowie called it wrong.

I was now on-deadline. I found a quiet corner table in Claridge's and began writing my story longhand in a notepad. Laptop computers were still a long way off.

And so were mobiles. I made a reverse-charge call on a payphone to the *Record*'s team of copytakers and dictated my story down the line to make the edition. This was another first.

My question must have triggered something because a Scottish date was hastily slotted into his tour itinerary. It was later confirmed that he would appear at Murrayfield Stadium in Edinburgh on 28 June.

The next time I got to ask Bowie a question was when I interviewed him backstage at the home of Scottish rugby just thirty minutes before he faced a 60,000-capacity crowd.

The copytakers could always be relied on to keep your feet firmly on the ground. I'd be midway through dictating what I regarded as a 1,200-word masterpiece, when Iain Barclay at the other end of the line would sigh in exasperation and ask: 'Is there much more of this?'

He was the classic wind-up merchant.

His partner-in-crime was Tommy McGee, who became the official biographer of Betty Grable, writing a successful book about the Hollywood queen called *The Girl with the Million Dollar Legs*.

He'd interrupt me when I was in full flow and say: 'This is pure rubbish. I'm nearly falling asleep. Nobody is going to want to read this stuff.'

But I didn't take it personally. They did it with all the writers, just to keep them on their toes.

Bernie was incredibly supportive and insisted that I had to be visible as the face of the paper's music coverage. And to show his faith in me, I was billed as . . . Scotland's No.1 Pop Writer. So no pressure then.

If I interviewed an artiste of the stature of Paul McCartney, Mick Jagger or Bruce Springsteen I'd get a picture taken with them . . . what in modern parlance you'd now term a 'selfie'.

There were two very good reasons for this.

Bernie was keen to show that while it was virtually impossible to break through the protective security cordon of publicists, managers and minders who surrounded every major act . . . the *Record* had direct access to the stars. You'd be amazed just how many so-called 'exclusive interviews' are cobbled together from press releases and spurious quotes planted by PR guys. Even more so today with so much information – or should it be misinformation – freely available on the Internet.

There were selfish reasons for doing it too. As a music fan I felt it was too good a chance to pass up. I make no bones about it. You might only get one opportunity to sit in a room with McCartney and talk to him about his life and career. You'd be insane not to have some kind of lasting record of it.

I was lucky . . . to date I've interviewed McCartney on four occasions and each time I asked for a quick snap. He was only too happy to oblige.

I also took my albums along and got them signed. Few of the London hacks would dream of doing such a thing. They were too cool for school and always thought they were much bigger stars than the stars they were interviewing.

I later shared an office with the TV editor who, when we had one of our frequent arguments, would say: 'Your fucking problem is that you're nothing but a fan with a typewriter.' It was meant as a venomous put-down. But I took it as the ultimate compliment.

For the next eleven years, writing about music for the *Record* would dominate my life.

I reported on some of the greatest gigs in rock history including Live Aid in 1985, Wham! – The Final in 1986, the Nelson Mandela 70th Birthday show in 1988 and the Freddie Mercury Tribute in 1992.

I travelled the word, got wined and dined by record companies and was given shelves full of free albums. At the end of each month, a few quid – my salary – was transferred into my bank account. Is it any wonder I loved my job? Well, I say job, but it seldom seemed like work. I was being paid for pursuing my hobby. Who came up with that one?

I got to meet many of my heroes, getting up close and personal with some of the most famous names in music.

And, I'd also cross swords with a few of them too.

SIDE 2
HEROES AND VILLAINS

Chapter 11
I Don't Want to Talk About It

THE WORD 'INTERVIEW' IS listed at the bottom of page 381 in the *Oxford English Dictionary*. The definition reads: 'An occasion when a journalist or broadcaster puts questions to a person'.

If only it were that simple.

Just to get to a point where you sit opposite an artiste and politely strike up a conversation can be fraught with danger. In this modern era, most cynical publicists want maximum coverage for minimum effort. You only get access to the stars on their terms and setting up a one-on-one meeting with a major celebrity often requires having to successfully plot a path through a minefield. But I'm fortunate in having a little black book of valued contacts. I have earned their trust. They know I shoot from the hip.

I wish I'd kept a tally of the interviews I've done over the years. They must number well over 1,000. There hasn't been a sustained period since the late 1970s when I've not pointed my tape machine at somebody or other.

My most memorable? The list would have to include Paul McCartney, Mick Jagger, David Bowie, Bruce Springsteen and Bono.

When you've chased a star of that stature to organise an interview – and things have gone well – it can give you an adrenalin rush that lasts for weeks. But what about when it all goes wrong? Where do I start?

I've had my fair share of calamitous chats where nothing has gone to plan. And the bigger the disaster, the more people want to know the names of the stars who gave me a hard time.

Taxi drivers in particular appear to have a real sadistic appetite for hearing all the gory details. I've lost count of the number of cabbies who've glanced at me in their rear-view mirror and said: 'Who was your worst-ever interview?'

Step forward Chuck Berry. I'd secured a rare interview with the American singer and guitarist while he was in Scotland to perform at The Magnum in Irvine in 1983. As one of the founding fathers of rock and roll, his classic songs including 'Johnny B. Goode', 'Sweet Little Sixteen' and 'Roll Over Beethoven' were a direct influence on The Beatles, Jimi Hendrix, Buddy Holly, The Beach Boys and just about anybody who's ever picked up a guitar. In 1961, The Rolling Stones launched their career with the single, 'Come On', a cover of his song. It was the band's first chart hit. So, to get the opportunity to talk to such a legendary music figure was a real exclusive for the *Daily Record*.

Chuck refuses to do a soundcheck so there was no reason for him to get to The Magnum early. The interview was arranged by his promotional team – who could not have been more cooperative – for 5.30 p.m. at the Excelsior Hotel at Glasgow Airport. And that gave me a real problem.

Before leaving the office, *Record* editor, Bernie Vickers briefed me: 'The King of Rock and Roll is back in Scotland. We're going big on this one. I want a great colour picture for page one to tee up your exclusive interview inside,' he said.

He was holding the front page for Chuck Berry. But with a 5.30 p.m. start we were up against the clock to make the first edition. Back then – long before the convenience of digital photography – snappers had to get their film to the office so it could be processed in the darkroom. And that took time.

To help speed things up, my photographer hired a motorbike dispatch rider. We hoped to quickly snap a couple of shots of Chuck, then hand the film over to the courier so he could head straight back and beat the rush-hour traffic. Well, that was the plan.

When we arrived at the Excelsior, I caught sight of Chuck disappearing into a lift to go up to his room. His tour manager was still checking in at reception so I introduced myself. He claimed to have no knowledge of any interview being on the itinerary. I showed him a fax confirming our chat.

'Chuck has gone upstairs for a nap. He likes to rest before a show. I don't know if we're going to be able to do this,' he said.

We sat in the hotel lounge and waited and waited for the next half hour. The tour manager reappeared and said: 'Chuck will be down in a minute. But you're gonna have to be quick. We're leaving for the gig.'

Another fifteen minutes passed before Chuck finally arrived. He was immaculate. His oiled black hair was slicked back into a D.A. He wore a shirt with pearl buttons and fastened with a bootlace tie held in place by a beautiful silver ornamental clasp. An embroidered waistcoat, faded vintage blue jeans and a pair of Cuban-heeled boots completed the look. But Chuck didn't want to talk to us. It was painfully obvious.

Our intention was to get the pictures done before I started the interview. Chuck took one look at my colleague who was surrounded by his camera gear and said brusquely: 'Who's he?' When I introduced my photographer, the singer got irritated and shouted: 'No photographs . . . I'm not dressed yet.'

My heart sank. I could see the motorcycle courier at the front door pointing to his watch as if I had not realised time was now against us. This was a fucking disaster.

'But Mr Berry, you look incredible,' I said, not patronising him in any way. It was true. He looked exactly like the guy you see duck-walking across the stage playing a guitar solo.

'No, you don't understand me,' said Chuck, pointing a finger to his head, 'I'm not dressed up here yet.'

My snapper walked off hoping that if he left us alone for a few moments his mood might thaw a little. I switched on my tape machine. I knew I had to steam in. There was no time for any pleasantries. I asked Chuck how it felt to be back in Scotland again.

'I don't know yet . . . I've just got here,' he said.

That was probably his most expansive answer.

For the next ten minutes he was monosyllabic, sullen and obstructive. I don't mind admitting it . . . I was floundering. I'd pitch a question, only to get a non-answer back. If he replied at all, that is. It was painful.

As part of my research, I'd read that he visited local children's homes teaching underprivileged kids how to play guitar and talking to them about his music. Chuck had got on the wrong side of the law on a few occasions, so working with the youngsters was part of a court order for him to help give something back to the community. I was very careful NOT to mention his well-publicised police rap sheet so I didn't antagonise him further. He'd been quoted as saying how much he enjoyed interacting with the kids.

It was my last roll of the dice to try to get anything out of him and a golden opportunity to blow his own trumpet about doing something good and worthwhile.

'How do you find teaching children? Is it very therapeutic,' I asked him.

He looked at me coldly and replied: 'I don't need therapy. Music is my therapy.'

I threw in the towel. Match abandoned. I'd so wanted to meet this giant of music . . . one of the true originators whose unique craft influenced and inspired so many of my heroes. It was a complete waste of time. The worst interview of my career.

Then, I let myself down. It was a rare moment when being a fan completely clouded my judgement. I had a glossy 10x8 publicity photograph and asked him to sign it for me. It was the classic Chuck Berry shot . . . legs splayed, wielding his guitar.

He grudgingly scrawled his name across it, dropped the pen into my lap and walked off. I realised I'd made a huge error of judgement. I'd been polite and most respectful towards him, but this horrible man had treated me like shit – for no reason – only for me to indulge him by asking for his autograph. I called it wrong and instantly regretted it. All these years on I could kick myself.

The picture is still in my filing cabinet. It's long been my intention to profit from him. The going rate for a signed print of Chuck Berry on Ebay is around £200. But I can't even be bothered to fish it out of the drawer, let alone list it for sale.

When we got back to the office, Bernie was still holding the front page. 'What have you got?' he asked.

'Absolutely nothing,' I told him. When I relayed the whole sorry saga he instructed me to write it up exactly as it had happened. It made the edition and we used a stock file pic of Chuck to illustrate the story.

A few days later I received a stinker of a letter from a member of a Chuck Berry appreciation society slaughtering me for not treating the King of Rock and Roll with more respect. He didn't mince his words. I got both barrels.

I fired off a lengthy reply detailing what had taken place and he wrote back again saying: 'Fair play . . . I know he can sometimes be very difficult.'

But I didn't take it personally. Chuck had a reputation for being a handful, and that's putting it mildly. Frank Lynch, boss of the Glasgow Apollo, once told me he'd been made to jump through hoops before the singer appeared at the venue in 1975.

'With Chuck you're talking about a real living legend. But fifteen minutes before showtime he announced: 'I'm not going on unless I get my £25,000 fee,' recalled Frank.

'I pleaded with him but he refused to take a cheque. He wanted cash. I got my team to run around our other venues – The Muscular Arms, Maestro's, The White Elephant and The Savoy – and grab that night's takings. Only when I handed Chuck a bag with twenty-five grand did he agree to go on.'

I have a tried and tested system I use before every interview. It's called . . . doing your homework. I read up on my subject carefully making notes of names, dates, times and points of interest. You don't want to be midway through an interview, particularly if the going gets tough, and throw a quote at an artiste only for them to claim: 'I never said that.' If you've got the source marked in your notes, you can at least mount a credible challenge.

Going into an interview being ill prepared is not just unprofessional, but also disrespectful towards the star you're about to talk to. Doesn't everyone do this? You'd be surprised.

I was part of a group of radio DJs who travelled to London to interview Jeff Lynne when ELO released their album, *Alone in the Universe* in 2015. As I was having a final read through my notes, a fellow DJ asked what I was doing. When I told him he said: 'What do you need notes for? I never bother.'

It showed. His opening question was when he asked Jeff if the lead single, 'When I Was A Boy', was a copy of a song by Julian Lennon. For a start, you'd never accuse an artiste of ripping off another, certainly not first off. And if you did, you'd maybe phrase it a bit more delicately. The ELO frontman replied that he'd never actually heard the song he was supposed to have copied. But the guy persisted. Jeff then just switched off and the interview hit the buffers, never to recover.

When it was my turn, Jeff quickly realised that I was au fait with his band's music and responded accordingly. I got a great interview where he talked about the history of the group, known originally as the Electric Light Orchestra, and how he formed The Traveling Wilburys with George Harrison, Bob Dylan, Roy Orbison and Tom Petty.

But, inevitably, there are times when you hit a bump in the road. When I met Damon Albarn of Blur, he seemed disinterested and didn't give anything away. At the end of the year – when I was putting together my 'best of' compilation – I wanted to include him. But I couldn't find a ten-second clip where he said anything worth repeating.

It was a similar story with Mick Hucknall of Simply Red who appeared full of his own self-importance. Not an enjoyable experience.

MC Hammer was another nightmare. He wouldn't sit still and danced up and down in his dressing room looking at himself in the mirror. He was more interested in the cut of his outsize 'parachute pants' than any of my questions.

All three interviews took place backstage at Wembley Arena in London. Maybe the venue is jinxed.

There were times when, despite all my best efforts, the odds were stacked against me. I was invited to London to interview Mariah Carey who was promoting a new album I've long since forgotten.

Her music is not really to my taste but the US diva won't lose any sleep over that. Mariah is one of the biggest music stars in the world, as her 220 million record sales will attest.

She is also now as much a part of the festive season as Rudolph the Red-Nosed Reindeer, thanks to her 1994 hit, 'All I Want For Christmas Is You'. In a poll of UK music fans, it was voted the most annoying Christmas song ever. But as it's gone twelve times platinum, chances are she won't lose any sleep over that either.

Mariah is beautiful, colourful and just about as famous as any living person can be. So an interview with her will fly into the paper . . . if I'm lucky enough to actually get one, that is.

When I'm escorted into her plush hotel suite, it's chaos. Mariah has a huge entourage and there are so many people fussing around her I can hardly get inside the room. She has somebody fixing her hair. Another applying her make-up.

'Juice . . . juice,' she says, and in a flash an aide appears at her side and holds a glass as she sips a drink through a straw.

I take a seat in the chair opposite Mariah but there is no small talk between us. She is too preoccupied giving orders to her promotional team. For all she knows, I could be the bloke who's come to empty the bins. I walk over to place my bag on a table so it doesn't get in the way during our chat, but return to discover my chair has been moved a further 10ft away from Ms Carey. As eye contact is always advantageous, I pull it back to the original position.

I nip over to my bag to retrieve my tape machine only to find her aides have pushed the chair back again. I'm now about 20ft away from Mariah. I don't know what they feared I was going to do. Bite her, perhaps. This was social distancing Mariah Carey-style more than two decades before COVID.

The interview was a real non-event. It's impossible to establish any kind of rapport with an artiste – not to mention very distracting – when you're surrounded by people whispering messages to each other or checking emails on their laptops.

It's very intimidating, too, knowing that if you were to ask something a little more probing, her publicist was poised to intervene and move the chat on to less challenging territory.

Mariah is a real pro. She has perfected the skill of talking a lot without actually revealing very much about herself. I'd maybe have got more out of her had I used semaphore signals to direct my questions.

In the aftermath of any interview your first thought is always . . . what's the top line? The eye-catching bit of previously undisclosed information you can build your article around. I racked my brain. There was none. Maria was nice and polite but she didn't say anything that would stop you in your tracks.

It's moments like this when the disposable nature of newspaper stories can work to your advantage. I found an Internet cafe nearby, hammered out my copy and it made the edition. Job done. I could move on and concentrate on my next assignment.

The US music scene would appear to have a non-stop assembly line in divas. I interviewed Natalie Cole, daughter of the late Nat King Cole, the legendary jazz singer and actor. We got together to promote her album, *Everlasting*, which included a great cover of Bruce Springsteen's song, 'Pink Cadillac', a Top 5 hit in the Billboard Hot 100. Before a question had left my lips I was taken to one side and forcibly told that if I mentioned her famous father – who died in 1965 when she was aged fifteen – the interview would be terminated.

He was off limits.

Four years later, I interviewed her again to promote *Unforgettable . . . With Love*, an album of her interpretations of a collection of Nat King Cole standards. This time, I was informed that if I questioned her about anything other than her father's classic catalogue of songs she'd leave the room immediately.

But it was the opposite with the wonderful Liza Minnelli. I met her at The Savoy Hotel in London in 1989 when she was promoting *Results* . . . a fabulous album produced by the Pet Shop Boys. Being granted an audience with the daughter of Hollywood screen icon Judy Garland was a real treat.

I was up against it though. Liza was doing a day of back-to-back interviews with the UK media and I was the final name on a list of twelve journalists. It was the worst slot imaginable, for after such a packed schedule, the danger was that Liza would be 'interviewed out' by the time I got to her. She'd have talked about her new record for hours on end and fatigue would inevitably have set in.

I had a trick up my sleeve. As we were introduced, I handed Liza a box from Harrods, tied with a pretty red ribbon, and said:

'I'm Scottish and we never go to visit somebody empty-handed. So I've bought you some cookies. You can choose any one you like except the oatmeal and raisin . . . that's mine. Put the kettle on and we'll have a cup of tea.'

Liza shrieked with delight and the interview was off and running. She was a real live wire and fascinating company . . . loud, outrageous and full of fun. When Liza recalled house parties with her favourite uncles Frank, Dean and Sammy, she was of course talking about the Rat Pack. Her mum Judy and film director father, Vincent Minnelli, allowed her to stay up late to entertain friends such as Humphrey Bogart and Lauren Bacall, Elizabeth Taylor, James Stewart, Ava Gardner and Tony Curtis. It was like coming face-to-face with an endangered species . . . one of the last true stars of that immortal glittering Hollywood era which stretched back decades.

I'd been warned off talking about her late mother who died in London in 1969 – after a troubled period in her life and career – aged just forty-seven. Frank Sinatra helped towards the cost of the funeral after her body was returned to New York, and more than 20,000 fans lined up to pay their respects. But you can always judge if it's wise to take the plunge during an interview. Liza and I were getting on so well, I decided to go for it.

She spoke from the heart about her mother's career both as an actress and singer. 'I had a very happy childhood. Growing up surrounded by all those Hollywood stars was wonderful. But I didn't see them as stars . . . they were just friends of my parents,' she told me. 'I think my mother would have been proud of my work and achievements. She always encouraged me.'

I interviewed Liza again in 2008 to preview her sell-out concert at the Clyde Auditorium. She invited me, my parents and two friends backstage after the show. Liza made a real fuss of my late mother who couldn't believe she was hugging Judy Garland's daughter and the Oscar winning star of the movie, *Cabaret*. The look on my old ma's face as Liza posed for a picture was a treasured moment.

I employed a similar tactic before travelling to New Orleans to talk to Celine Dion. During my preparations for our chat, I sourced a film clip where the Canadian superstar talked warmly about a previous trip to Scotland. She revealed she'd become addicted to the homemade butter cookies placed in her hotel suite. I did a bit of detective work and discovered she'd stayed at One Devonshire Gardens, a five-star boutique hotel in Glasgow's fashionable West End. I had a quiet word with the manager and he very kindly got his chef to make a special batch for Celine.

What the singer was actually referring to was traditional Scottish shortbread. I still don't know how I got the box all the way to The Big Easy without the contents being smashed to smithereens. Celine was knocked out when I presented it to her backstage at the New Orleans Superdome. It really got my interview off to a flying start.

But there are times when interviews can go tits up for the most inexplicable reasons. Facing Brian Wilson being a classic example.

It's confession time. My prime motivation for organising an interview with the music icon was for purely selfish reasons. I wanted to get my Beach Boys box set signed and touch the hem of the great man's garment.

Brian had not set foot on UK soil for more than twenty years, but in 2002 he toured here to showcase the album, *Pet Sounds*. I planned to interview him as the music correspondent for *Scotland Today*, on Scottish Television. I received word from the singer's camp that for a TV interview he would need a make-up artist. This was a problem. I had no budget for such 'luxuries'.

I asked one of the young women in the office, who was a Beach Boys fan, if she could help me out. We set up in the main dressing room of the Clyde Auditorium in Glasgow, where he was performing *Pet Sounds* in its entirety.

I knew the singer – whose mental health issues are well known – could be a tough interviewee. But, as usual I did my homework, and was armed to the teeth with all the information I needed.

The first shock was when Brian walked in. He looked enormous. The singer is a very tall guy – I'd guess around 6ft 3in. – and his silver puffer jacket made him look even bigger. He also wore huge black wrap-around ski shades that gave him the appearance of a superhero from a Marvel comic book.

My colleague opened her make-up bag and began applying some powder to his face. All her attempts at engaging him in friendly conversation were ignored. His facial features seemed frozen and expressionless. I introduced myself but did not get much feedback either.

When Brian sat down, my cameraman swung into action. He asked if he could clip the mic on to the singer's collar after hiding the wire by running it up inside his jacket. But Brian didn't want to unfasten the zip so the only alternative was to pin it on and let the wire hang loose. It was not a good look. He then asked Brian if he planned to take off his ski shades. The singer chose to keep them on.

I kicked off the chat but it was like pulling teeth. His answers were only a few words long. It was also difficult to work out whether he had finished a sentence or not.

I focused on *Pet Sounds*, his musical masterpiece written, conceived and recorded in 1966 when he was just twenty-three years old. His collection of songs is frequently named the greatest album of all time in music press polls. Why did he think it was given such an accolade?

'Because it's a great album,' he said.

But what makes it such a great album?

'The songs.'

What makes the songs so special?

'The melodies. The lyrics.'

And so it went on. I had prepared enough questions for a half-hour chat but, five minutes in, I realised the interview was a complete dead loss.

As a TV interview it wasn't quite the disaster it appeared. By the time I'd edited his words and laid them over some footage of The Beach Boys in concert, it would sound like we were getting on famously. A few moments later I decided to abort.

I made a last-gasp bid to tease something out of him, more in desperation than anything else.

'It's the first time you've been in Britain in more than twenty years,' I told him. 'You've been an influence on so many artistes in this part of the world. Do you plan to check out any of the current crop of great bands like Blur or Oasis?'

Brian peered at me from behind his ski shades. It must have lasted for forty-five seconds, which is a lot of dead air if you're on camera. He stroked his chin, looked me up and down again, and said: 'No, not really.'

It's a wrap, as they say in TV-land. The time code on the tape said . . . six minutes and twenty-five seconds.

The concert later that night was a total triumph. To witness him recreate the musical intricacies of *Pet Sounds* – with his brilliant band, the Wondermints – was stunning. I saw a true genius at work.

After the gig, Brian hosted a meet and greet for media and fans backstage. As he signed autographs and posed for pictures, you couldn't shut him up. He talked non-stop.

I got to interview the great man on three more occasions and didn't fare much better. What made it even more galling was that I'd then switch on MTV or VH1 and see him talking incessantly about the making of *Pet Sounds* or *Smile*.

When we met, I don't think Brian was being difficult, obstinate or disinterested. There is clearly a window in each day when the great man is in 'interview mode'. So far, we've just not been able to synchronise our watches.

Chapter 12
Rebels with a Cause

I TRIED TO CHOOSE my moment. But any attempt to lessen the impact of a near nuclear explosion proved fruitless.

'You're doing what?' shrieked my mother. 'Wait until your father hears about this.'

I'll never forget the look of sheer outrage on her face. It was December 1977, and I'd gently let slip the ticking time bomb that I wouldn't be joining the rest of the family for Christmas dinner.

'Why, are you working?' she asked. Well, sort of.

Instead, I calmly explained, I was going to see The Sex Pistols play a secret gig in Huddersfield. As my folks would be sitting around the table in their Christmas party hats, I'd be celebrating the festive holiday with Johnny Rotten, Steve Jones, Sid Vicious and Paul Cook 240 miles away.

The Pistols were planning a gig – beneath the radar – in a club called Ivanhoe's. The location was kept so well under wraps the tickets, priced £1.75, simply said: 'Sex Pistols at ?????'

The promoters, Bankhouse Entertainments, were so fearful they also printed a bogus date just to throw the authorities even further off the trail. They didn't want anyone in the council to have prior warning that the band were due to appear at the venue.

A mate who was a promo rep for Virgin, the Pistols' record label, had been tipped off they were booked for the venue on 25 December. The show was one of just eight scheduled dates on their 'Never Mind The Bans' tour. Four gigs had already been cancelled after being shut down by the police.

We headed south on the M6 and made a pit-stop for an alternative Christmas lunch at a Little Chef. The place was deserted. The cook had to virtually chisel off two beef link sausages that were welded to a grill tray – after lying under heat lamps since early that morning – before slapping them on to a stale bread roll.

I imagined my mum saying: 'It's no more than you deserve.'

We arrived at Ivanhoe's to discover the Pistols had thrown a surprise Christmas party in the afternoon for the children of firemen who were on strike. Singer Johnny Rotten played Santa Claus and handed out 'Anarchy In The U.K.' T-shirts and *Never Mind The Bollocks* skateboards to the kids. The band had entertained the youngsters with their usual set which included controversial songs like 'Holidays In The Sun' and 'Bodies'.

I was introduced to Johnny backstage. He'd changed into his civvies – a Chinese-style straw hat, punk mohair jumper and leather trousers held up by padlocks and chains. Despite his volatile reputation he made us feel welcome and was grateful we'd travelled down from Scotland to see the group.

But bassist Sid Vicious more than lived up to his true punk persona. He was snuggled up on a sofa with his US girlfriend Nancy Spungen and snarled at anybody who came within a three-foot radius. I asked him for his autograph but he told me to 'fuck off'. Sid looked like he'd been on something much stronger than mulled wine.

When the Pistols took the stage for the evening show in front of 300 fans they were sensational. They kicked off – and ended – a seventeen-song set with 'God Save The Queen', as Her Majesty's Silver Jubilee year drew to a close.

Johnny wore a 'Never Mind The Rich Kids, We're The Sex Pistols' T-shirt – a reference to the new group formed by Scots musician Midge Ure and the Pistols' original bass player, Glen Matlock, who'd been fired several months earlier.

Powered by Steve Jones' guitar and Paul Cook's drumming they created absolute chaos in the tiny club, careering through key songs from their album, *Never Mind The Bollocks*, including 'No Feelings', 'Pretty Vacant', 'Submission' and 'EMI'. So much for music industry rumours they couldn't play.

Rock photographer Kevin Cummins, who worked for *NME*, shot the group on stage. His pictures were published in a beautiful coffee table book called *The End Is Near 25.12.77*. You can clearly spot me, from my vantage point standing on a table, in several of his best snaps.

Movie director Julien Temple also filmed the gig. His footage was later used in a BBC documentary titled *Never Mind The Baubles*.

My decision to body-swerve the family Christmas dinner proved an astute choice for I saw the Pistols at the absolute peak of their musical powers and punk notoriety. Years later, when Johnny appeared on my radio show, he hailed the gig at Ivanhoe's as one of the greatest of his band's short and controversial career. It also took on an added historical significance when it became their final performance on UK soil.

Just two weeks later the Pistols imploded during an ill-fated American tour. Their final gig at the Winterland Ballroom in San Francisco ended in turmoil. Johnny baited the crowd saying: 'This is no fun at all. A-ha-ha. Ever get the feeling you've been cheated?'

They would not play together again until they reformed eighteen years later on their money-spinning 'Filthy Lucre' tour. But good as they were – with Glen Matlock back in the line-up – they never quite captured the incendiary edge of that Christmas Day performance. I was lucky to catch the Pistols at Ivanhoe's, a gig that became such a defining moment in their history. And I'm pleased to say, my dear old mum even forgave me. Eventually.

In the years that followed I interviewed Johnny – who reverted to his real name John Lydon – several times when he formed his own band, Public Image Limited. I've got to know him well and he's appeared as a frequent guest on my show on BBC Radio Scotland. I've got nothing but total respect for Mr Lydon. Love him or hate him, he always calls it as he sees it.

In our recent chats, I got a real insight into the man behind the punk image. John talked very movingly about caring for his wife, Nora, who suffered from Alzheimer's disease. The singer put his music career on hold to look after the woman he married forty-four years ago. He was constantly by Nora's side at their home in Venice,

California, and wrote the song, 'Hawaii', about his love for her. It was on the shortlist to be Ireland's official entry in the 2023 Eurovision Song Contest, although ultimately wasn't selected.

'Nora wakes up every morning – which is usually at 6 a.m. – and she'll lean over, stroke my nose and say: "Hello, Johnny,"'he told me during one chat. It's just lovely. I'm lucky she still knows who I am. That's vitally important. I'm fully aware that as this goes on that will become less and less. But I really do enjoy the moment when she wakes. It spurs me on for the rest of the day.'

Sadly, Nora lost her battle with Alzheimer's – aged eighty – on 6 April 2023. John said that despite her illness, their life together had been 'worth every moment.' Having gone through a similar process as the full-time carer for a beloved family member, I was able to identify with the impact Nora's illness had on his life. I remain a huge fan of John Lydon, the musician. But I'm an even greater admirer of John Lydon, the man. More power to him.

I was drawn like a magnet to some of the most notorious rebels in rock. Mixing it with the bad boys was a real journey into the unknown. You never knew what to expect. That was the appeal.

I still look forward to verbally jousting with Liam and Noel Gallagher of Oasis. Talking to them is always eventful. When you sit down with either of the brothers there is never a dull moment.

Liam and Noel are what in media terms are known as 'good copy' and you always come away with some great quotes or controversies. Their volatile relationship also pays dividends for they rarely – if ever – agree to do interviews together.

If Noel says black, Liam would invariably say white. If you were lucky you'd be given twenty minutes with Liam, then another twenty with Noel. And one would contradict the other. I love talking to them.

My first encounter with Oasis was when they played two gigs at Irvine beach in Scotland on 14 and 15 July 1995. The shows – in a 6000-capacity circus big top – were part of their '(What's The Story) Morning Glory?' tour.

I covered the event for the *Sunday Mail* and Scottish Television, and through no fault of mine we got off to a rather rocky start. I was lined up to interview Liam and got to the site forty minutes before my pre-arranged time slot. But Oasis had finished their soundcheck earlier than expected and when I wasn't there for our chat the singer thought I'd blanked him and not bothered to show up. I arrived to see the band being driven back to their hotel in a minibus with Liam giving me the finger and shouting through the window. Now, I'm no lip-reader, but I don't think he was passing on his best wishes.

I put a call in to their plugging company in Manchester and told them to sort out the mess. They managed to reschedule the interview two hours later.

When I turned up at the Darlington Hotel in Ayr, Liam – accompanied by guitarist Bonehead – could not have been nicer. We got on like a house on fire. In those very early days of Oasis, Liam was already struggling to come to terms with such instant success.

'All the fame and that, some of it is boring. It does your head in. It's not real,' he told me. 'I'll go with the fans. I'll sign anything. But little things about it – bits and bobs – just don't suit me. When you start out you've got to do the whole circuit. But as you get on – and get bigger – you can pick and choose more. I don't want to play GMEX and these big arenas like Sheffield, y'know what I mean? I'd rather start in a tent and just go . . . like a travelling little circus and put it wherever. Start off with 6,000 people and do two nights. That's just the way.'

But the band's meteoric rise would prove otherwise. Just twelve months later, Oasis played two massive outdoor shows at Balloch Country Park, on the banks of Loch Lomond, to an audience of 40,000 people each day. So much for Liam's assertion the band had no desire to play large venues.

But why did he and Noel seem to walk this perpetual knife-edge between love and hate?

'Because we're brothers. I'm totally different from him and he's different from me,' he said. 'I've got my views on things and he's got his on his. Know what I mean? We don't fight. We argue. He's worse than me. Everyone makes out it's always me.'

There is no such thing as a boring Oasis interview. You'd need to make an effort – and employ real skill – to talk to either Gallagher brother and come away with nothing.

I flew to the US on 19 April 2000 to interview them when they were appearing at the ornate Fillmore State Theatre in Detroit with their special guests, Travis. Once more, it was a 'two-for-one' deal and I got twenty minutes with Liam, then Noel on the tour bus. I planned a story for the *Sunday Mail* plus a feature on Scottish Television to preview their headline date at Gig on the Green in Glasgow later that summer.

I caught Liam in a very reflective mood. Our chat came just a few months after he and his wife, Patsy Kensit, celebrated the birth of their son, Lennon. The singer revealed he'd become a very hands-on father and was enjoying his new role.

'Did I have any reservations about the experience of parenthood?' said Liam, 'Not really, no because I don't look too deep into it, y'know what I mean. I can't explain it. It was just a good experience. The best I've ever had. He's a child at the moment. A baby. I was at the birth. It was exciting and scary because I wanted everything to be fine . . . everything to be all right, an' that.

'I'll tell you what WAS scary . . . wearing that green outfit. I was like Andy Pandy. But I've taken to it like a duck to water. I do everything . . . all the nappy changing, all the feeding. When I'm there I try to put the time in. I love it.'

As the interview progressed, Liam revealed he had a new-found responsibility as a parent. I wondered if pop music now seemed a little insignificant.

'Not really, because you've to put food on the table. You've got to put milk in his bottle and I need to get that . . . so I've got to play in my band,' he said. 'I've got to do this. Do my band for me, first of all to keep me sane, and hopefully also make a few quid out of it then have a nice life.

'It's great to have some money. I don't class myself as rich. It's good to be paid for something that you do . . . when you do it well.

'I don't get money for nothing, y'know what I mean. It's hard earned. Material things aren't really important to me. I've got one car and one mountain bike . . . and I've got about eight scooters. But I collect them.'

I asked Liam, if the house was burning down – apart from his wife and child – what's the first thing he'd grab as he fled to safety?

His answer was classic.

'Myself. Apart from that, my two cats. I never used to be a cat lover . . . I was more a dog lover,' he revealed. 'But this dog I had was a bit not well so I had to carry it around the park. It wouldn't move so I gave it to the vet and then I bought two cats. They're called Mick and Keith and they're tops. I'm the Barbara Woodhouse of rock and roll.'

Noel is also very quotable. I've talked to him many times and he is very entertaining – and illuminating – company. He gives it to you straight, something of a rarity in the music industry.

One interview that really stands out took place just a few months after my trip across the Atlantic. I sat down with Noel backstage at Gig On The Green in Glasgow on 26 August 2000 and midway through our chat, things got a little interesting.

It seemed the obvious question to ask him . . . why didn't he just walk across the stage, put his hands around his brother Liam's neck and throttle him?

We talked after the band had played two shows at Wembley Stadium in July, the second of which Noel described as 'a nightmare, a disgrace and the low for me in all the Oasis years'.

The now notorious concert – on 22 July – was a complete disaster. For reasons best known to himself, Liam sabotaged virtually every number by swearing or ranting incoherently instead of singing the actual lyrics. He also deliberately baited and antagonised his brother throughout the sixteen-song set.

Liam told the capacity 75,000-strong audience: 'If you think I'm over the moon to be here you're fucking tripping. I'm no fucking celebrity. I ain't no fanny. I ain't no dickhead, man. I'm a rock star and I don't fucking arse about.'

Rumours circulated that his anger was fuelled by a bitter bust-up with Patsy. To make matters even worse, the show was being beamed live on Sky One to a vast TV audience.

It was car-crash television, with the highlights – if you can utilise that term – captured forever on a YouTube link titled:

'Oasis: Their Worst Gig Ever – Explained and Subtitled' which has notched up more than 750,000 views. Like me, viewers must have cringed as Noel battled to keep the band together.

Cards on the table, I would have happily throttled Liam. So why didn't Noel? As ever, the guitarist didn't mince his words. He told me: 'If I'd gone over and smacked him in the mouth that's his way of winning the argument because he's made me lose my cool. And I refuse to lose my cool.

'I would never act like that in front of 75,000 people. And not in front of the millions more who were watching at home on television. We were just trying to do a gig, man. I couldn't let him think he'd won.'

And with a wry smile, Noel added: 'But you know, I rise above these things man. I get into my Zen Buddhist zone. I'll go to heaven and he won't. And that's the end of it.'

It's always a pleasure to spend time with Alice Cooper. As rebels go, they don't get much bigger than the US superstar who's been causing mayhem on concert stages for more than fifty years. In 2017, I helped organise an award for the singer known as the Godfather of Shock Rock. He was honoured by music-biz charity, Nordoff Robbins (Scotland) to commemorate the forty-fifth anniversary of his UK debut gig at Green's Playhouse in Glasgow on 10 November 1972. Veteran morals campaigner, Mary Whitehouse, petitioned the government to ban him from setting foot on British soil, claiming his outrageous act would corrupt the youth of the nation.

We presented Alice with a Tartan Clef in recognition of his outstanding contribution to music.

'She was our greatest ally,' said Alice, with reference to Mrs Whitehouse. 'Her campaign helped get me two million record sales.'

When we met, he had vivid memories of that historic gig in the city: 'You must remember one thing. There was no Internet or social media at that time . . . it was all urban legend,' Alice recalled. 'You have this guy called Alice Cooper who has snakes, baby dolls chopped up all over the stage and a guillotine or electric chair to execute him at the end of the show.

'It was like this American Frankenstein coming to take over the youth. Well, the youth were the ones who got it. They said . . . this is funny, this is good, my parents hate it but I love it. There was nothing in my show that was bannable. There was no nudity or bad language. It was just this character who was definable . . . and that's what scared everybody.

'The kids didn't want soft rock. They wanted Alice Cooper to be hard rock. They wanted a punch in the face with the music. So we got along very well with that audience.'

I was in there when Alice played at Green's. The stage set resembled a garbage-strewn New York back alley – inspired by the musical *West Side Story* – and he performed with a 20ft long boa constrictor named Eva Marie Snake wrapped around his body. At the end of the show, an executioner led him to the gallows to be hung by the neck. The Glasgow crowd went crazy. We'd never seen anything like it. Neither had anybody else on this side of the Atlantic.

Alice revealed that his image – the garish panstick make-up and thick black eyeliner – was inspired by the 1962 movie, *Whatever Happened to Baby Jane?* starring Bette Davis and Joan Crawford.

He was determined to make an impact and it paid off.

'The world was full of rock heroes . . . The Beatles, The Rolling Stones, The Dave Clark Five and all these great British bands,' he told me. 'There were NO villains. We had tons of Peter Pans but we had no Captain Hook. I looked at the whole scenario of rock and roll and said: "I will gladly be that villain".

'I don't want to be a hero. I wanted to be Vincent Price or John Carradine . . . the dark lord of rock and roll. But it also had to have a sense of humour to it. And you had to have GREAT songs in order to make any of this work. So the music always came first, then the image and the show. Without that you just have a puppet show up there.'

Alice worked with the famed US-Canadian magician and illusionist, James Randi, to perfect the outrageous stunts in his stage act. His favourite mode of death was the guillotine.

'It's a great prop and the most effective one for the audience because it looks so real,' said Alice. 'That steel blade weighs 40lbs.

It's not plastic or rubber. It misses me by a fraction every single night for the last forty years. But I've felt it get very close.

'You actually see the head come off . . . and when they pull it out of the basket it's as shocking as it can be.'

Alice confided that he DID have a few very close brushes with death during his show.

'The hanging was a different thing. The trick is that there's a piano wire that comes down and it latches on to a hook and brace I'm wearing under my costume that you don't see,' he revealed.

'It's one inch shorter than the hangman's rope. When the floor drops out the rope DOES grab your neck . . . but the piano wire catches so it won't actually strangle you.

'One night, during a show in London, the wire broke. When I felt the rope too tight there was a natural reaction – I slammed my head back – and it went over my chin. If it would have caught it, I'd probably have broken my neck.'

I've interviewed Alice on numerous occasions. His stories of hitting the bars on Sunset Strip with The Hollywood Vampires – the notorious drinking club led by John Lennon, Ringo Starr, Harry Nilsson, Keith Moon and Micky Dolenz – are mind-boggling. So are his tales of spending time with legendary comedian Groucho Marx and surrealist painter, Salvador Dalí.

Alice quit booze and drugs when his wild lifestyle threatened to kill him. He's been clean since the mid-1980s and helps counsel other rock stars who have addiction problems.

During our chat in 2017, Alice confided that there was one person who makes sure he keeps his feet firmly planted on the ground . . . his mother, Ella Mae.

He was born plain Vincent Damon Furnier – the son of a clergyman – in Detroit in 1948.

'My mom is ninety-three and she still calls me Vince . . . she's the only one who does that,' he admitted. 'She'll say: "Hey superstar, take out the garbage." That's mom for you.

'The time when she finally knew I was in showbusiness was when I brought home a picture of me and Frank Sinatra. That was her guy. Frank treated me like everyone else. He said: "It's pretty unique what you're doing. I don't think you'll ever sing better than me. But your show is interesting." He was a good guy.'

Marilyn Manson owes an enormous debt to Alice Cooper who paved the way for his rather more sinister brand of shock and roll. When I interviewed the US star in 2007, it was one of the most bizarre encounters of my career. I spent months trying to confirm an interview with him. Plans were made, then cancelled at the eleventh hour, only to be rescheduled yet again.

When I got the thumbs up, I flew to Hollywood and booked into The Standard hotel on Sunset Strip. Then I played a waiting game – sitting by the phone for hours – for a call to say I'd finally been granted an audience.

A promo guy from his record label picked me up in a cab and took me to a house near the famous Capitol Records building. The lane behind his home was eerie – with no cars or pedestrians – and there was little sign of life anywhere in the surrounding buildings. I was shown into a house that was virtually pitch-black, as if some-one had unscrewed every bulb from the light fittings. It gave me the creeps.

I sat down on a sofa in a room that was again so dark I couldn't read the notes for my interview. It was very intimidating.

I waited in silence for thirty minutes. Nobody came near. Nothing happened.

As my eyesight eventually got used to the dim light, I could make out artefacts such as a giant wooden crucifix, a model of rapper Eminem wielding a chainsaw plus various mutilated dolls and items of religious paraphernalia. It confirmed that the Marilyn Manson you saw on stage was an extension of the man himself.

Then, Manson – as he prefers to be called – walked in and sat down. He was dressed from head to toe in black and wearing a cowboy hat and wrap-around sunglasses. He was on the sofa next to me and I could barely see him. But then, I got the biggest shock of all. He was the perfect host. And highly articulate. A very clever guy.

It was still so dark I couldn't read my questions, so I had to busk the interview. Manson was such a great talker that it went smoothly. We talked about his forthcoming appearance at Gig On The Green and he revealed his girlfriend, actress Evan Rachel Wood, was planning to join him on stage. Well, not quite.

Manson told me: 'I've built a robot replica of her. She brings me absinthe on stage, like any wonderful girl should. There's a very sentimental moment where I slice her head off and perform my sarcastic version of *Hamlet* with it. She's very lifelike. Backstage, people stumble across her and say: "Hello Evan". And of course, it's not her. The response is a strange mix of confusion and amazement.'

The singer was later accused by the real Ms Wood of sexual assault and abuse during their five-year long relationship

When the interview took a more serious tone, I wondered how Manson would react.

In 1999, he was blamed for inspiring the Columbine High School massacre when two students – said to be fans of the singer – shot thirteen of their fellow pupils dead. In a separate incident, just one month before our meeting, a fourteen-year-old wearing a Marilyn Manson T-shirt, shot four people before killing himself at a school in Cleveland.

While Manson sympathised with the victims, he took no blame for either crime. He fought his corner incredibly well and told me: 'If a kid wants to be violent all they need to do is join the army. I'm not responsible for any of this. I just want people to feel emotion . . . good or bad.'

He then revealed he would like to appear in a TV reality show based on his rather unusual lifestyle. 'I'm guilty of watching reality television as much as the next person,' he said. 'It's really shocking how fucked up people are. I've been offered a lot but have always turned them down. But I'd definitely do one if it involved machine guns and hookers.'

My time was up. Manson signed a copy of his autobiography and happily posed for a quick snap. He was a perfectly genial if rather unorthodox host. I liked him enormously. He came across as a very intelligent and driven individual.

He wished me good luck and disappeared back into the darkness.

A few months later, while on an assignment in Osaka, Japan, I spotted him walking down a street with some female Goth fans. We momentarily exchanged glances but I walked on.

When I met him again backstage in Glasgow I mentioned it.

'I saw you. Why didn't you stop and say hello,' he said.

I never thought he'd remember me.

There was one final twist in the tale, however. Word is there were two items on his dressing room rider at Gig on the Green that raised a few eyebrows. Included in the usual range of drinks and foodstuffs was a large plastic basin and a bag of cat litter. There was speculation that Manson had a real aversion to using those portable chemical toilets backstage at music festivals. Few could blame him. I'll leave you to draw your own conclusions.

Chapter 13
I'm Happy, Hope You're Happy Too

I'D NEVER HEARD DAVID BOWIE sound so full of life.

'There's one thing I want more than anything,' he told me. 'I desperately want to live forever. I want to still be around in another forty or fifty years.'

The singer always looked forward with a perpetual fascination for whatever challenges lay ahead. By refusing to allow himself to get weighed down in the nostalgia for his incredible musical achievements, he never stood still . . . constantly moving on to his next project be it an album, concert tour or acting role. So, during one of my final interviews with Bowie, it came as no surprise to discover his focus was on the future.

I interviewed Bowie seven times and became the Scottish journalist he got to know best. Meeting him was always a very rewarding experience. And for an artiste who was a true pop icon, he was always so honest and down-to-earth. But on this occasion Bowie really opened up and spoke with a remarkable candour I had not heard before.

When we talked – in 2003 – he was promoting his new album, *Reality*, the twenty-fourth release of his career. Bowie was fired up and loving life. His enthusiasm was infectious. I put that down to the events of the previous three years. The singer and his beautiful Somalian wife, Iman, had their first child, a daughter named Alexandria in 2000. The new parents settled into family life in a $4 million apartment at 285 Lafayette Street, in the fashionable

SoHo area of Manhattan in New York. The luxury condominium had its own quirky bit of NYC history. It was located in a building that was formerly the site of the Hawley & Hoops chocolate factory built in 1886.

The singer was able to enjoy relative anonymity when walking in Washington Square Park nearby or browsing in local bookstores. 'He felt at home among New Yorkers too cool to act starstruck at celebrity sightings,' wrote Will Brooker in the book, *Forever Stardust: David Bowie Across the Universe.*

Alexandria had inspired several of the key songs on *Reality* and the singer confided he got as much pleasure taking his daughter to the park as he did from wowing audiences in stadiums around the world.

During our conversation, Bowie – who was usually very guarded about his private life – really opened his heart about the child who had brought him so much happiness. He said: 'I just want to be there for Alexandria. She's so exciting and so lovely . . . so I want to be around when she grows up.

'I think: "When am I gonna let go of her?" When she's twenty? Nah, I wanna see her get married.

'When she's thirty? Nah, I wanna see what she's like as a mother.

'I don't want to let her go. If I didn't have my little three-year-old running around, I wouldn't be writing songs in quite this way. Seeing in her eyes all the hope and joy and optimism of the future, I have to reflect that in what I'm doing.'

It was refreshing to hear him talk with such affection about how his life had changed.

Bowie had real regrets that he'd largely missed out seeing his son Joe – from his first marriage to Angela Barnett – grow up. His non-stop touring schedule and wild lifestyle meant he wasn't around for the boy – whom the couple initially named Zowie – during the most formative years of his childhood. He was determined not to let the same thing happen with Alexandria.

What did he discover about fatherhood second time around?

'That being there for your child is a good idea,' he said. 'I missed so much of Joe's life. It was just bad luck he had a dad who had to be out on the road for his own career ambitions. It's a shame. In a way, I've never forgiven myself for that. But on the other hand, that's life. Joe and I have long ago reconciled ourselves about that. We get on great.

'Now I love being with both my son AND my daughter. It's just wonderful.'

With a supermodel wife, secure domestic life and a reputation as one of the most innovative figures in music history, I remarked that he was a very lucky man.

'I am, I am,' he agreed, 'It's like the story where the hotel waiter said to footballer George Best: "Where did it all go wrong?"'

'In my case, it's where did it all go right?'

Bowie revealed that he could wander around his neighbourhood virtually unrecognised, in stark contrast to his previous life in his native London where paparazzi photographers stalked him wherever he went. His new, more laid-back lifestyle was reflected on several of the songs on *Reality* whose lyrics contained references to local Manhattan landmarks like Riverside, Battery Park and the Hudson River.

'I am anonymous in New York and it's one of the major attractions of living there,' he said. 'In Paris, Los Angeles or London it's never that easy to get around. What do I do on a normal day? Well, what do YOU do? I do some shopping, meet the wife for lunch or go to the park with Alexandria.

'Or else I might go do some recording in my studio or see a movie at the Angelika cinema in nearby Greenwich Village.

'It's easy to get about. Nobody looks at me twice. In New York, they don't feel they have possession of you. They let you get on with your life.

'Whereas in London it's all, "David, David, gimme your autograph." And me saying: "Oh please, leave me alone. I've got three shopping bags, it's raining, I haven't got a coat and I'm trying to get home." It's not like that in New York. It's more, "Hi Dave". That's all you get at the most.

'But it's exactly the same for Moby or Lou Reed, who live in my area. You see them all the time on the street. We're all just people who live around town.'

The most revealing moment of the interview was when I asked him about the tragic events of 11 September 2001. Bowie revealed that his SoHo apartment had spectacular views of the Twin Towers of the World Trade Centre. It was one of the main reasons he bought it. When I asked how he felt when his adopted home came under attack by terrorists, he spoke straight from the heart.

'It was traumatic and very, very disturbing. What made it worse was that I was in Woodstock, upstate New York, recording my previous album, *Heathen*,' he recalled. 'Iman and Alexandria were at home in the apartment. That was the most terrifying thing. After the attack, the phones all went dead. You couldn't get in or out of New York. We were cut off from each other.'

He then relived the terrifying moment Iman described the attack on the second tower by al-Qaeda. He admitted he felt completely helpless because he wasn't there to protect his wife and child.

'Iman was standing at our kitchen window and we were on the phone to each other,' he recalled. 'She said: "You won't believe what's happening. A plane has gone into one of the towers." Then she said: "Oh my God, another plane has just gone into the second tower." I shouted, "Get out of there. Get the baby, get a pram and get out . . . you're under attack." I just knew immediately it was a terrorist attack.'

When he finally managed to return to Manhattan he saw the full impact of the atrocity. 'What I ended up seeing from our window was a big hole in the sky where those buildings had been,' he said. 'There was a thin film of ash over the house and all the furniture.'

A month later, Bowie performed in the fund-raising Concert For New York at Madison Square Garden to pay an emotional tribute to the first responders from the New York City fire, police and ambulance departments. With fellow Brits, Paul McCartney, Mick Jagger, Keith Richards, Elton John, The Who and Eric Clapton, he joined forces with US artistes Billy Joel, Jay Z, Bon Jovi, Destiny's Child and James Taylor in a show of solidarity.

Bill Clinton, Robert De Niro, Billy Crystal, Leonardo DiCaprio, Harrison Ford, Susan Sarandon and Richard Gere were among the show's guest presenters.

To interview – and get to know – one of the biggest stars in rock history was a real privilege. The first time came in 1983 when I was shown into his dressing room backstage at Murrayfield Stadium in Edinburgh. His 'Serious Moonlight' tour marked a re-emergence by a performer who'd consistently pushed the envelope musically with every album he'd released since *David Bowie-Space Oddity* in 1969.

He looked incredible with his Princess Diana-style bleached blonde hair and powder blue suit which became his trademark around the release of 'Let's Dance', the most commercially successful record of his career. He talked about the pressures of stardom and why he was now much more relaxed – both personally and creatively – after portraying other characters such as Ziggy Stardust, Aladdin Sane and The Thin White Duke. It would be the first of seven interviews with him over the years. He was always full of surprises.

None more so than when he unveiled Tin Machine – a heavy metal group he formed with guitarist Reeves Gabrels and Tony and Hunt Sales, on bass and drums respectively – in 1988. Bowie toured with the brothers when he played keyboards in Iggy Pop's band during gigs to promote his album, *The Idiot*. He confounded critics and fans alike, with some complaining his new heavy rock sound made their ears bleed.

I met the group during rehearsals at Factory Studios in Dublin as they prepared for a UK tour. Bowie brushed aside any criticism, insisting he was fully committed to the band and that it wasn't some kind of offshoot vanity project.

Tin Machine hit the road in 1989 and played several venues off the beaten track including a surprise date at The Forum in Livingston. To prepare for the shows, Bowie revealed he'd also embarked on a strict fitness regime to get in shape for the tour. It worked, for while making his debut at Barrowland in Glasgow, the then forty-three-year-old singer stripped off his shirt to reveal a muscle-bound torso that was the envy of guys half his age.

I caught up with him again backstage at Ingliston Exhibition Centre, near Edinburgh on his 'Sound and Vision' tour in 1990. In the previous months he'd asked fans to vote for their favourite hit songs and pledged to perform the most popular choices for the final time.

His embarrassing 1967 novelty single, 'The Laughing Gnome', topped one poll. 'But there's no way I'm going to be playing that. I don't see it being in the set, somehow. Do you?' he said, laughing.

When we got together at the SECC in Glasgow in 1995, the show was surrounded by controversy. Bowie was a great admirer of Morrissey, former frontman of The Smiths, and invited him to be his special guest on a sell-out UK tour. The previous night, at Aberdeen Exhibition Centre, Morrissey – who was a lifelong Bowie fan – went AWOL before the show. He claimed he was ill and his sudden disappearance really left the singer in the lurch.

The story hit the headlines and there were reports that the tour had been plunged into turmoil with angry fans storming out and demanding refunds. When I interviewed Bowie for Scottish Television, my first question was to ask him what lay behind Mozz's sudden 'vanishing act'. His answer was totally nondescript. I was surprised that he was not more expansive about the incident and he skilfully avoided saying anything critical about him.

The chat quickly moved on to his own music where he was much more forthcoming, and the interview went well.

But as the camera crew were packing up their equipment, Bowie's publicist returned and said he wasn't satisfied about how the singer had dealt with the Morrissey issue. As a favour, he asked if I would be prepared to pitch the question to him a second time so he could set the record straight a little more decisively. When Bowie reappeared it was obvious he had been well briefed. He chose his words carefully.

'I was quite flabbergasted at the couple of tabloids that really seemed to have had their knives out for me this year. It's par for the course really . . . it goes with my territory,' he admitted. 'What I think was so unfortunate was that Morrissey came down ill in Aberdeen and the papers had it that the Bowie tour plunged into turmoil and angry fans stormed out. And that nobody knew that Morrissey wasn't going to appear.

'What happened is that forty-five minutes before the show we were suddenly told that Morrissey wasn't going to be working that night. In fact, I think he went back to London. The promoter immediately told the audience and, in all honesty, there was hardly a murmur from the crowd . . . and 422 disgruntled Morrissey fans asked for their money back, leaving many, many thousands to watch the show.

'I think I'm old-fashioned to believe that a standing ovation generally means that the audience like the show. Which is very far away from the story that appeared in the press.

'I don't think you can do much about changing those situations other than me telling you what it's really like. That's all I can do. And I hope Morrissey gets better.'

But despite his more diplomatic comments, I could sense he was still seething.

On the tour, Bowie was also criticised for turning his back on some of his biggest hits preferring to feature songs from his latest album, *Outside*.

The singer made no apologies for going his own way, as he always did. Had he been let off the leash?

'For me it's thoroughly enjoyable I'm playing all the music that really interests me at the moment. That's the kind of show I want to do,' he said.

'I don't think I feel like I've been let off any leash. This last five years I've made probably some of my best albums – *Black Tie White Noise*, *Buddha of Suburbia* and now, *Outside*.

'I'm really in a very creative mode.'

He also politely put me in my place when I asked if his age was now a disadvantage when competing with new bands like Oasis and Blur.

'I wouldn't tell that to Neil Young if I were you,' he said. 'They're only as young as a band who starts up. I was that age when I was that age. Everybody is nineteen once. But only once.'

Two years later, Bowie invited me to Brixton Academy in London during production rehearsals for his 'Earthling' tour. The venue was just a short distance from No.40 Stansfield Road, the terraced house where he was born in 1947. He'd recently celebrated his landmark fiftieth birthday, so I light-heartedly mentioned his age once again.

If life begins at forty . . . does it gather momentum when you get to fifty?

'I suppose that I'm so absorbed in the work that I do that time ceases to have much of a function for me,' he admitted. 'I don't really notice them [years] slipping by. I'm just a walking bundle of energy. A glass of water . . . half full.'

Sitting on the edge of the Academy stage, we were surrounded by a set decorated by inflatable eyeballs with distorted pictures of his head projected on to them. It looked amazing, if slightly unnerving. That was probably his intention. Bowie revealed that after portraying such diverse characters in the past it was just as exciting to simply be himself again.

'I think I've probably been doing that for quite a long time now. The characters really dropped off in the late seventies,' he said. 'There's always been a strong degree of theatricality in what I do because I find it irresistible. I just like it. I like to make the stage as interesting as I hope the music is. And this present tour is really no exception.

'I've been working with a visual artist called Tony Oursler who has created some very strange kinds of faces – disembodied heads – which are very bizarre.'

I told Bowie I was a collector of memorabilia and asked if he had managed to hold on to any of the artefacts of his colourful career. He revealed he still had many of his handwritten lyrics, costumes and props and they were all safely stowed away.

He told me: 'I've had a lot of stuff stolen from me over the years because I wasn't too good, unfortunately, about looking after anything that I had. But I don't run around looking for it. So, if I'm doing tours, I tend to keep all the stuff.

'I've got most of the clothes . . . being a bit of a dandy, being a bit of a fop. I tend to have kept all the frocks.'

Such foresight would prove to be beneficial when the Victoria and Albert Museum staged David Bowie Is, in London in 2013. The exhibition showcased his extensive archive and it broke box-office records before touring the world. Now, the V&A plan to open The David Bowie Centre in Stratford in 2025. They have been gifted more than 80,000 items – costumes, album artwork, lyrics, set designs and letters – by the late singer's estate. The free-to-view permanent exhibition – in a new purpose-built building – will span all six decades of Bowie's career.

Bowie hit the Barrowland Ballroom on his 'Earthling' tour on 22 July 1997, in what was arguably THE greatest ever gig at the legendary Glasgow venue. He walked onstage to a hero's welcome and opened with a solo version of 'Quicksand', before his band joined him.

His twenty-two-song set included classics such as 'The Jean Genie', 'Under Pressure', 'The Man Who Sold The World' and 'Stay'. I met him in the dressing room after the gig and he kindly autographed my poster from his appearance in *The Elephant Man* on Broadway . . . proudly showing it off to his fellow band members.

Then he surprised me, yet again.

The singer and his wife Iman had checked into the chic One Devonshire Gardens hotel in the city's West End twenty-four hours earlier. I couldn't believe it when he revealed they'd gone for a stroll in the area to take advantage of the summer sunshine. Bowie and Iman walked arm in arm straight past the front door of my flat.

I later discovered a neighbour had spotted this striking figure with spiked red hair and a goatee beard, who resembled David Bowie. But why on earth would the singer be in our street? So she didn't give him a second glance.

When I told her she HAD seen Bowie she couldn't believe it.

'We walked along the terraces down to the Botanic Gardens, bought a couple of cones from the ice cream van outside the gates, and sat down on the grass to relax and soak up the sun,' he said. 'A few people spotted us but they were pretty cool. They just wanted to say "Hi" and were very nice.'

My final encounter with the great man was when we talked at the SECC in Glasgow before his gig on 28 November 2003. I'd been tipped-off the singer was going to surprise the 8,500-capacity sell-out crowd by revealing that he'd signed up to headline T in the Park the following summer.

'I've never played a music festival in Scotland before and T in the Park seems to be the big one,' he told me backstage. 'It's always great to be a part of these multi-band events. I plan to get there early to check out a few of the other acts who are on the bill too. I don't think I've had anything other than good times when I've been to Scotland generally, not just Glasgow. Nobody seems to have much of a side up here. What you see is what you get.'

The gig was sensational as Bowie opened with 'Rebel Rebel' and then powered through hits like 'All The Young Dudes', 'Life On Mars?', 'Ashes To Ashes', 'Starman', 'Let's Dance', 'Heroes' and 'Suffragette City'. Midway through the gig he was forced to stop the show as a fight broke out near the stage. As he raced to his limo at the end he spotted me and said: 'Only in Glasgow . . . only in Glasgow'.

His performance whet my appetite for T in the Park. But, sadly, Bowie never made it. In June 2004, he headlined the Isle of Wight Festival, which became his final show on UK soil. Later that month, he experienced chest pains at a gig in Germany and suffered a heart attack. All future shows were cancelled.

In the years that followed he limited his live appearances and his last-ever stage performance was a guest spot at a charity event in New York in 2006. Sadly, there was worse to come. In 2013, Bowie released *The Next Day* – his first album in a decade – and a few months later was diagnosed with liver cancer. His condition was kept a close-knit secret known only to his family and friends.

He continued to work – where his illness allowed – and completed his twenty-sixth and final album, *Blackstar*. It was released on 8 January 2016 – his sixty-ninth birthday – and he passed away just two days later.

The album debuted at No. 1 in the UK, the USA, and several other countries as fans around the world mourned the loss of one of rock's most innovative performers. I couldn't believe Bowie was gone. I still can't. It was months before I could even bring myself to watch the video for 'Lazarus' . . . the single that became his swansong.

According to his long-time producer Tony Visconti, the track was a self-epitaph.

The last scene in the video where this frail – and as we now know, cancer ravaged – figure steps back into the wardrobe and pulls the door closed with one finger still brings a lump to my throat.

Was Bowie's final artistic statement to almost choreograph his own death?

But David Bowie left me with many fond memories, a cupboard full of precious pop memorabilia and some of the greatest albums ever recorded.

I feel honoured to have grown up in the same era in which he was an influence on so many people and broke down musical and cultural barriers with his abundance of talent.

He was the ultimate Starman.

Chapter 14
I Went Down, Down, Down . . . and the Flames Went Higher

JOHNNY CASH. THE MAN in Black. Never had that famous nickname described him better. Black hair. Black shirt. Black jeans. Black cowboy boots. Black mood. Johnny was furious. The US music legend stepped forward to confront me, making no attempt to conceal his anger.

'Why would I wanna do that?' he growled. 'I'd feel foolish.'

I stood rooted to the spot in fear. Johnny was going to kill me for sure. As his piercing eyes drilled into mine, I felt the life drain out of me. This was the guy who'd shot a man in Reno, just to watch him die, if we're to believe his classic song, 'Folsom Prison Blues'.

Despite being ravaged by booze and drugs Johnny remained an imposing figure. He'd snap me like a twig. Big deal if he got banged up for murder. Johnny was already a hero in Folsom and San Quentin.

As any hardened con will tell you, there's good jail time, bad jail time and Johnny Cash jail time. At worst, he'd get another hit song out of it.

'I Throttled A Scots Hack In Mayfair' may not have the same poetic lyrical hue or shortlist him for a Grammy for Best Songwriter, but that wasn't uppermost in Johnny's mind right now. He wanted answers. And I didn't have any.

'Why would I wanna do that?' he barked a second time.

I took a deep breath, opened my mouth and meekly said: 'Why don't we go to the coffee shop? It's quiet in there,' before turning on my heel and heading for the door.

Johnny followed. Reluctantly.

As interviews go, we'd definitely got off on the wrong foot. Things could only get better. Wouldn't they?

The call came to talk to Johnny when he was booked to play a concert at the Glasgow Apollo in 1984. Ticket sales were a bit slow. Johnny, whose relationship with the press was best summed up as 'prickly', was prepared to do a rare interview if only to generate some much needed action at the box office. There was pride as well as dollars at stake. Johnny had opened the now legendary Apollo with two historic gigs on 5 and 6 September 1973.

But I had a professional dilemma. The very mention of the name Johnny Cash would be met with blank indifference from my editor. He wanted a splash of colour in his paper. Adam Ant, Wham, Boy George, Spandau Ballet, Kid Creole and the Coconuts . . . they put a smile on readers' faces.

Simon Le Bon didn't sound like a tubby bloke from Birmingham. His very name was exotic. He wore a bandana and no socks. Simon had his own yacht. In the eighties, that stuff sold papers.

Johnny Cash, the 'Man in Black', belonged to a forgotten, mono-chrome era when you still got inky fingers reading the news pages or racing forms. It would be many years before black became 'the new black'.

'It's a waste of time. I'll never get an interview with Johnny Cash in the paper,' I diplomatically told the singer's PR. He ignored my polite refusal and made his pitch.

'It's a great story,' he said, 'Johnny has spent months drying out in the Betty Ford Clinic in California. He was swallowing handfuls of pills. Downing two bottles of liquor a day. Beating up his wife. He's had half his stomach removed in a life-saving operation. His career was down the toilet. No record company or TV show would touch him. But he's back. It's a great story.'

He was right. A music legend who'd conquered his demons and stepped back from the brink. In tabloid terms it was a great story. Readers loved that stuff too.

Still, I wasn't sold. Johnny, monosyllabic in interviews at the best of times, was hardly going to revisit the darkest recesses of his tortured life just to fill two pages of copy sandwiched between the TV listings and the Quickie Crossword.

'He'll tell you all about it. It's all part of the healing process. Johnny wants his Scottish fans to know he's been saved. It's a new beginning,' said the PR with an almost evangelical zeal.

The interview was set for the plush Mayfair Hotel in London the following week. Knowing the job would be a tough one, I read up extensively on Johnny. I then faced the most difficult part of my preparation for any assignment . . . briefing the photographer.

I've worked with many talented photographers over the years. Guys with real flair for a great picture, whose shots leap off the page elevating a feature to a higher level. But, and I have to be fiercely brutal here, most snappers have a whole different mindset from the common man. It's almost as if there's the world we live in, then an alternative universe which spins on a different axis – slightly off-kilter – that they call home.

There's a well-told music industry joke that goes: 'What's the difference between a drum machine and a drummer?'

Answer – 'You only have to punch the rhythm pattern into a drum machine once.'

That could also apply to photographers. No matter how many times you tell them the interviewee is a superstar, they've always got to come up with an 'angle'. So it's no coincidence scores of sober features have been accompanied by pools-winner-style snaps.

With Wikipedia still light years away, I gave the photographer a quick crammer course on the life and times of Johnny Cash, specifically highlighting the fact the singer would be dressed from head to toe in black.

We were under pressure to add some colour. It was imperative we found a bright backdrop – a stained-glass window, striking mural or strategically placed tropical potted plant – as a set design for our snaps. The 'bull picture', the main shot on a feature spread, had to light up the page.

I also warned him that as my line of questioning would be tough – focusing on the most harrowing period of Johnny's tortured life – it was advisable to do the photos first. I wanted something 'in-the-bag' in case there was a detonation on a nuclear scale. How prophetic!

'Leave it to me. I'll sort something out,' said my trusty snapper, 'You want colour . . . I'll give you colour.' Little did I know those fifteen seemingly insignificant words would come back to haunt me.

The lift door opened and Johnny Cash stepped out into the hotel foyer flanked by his entourage. Whatever had gone on in the Betty Ford Clinic, he'd clearly been through the wars. You could see it instantly. His rugged features had the grey pallor of a POW who'd just been released from a solitary confinement punishment detail in 'The Hole' in Stalag 13. An outsize, flowing black artist's smock gave his ravaged frame a bulked-up look.

If Desmond Morris had been interpreting Johnny's body language, his analysis would definitely have said: 'Don't mess'.

I introduced myself. Johnny barely acknowledged me. It was clear he didn't want to do the interview but had been press-ganged into it. My reading of the situation was, let's make this as quick and painless as possible.

I suggested doing some shots first, to get them out of the way. I threw the floor over to my photographer. If I'd pulled out the pin from a hand grenade the explosion would have been a mere dull thud compared for what was to come.

'Hello, Johnny, I don't know if you know . . . but we print in colour,' said my snapper.

It was true. The *Record* had been the first newspaper to introduce full colour presses in the UK and Europe.

'I've got a great idea for a nice, colourful picture,' he enthused. 'I've had a word with the Duty Manager and he's given us the okay to do a few shots in the hotel kitchen. I thought I could get you to wear a white chef's hat and mix some eggs in a frying pan to make an omelette. Bags of colour. It'll look great. Make a smashing snap.'

Suddenly, my life went into slow motion. Hotel guests around us began talking at 33rpm. People moved across the foyer like the gloop in a lava lamp.

'Why would I wanna do that?' growled Johnny. 'I'd feel foolish.'

The idea originated with the photographer. But Johnny fixed his stare on me and wanted answers. While reading up on his chequered career had I missed something?

Had Johnny just published his first cookbook? Was his comeback TV special due to be screened on the Food Channel? Could you buy J.C. monogrammed oven gloves or kitchen utensils from the merchandising stall at his concerts? What was the 'angle'?

An already difficult situation was now virtually irretrievable.

'Let's just do the interview first,' I suggested trying to salvage something from the wreckage. We headed for the deserted coffee shop.

There's something very comforting when you hear the 'click' as you press the Play/Record buttons on your Dictaphone. It formally declares you're now in work mode. The interview has begun. We're off and running.

'How does it feel to be on the road again? Is it good to be back in Britain? How's your new album coming along'?

Johnny was remarkably lucid, almost conversational. Surprising in the circumstances. All was not lost. Maybe!

Five minutes in, I felt bold enough to redirect the dialogue to Rancho Mirage, California, the location of the Betty Ford Clinic. It was time to put some real meat on the bones.

'Johnny, the fans in Scotland love you so much. They've really taken you to their hearts. So imagine how shocked they all were to hear you'd gone through a rough time. How's your health these days?'

I was speaking on behalf of a nation. If Johnny felt pain, we all felt pain. The Scots stood shoulder to shoulder with him in this battle for personal redemption. I fixed Johnny with the most sympathetic look I could muster, sat back and prepared myself for the best – or worst. It could go either way.

His PR guy had been one hundred per cent correct. Johnny wanted to talk about this darkest period of his life. The words came tumbling out . . . every one possessing a cathartic and cleansing power.

Until now, the Betty Ford Clinic had been this almost mythical place where celebrities go to get straightened out. But what exactly goes on there? Johnny began to tell me.

He woke up at 6 a.m. Made his bed. Tidied his room. Read the Bible. Fixed breakfast. Went to a therapy session. Shared the experience of past traumas with fellow patients. Received expert psychiatric care.

I discreetly shot a glance at the cogs on my cassette tape. They were still turning. Johnny was giving a guided tour of what went on behind the security gates of the clinic. This was pure gold.

They say every addict has got to reach rock-bottom before starting the long climb back to the mountain top. Johnny sank into his chair as he recounted the most harrowing times of his drug and booze fuelled addiction. It made for painful listening. He was still hurting. Revisiting such a dark place was taking its toll. Johnny's black mood was getting blacker with each sentence.

Then it happened . . . the eruption.

Johnny's face contorted with rage. It was like a scene from a *Tom and Jerry* cartoon when the cat gets mad. From the neck up – like water rising in a bathtub – Johnny's face began to change colour from a deathly grey to a purple rage. He let out a pained roar – eyes bulging from his head in fury.

I was aware of my trusty photographer crouched on the floor at my elbow. He'd been snapping a montage of shots while Johnny regressed into the black hole of addiction. Just as he'd confronted his darkest inner demons, reached his private hell, the photographer said the fatal words: 'C'mon Johnny, give us a smile. Show a wee bit of enamel.'

Johnny started growling in an unfamiliar language akin to fluent rhinoceros. It sounded like something I'd once heard on a safari holiday in Kenya. Whatever tongue it was . . . it wasn't good.

'What I'm talkin' about. Where I'm goin' back to. A bad, bad time in my life. It doesn't make me wanna fuckin' smile,' snarled Johnny.

Oh, fuck. Please God, no. He'll kill us for sure. We're fucking dead. Beam me up, Scotty. Perm any three from five. My life went back into slow motion again. What made a bad situation even worse was that the photographer, while rewinding his film and dismantling his lenses, seemed completely oblivious to the fact Johnny was a tad upset.

The interview was over. Stone dead. The only crumb of comfort was I'd got enough gold on tape for an insightful feature. Now, I just wanted to get out of there alive.

In a vain attempt to lighten the mood I asked Johnny if his busy schedule had allowed him a few hours off to see the sights in London.

'Has it been all work and no play?' I said, quickly realising Johnny doesn't do small talk either.

His grudging reply was he'd gone with his wife, June Carter, to see the musical *Pump Boys and Dinettes* in the West End. In my time as a broadcaster there was a huge sign on the wall of Studio A at Radio Clyde that read: 'Before engaging mouth, make sure brain is in gear'.

Wise words. Oh, how I wish I'd heeded them.

'That's amazing,' I gushed, I went to see *Pump Boys And Dinettes* a few weeks back. I go to musicals all the time. Love 'em. I don't know what you made of it – but I thought the acting was awful, it had shit songs, the stage set looked like it had been assembled from a B&Q flat-pack and the plot, if you can call it a plot, was piss poor. In fact, I thought it was so duff I left at the interval and went for a pizza.'

Johnny drilled me with those piercing eyes again and said through gritted teeth: 'Well, I kinda enjoyed it. But maybe that's because my daughter, Carlene Carter, was the star of the show.'

So she was. The blonde girl at the front. Gingham shirt. Dancing. I thought I recognised her.

Johnny wanted more answers. I didn't have any.

Scotty, for fuck's sake, beam me up.

Chapter 15
The Twins . . .
There's Two of Them

'I ALWAYS KNEW THERE was something funny about that pair of bastards. They better never show their fucking faces in Scotland again.'

The female counter-staff in the *Daily Record* canteen were always a solid barometer of the public mood. As I paid for my steak pie and chips, the thought suddenly crossed my mind . . . have I gone too far?

A few hours earlier, the paper had hit the streets with an exclusive story that marked one of my finest hours as a music journalist.

'Proclaimers Sensation . . . turn to Page 7' screamed the headline next to the masthead. In a piece of investigative journalism BBC1's *Panorama* would have been proud of, I told how the duo – so-called twins Craig and Charlie Reid – had conned music fans and the public alike. Finally, it was there in cold, hard print . . . The Proclaimers were a fraud.

But first, allow me to backtrack a little.

On 30 January 1987, the twins boarded a train at Waverley Station in Edinburgh to travel down to Newcastle to appear on TV pop show, *The Tube*. They'd been given a coveted slot on the programme – hosted by Jools Holland and Paula Yates – after sending a homemade video of their song, 'Letter From America' to the producers in a bid to whip up a bit of interest in their music.

It worked, for within three hours of Craig and Charlie making their television debut, life would never be the same again.

'At that point we'd had a little bit of record company attention but nobody was really biting,' recalled Craig. 'We always assumed if we ever signed a deal it would be on an indie label. That was the level we'd get to. We never thought we'd reach a mass audience.'

Paula introduced the twins by saying they were one of the few new Scottish bands that didn't try to sing in a fake American accent. What happened next was one of those rare punch-the-air TV moments. The duo performed 'Throw The "R" Away', a superb song that told how they'd flattened all the vowels to make sure their words didn't grate on Saxon ears. The studio audience at Tyne Tees Television – most of whom probably had indecipherable Geordie accents themselves – seemed bemused.

But they made a real impact, such was the influence of *The Tube*, then the UK's premier live TV pop show.

'When we got off the train at Waverley on the way home, we walked along George Street to our flat,' said Charlie. 'A guy came running out of Mad Dogs bar and shouted: "I saw you on the telly . . . you're the guys off *The Tube*." It was only three hours later, so it was as quick as that. It was instantaneous.'

Within months, The Proclaimers had signed a major deal with Chrysalis Records and were in the studio recording their debut album, *This Is The Story*.

A few weeks later – on 19 November – DJ Steve Wright introduced their debut appearance on *Top of the Pops* with the single, 'Letter From America', that rose up the charts to reach No.3. It was produced by one of their music heroes, the legendary Gerry Rafferty.

But despite their success, I felt it was my duty as a true music fan to put an end to this charade. In my story for the *Daily Record* I claimed the duo were not what they seemed. I reported they were actually two out-of-work Cockney actors from the East End of London who'd been struggling for several years to make a break-through. My story revealed how they'd taken drastic action in a desperate last-gasp bid to achieve pop stardom.

In the mid-1980s, Scotland was at the epicentre of a music explosion. This pair of blatant opportunists had watched acts such as

Simple Minds, Altered Images, Del Amitri, Orange Juice, Deacon Blue and Aztec Camera all crack the pop charts. So they decided that if they passed themselves off as being 'Scottish' it could perhaps fast-track them to fame and fortune.

They were prepared to go to any lengths to make it happen. I claimed they'd attended a top Harley Street plastic surgeon and went under the knife in a series of painful operations to make them look like twin brothers.

We printed a photograph of a Pearly King – wearing horn-rimmed spectacles and a flat cap and suit decorated by hundreds of mother-of-pearl buttons – showing how 'Charlie Reid' looked after his facial surgery. I also revealed that both actors had approached singer Kenneth McKellar – best known for his recording of the classic, 'Song Of The Clyde' – to perfect their Scots accents. His credentials were absolutely impeccable. Kenneth worked closely with them as a voice coach for several months so each could perfect a defined Celtic brogue.

'I thought they were a COMEDY act . . . that's why I agreed to help,' said a visibly shaken Kenneth.

'When I saw them performing their single, 'Letter From America', on *Top of the Pops* I realised that I'd been duped. In real life, they sound like Derek Jameson.'

I explained too that they'd been skilfully steered to stardom by their ruthless manager, Rolf Paoli, renowned for his use of underhand tactics.

When the *Record* hit the streets the story did indeed cause a sensation. It became what in newspaper terms is known as . . . 'a talker'. A real water-cooler moment, long before these plastic contraptions had been installed in offices up and down the land.

Some people were stunned.

But it certainly pays to read the small print. Our publication date was, as you've probably guessed . . . 1 April.

In the following day's edition, we printed a retraction telling readers it was all a big joke, hoping they'd had a good laugh at my preposterous tale. But once the snowball starts rolling down the hill and gathering momentum, it's almost impossible to stop it.

The real Proclaimers were on tour 9,000 miles away in Australia when the story broke. A few days later, I received a message from their manager – the real-life Rolf Paoli, whose name was of course, an anagram of April Fool – in Melbourne saying:

'What the hell is going on?'

Somehow, they'd heard about my ridiculous exclusive Down Under.

I'm pleased to say the twins took my scam with good humour. When they were back home in Edinburgh there were a few occasions when they were the target of angry white-van-man drivers who'd shout out: 'Fuck off back to London . . . ya pair of English bastards.'

But in every bit of fiction is there really always a grain of truth? It would seem so. Years later, Craig and Charlie visited a radio station in Stoke during a promo tour. The interview was going well until the DJ said: 'And tell me . . . how did you two guys meet?'

You couldn't make it up. Or could you?

How I missed out on winning the Pulitzer Prize for such an accomplished piece of fearless journalism is nothing short of a scandal.

But the truth can sometimes be even stranger than fiction. I scored an exclusive with another story that turned out to be so outlandish, you'd have sworn it was also an April Fool.

It was late on a Friday night and I was trying to get out of the office after a hectic week on the *Record*. A guy called my number and introduced himself as the manager of a new rock band he was trying to drum up some publicity for.

He immediately launched into his sales pitch. They had just released a single recorded with top British producer, Vic Maile, who over the years had worked with The Who, Jimi Hendrix, The Kinks, Fleetwood Mac, The Animals and Led Zeppelin. Maile was a very big name to drop.

But then my ears really pricked up. 'The band are called The Scrubs . . . they take their name from Wormwood Scrubs high security prison in London,' said James Campbell, a Scot from Allanton in North Lanarkshire. 'There are six people in the line-up. Three prison warders and three convicted murderers, who are each serving life sentences.'

Now, he'd really got my attention.

James was a fast-talking fixer who had many different strings to his bow. Most notably, he was the PR manager for another pair of twins . . . the Krays, brothers Ronnie and Reggie. They had ruled the East End of London, owning nightclubs and operating protection rackets and they'd also forged links with the Mafia in America.

In 1968, the Krays were sentenced to thirty years imprisonment for murder by High Court judge, Mr Justice Melford Stevenson. It was the longest sentence ever handed down at the Old Bailey. James was signed up to promote their highly lucrative business interests from behind bars. When he had his first meeting with Reggie in HMP Lewes in Sussex, he told the press:

'He wasn't as big as I'd imagined but when he shook my hand and looked me in the eye, I understood why he scared people. Soon I was also travelling to Broadmoor secure mental hospital to visit Ronnie. It became my job to make sure the only people making money from the Krays were the Kray family.

'They made tons of money, but they were a bit like Robin Hood . . . they gave a lot of it away. I used to tell them no, don't do that.'

James seemed to have all the right connections. So much so, that he claimed organising a face-to-face interview with The Scrubs would not be a problem.

A week later, I travelled to Wormwood Scrubs with my photographer to talk to the band. We were escorted into the jail's infamous D-Wing, dubbed 'The Nut House' because it had held some of Britain's most notorious killers. Previous inmates included the 'Yorkshire Ripper' Peter Sutcliffe, the 'Black Panther' Donald Neilson, and a group of IRA bombers.

We were introduced to the three prisoners who had formed the band – J.C., Joe and Thinh. They were incarcerated alongside Winston Silcott, who'd recently been given a life sentence for the murder of policeman Keith Blakelock during the Tottenham riots, and Jeremy Bamber, who was serving twenty-five years for killing five members of his family.

As we were led in by the prison warders – Dave Bruce, John McCarroll and Tug Wilson – the atmosphere was chilling. To an outsider, it was a harrowing sight with rows of reinforced metal cell doors running the full length of three main landings where inmates were locked up for seventeen hours out of every twenty-four. Some had identification cards with the word 'LIFE' starkly printed on them in block letters that seemed to underline the feeling of confinement. It was a bleak, depressing scene.

When I sat down to talk to J.C., Joe and Thinh they played me the single appropriately titled, 'Time For You', released on the indie label, Flick Knife Records.

As I listened to the song they stared self-consciously at the floor and looked like any other unknown rock band seeking a bit of feedback for their music. It had been recorded in one day by a mobile studio set up by producer Maile in the prison's recreation hall. It was a heavy-metal rocker that would have given Motorhead the chills and was not for the faint-hearted.

In prison parlance it was hoped that the single would become 'a nice little earner', for all royalties were to be donated to the jail's charity that raised £10,000 annually for the local community. If nothing else, the project had helped boost morale in the dismal D-Wing.

The other inmates had staged a competition to find a good name for the group. The top three contenders were . . . Band On The Run, Murder Incorporated and The Stranglers!

'This is a way for us to keep body and soul together and if we can raise some money for charity . . . great,' guitarist J.C. told me. 'We consider ourselves very lucky and we make the most of it.'

The Scrubs were permitted to rehearse for a total of one and a half hours each week, between their regular prison jobs in the tailoring shop or studying Open University courses. But what would they say to people who think that as convicted killers they should be locked up and the key thrown away, instead of being turned into pop stars? It was a question they were anticipating.

'We have done terrible things – that's why we're here,' said J.C. 'There's no justification for what we've done and there never will be. But everyone's case is different. The general public tend to lump us all in together. We're not saying we're Mr Nice Guys, don't get me wrong, and we're not doing this to make stars out of ourselves. We're simply doing this for charity, to make money for needy causes. And maybe through that we can give something back to society. It might not be much, but if we can help somebody, that's great.'

Bandmate Joe was even more forthright when he told me:

'We've had letters from people saying: "They're killers and animals . . . DON'T turn them into pop stars". But we've also had many letters of support and encouragement from the public. I don't think people realise the punishment of being put in prison – the sheer detachment from society and the stigma put upon you – but everyone in here is different.

'Of course, we deserve to be here but that doesn't necessarily mean we have been murderers all our lives – it may just have been one isolated incident. So we view our record as merely a way to speak to people on the outside, and perhaps do a bit of good for the community around us.'

And The Scrubs appeared to be getting their message across. They revealed that they had a fast-growing fan club with members in such far-flung places as America, Australia and Europe.

James Campbell – ever the optimist – had total faith in the band and there was a real enthusiasm on D-Wing that the record could break out of jail and into the charts.

'Musically, they stand up on their own and I think they compare favourably with bands like ZZ Top and AC/DC,' he said. 'It's also quite easy for me to have a good working relationship with them. At least I always know where they are.'

This ambitious liaison between prison warders and convicted killers was definitely one of those rare occasions where truth really was stranger than fiction. Everybody in the whole cell block, WAS dancin' to the jailhouse rock.

Chapter 16
Satellite City –
17 January 1978

As the final minutes on the clock ticked down, the game was on a knife-edge with the score locked at 2-2. We had gone ahead twice and done well to mount a serious challenge but the realisation began to sink in that we were facing a team of magicians. The Brazilians played barefoot and they stroked the ball around with pinpoint accuracy. One goal was all that stood between us, and a famous victory.

There was much more than just personal pride at stake. Simple Minds carried a nation's hopes on their slender, rock-star shoulders. Suddenly chart statistics and record sales paled into insignificance. If we could beat the Brazilians – on home turf – the bragging rights would be incalculable.

I've had some great adventures travelling the world with Simple Minds, and flying down to Rio de Janeiro in January 1988 has got to be one of the most memorable. The band had been invited to appear at Hollywood Rock, a series of outdoor concerts – also starring Supertramp, Duran Duran, The Pretenders, UB40, Robert Palmer, Simply Red and Johnny Marr – in the square at the Sambadrome, a venue purpose-built for the annual carnival.

From the moment we set foot on the Copacabana we were bitten by the football bug. Along the entire stretch of the beach there were countless football matches or hands-free volleyball games – what we'd call head tennis – being played from dawn till dusk. The skill factor in even the most casual encounter between two kids' teams was off the scale.

Pelé – hailed as the world's greatest footballer – had an apartment overlooking the Copacabana with a massive roof terrace covered in AstroTurf so he could go up and kick a ball around.

Within days we'd raided sports shops buying Brazil strips, the classic yellow shirts worn by the national team. I'd not kicked a ball since 1981 after having broken my left leg twice within the space of three years playing football. I'd actually chucked my boots in the bin so I wouldn't be tempted to take to the field again. The thought of sitting in plaster for a third time, for months on end, was something I was keen to avoid.

But when the concert promoter organised a football tournament, all logic went out of the window. The Brazilians had thrown down the gauntlet. We were driven to his palatial pad – that had its own football pitch – on the outskirts of the city.

It's not often Jim Kerr is lost for words, but when he stepped off the tour bus and a TV reporter thrust a microphone under his nose and said: 'What can you tell me about your team selection for today's game?' the singer was caught on the hop.

'We're just here to have a bit of a kick around,' he replied.

He was well wide of the mark. The Brazilians were taking things much more seriously.

We were drawn against The Pretenders, a team that included former Smiths' guitarist, Johnny Marr, who had trials with Manchester City as a teenager. The game – a straight twenty minutes – was fiercely contested but we beat them 5-2.

In the other tie, the Brazilians faced UB40. The scores were level at 1-1, before the home side moved up a gear and banged in another three goals. It was a clinical finish. I remember thinking, shit . . . we've got to play them next in the final.

We also had a good team with Jim, guitarist Charlie Burchill, keyboard player Mick MacNeil and drummer Mel Gaynor. I played up front with Rab Clark, a mate from Glasgow, and tour manager, Paul Kerr – Jim's brother – who'd been tracked as a youngster by Liverpool F.C. But there was one problem preventing us from achieving our goal . . . we were having difficulty breathing.

The game was played under a blazing sun in eighty-degree heat. It was like running around in a sauna. When I looked at the Brazilians they didn't appear to have a single bead of perspiration between them. They were laughing and fucking joking. I couldn't catch enough breath to even shout to a teammate.

Then the temperature increased. As Paul was shielding the ball, a Brazilian player went in hard from behind. He reacted and elbowed him in the face to get clear.

In today's modern football era – tightly governed by VAR – the adjudication would probably have been a straight red card. All hell broke loose. The home side piled in – we retaliated – and a mass brawl broke out. The referee blew his whistle and the match was abandoned for fighting. The TV reporter was commentating on the melee as his cameraman filmed all the action. It was bedlam.

Back in the dressing room, with tempers still frayed, the Minds' manager, Bruce Findlay managed, somehow, to defuse the situation. It was agreed we'd return to the pitch and play out the remainder of the game. With just minutes left, the Brazilians broke up field and made it 3-2.

Defeated but not disgraced. That was the official line from the band. But I think we'd earned the respect of the Brazilians who knew they'd been in a real tussle with the 'Gorbals diehards'. The story hit the TV news and the pages of the morning papers.

Simple Minds also made a big impact musically in Rio. The gig was a triumph as they played to a capacity audience, most of whom were seeing the band for the first time.

For a laugh, Jim invited Rab Clark and me to join him on stage for a spirited rendition of 'Alive and Kicking'. What the audience made of our 'singing' God only knows.

Jim visited a favela, a slum area up in the hills where people lived in abject poverty, overlooking the opulent city below. He was accompanied by a number of security men for fear he'd be kidnapped by local drug gangs. But the people in the shanty towns were delighted to welcome him into their homes and made him feel at ease.

The only anxious moment came when a teenage boy raced out of a shack towards them. There was no danger . . . he had a copy of the band's album, *New Gold Dream (81-82-83-84)* and asked Jim to sign it.

When I went on the road with Simple Minds, I invariably shared a room with the singer's late father, Jimmy, who was one of my dearest friends. I loved the man. Our party was booked into the five-star Rio Palace Hotel on the Copacabana. The place was so upmarket Frank Sinatra was paid $1million to appear in the ballroom in 1980. Ol' Blue Eyes opened his show – in front of an intimate audience of just 700 people – with 'They've Got An Awful Lot Of Coffee In Brazil', a song he'd first recorded in 1946.

Jim very graciously swapped rooms with us. We were given his luxurious penthouse suite overlooking the beach . . . and he took one of our single rooms at the back of the hotel that looked into a noisy bus garage.

A few days later, any suggestions the arrangement could be reversed were soon dismissed by his old man, 'Get to fuck. You're here to work . . . we're here on our holidays,' he said, laughing. And just to rub it in, Jimmy would sit out on the veranda in his towelling bathrobe – looking like an old Mafia don – eating fresh fruit or handmade chocolates, a gift from the hotel manager who still believed the 'James Kerr' occupying the suite was the singer.

When the band were busy doing interviews and photo sessions, the two of us explored Rio, walking the length and breadth of the city like a couple of locals. The crew dubbed us 'Compo and Clegg' after the old duffers from the BBC TV series, *Last of the Summer Wine*.

The highlight was undoubtedly when we visited Christ the Redeemer – the 100ft high statue of Jesus – built on top of the Corcovado Mountain. It is one of the new Seven Wonders of the World and the panoramic views of the city below were breathtaking.

But I could see something was troubling Jimmy, a former builder. He looked quizzically at the statue and said: 'I wonder if they brought the concrete up pre-mixed . . . or did they mix it on the site? I think there would be such a big volume they must have brought it up pre-mixed and poured it in.'

Once a builder . . . always a builder!

We all wanted to meet Pelé. That would have made the trip really unforgettable. A few feelers were put out to see if it could be arranged. Unfortunately, Brazil's three-time World Cup winner was away on business.

Jim did get to spend time with him many years later, however, when the band headlined a massive gig at the Brandenburg Gate in Berlin to launch the 2006 FIFA World Cup in Germany. Pelé introduced them and spent a few moments backstage deep in conversation with Jim. The group were dying to hear what they'd talked about.

Later, Jim went on the wind-up and told them:

'Pelé said that even though he lived thousands of miles away in Brazil, he'd heard I was the star man of the school team at Holyrood Secondary in Glasgow.

'He told me I was a household name in Rio . . . and that they were all talking about how great a player I was up in the favelas.'

It was a great line. Total bollocks, of course. But firm proof that when you have to choose between the truth and the legend – choose the legend.

We did meet another famous name of a very different sort on the Copacabana . . . Ronnie Biggs, the Great Train Robber. One of our crew spotted him in a cafe on the beach and struck up a conversation.

Ronnie was part of the gang who stole £2.3 million – about £30 million today – from a Royal Mail express heading from Glasgow to London in 1963. He was still on the run from Scotland Yard more than twenty-five years after he'd been sprung from Wandsworth Prison, scaling the wall with a rope ladder.

Ronnie was popular with tourists, particularly Brits. He fronted a nightclub for a local businessman and invited the band to drop in after their gig. For some bizarre reason, I had a hunch we'd catch up with Ronnie in Rio. So I took a bunch of glossy Virgin Records publicity photographs of him singing with The Sex Pistols on the hit single, 'No One Is Innocent', with me. He signed the lot of them.

Jimmy and I had both read several books about the Great Train Robbery and we spent a couple of hours getting the inside story from him. Ronnie was more than happy to talk about his exploits.

'I shouldn't even be talking to you two because the last Jocks I got friendly with tried to take me back to Britain against my will,' joked Ronnie, in a reference to a failed attempt to kidnap him in 1981.

A gang of mercenaries led by a Scot, John Miller – a former SAS soldier – abducted Ronnie and set out to drag him back to the UK to claim the reward money. But their plan was scuppered when the yacht they were sailing in suffered an engine failure. After the crew put out an SOS, they were rescued by coastguards fifteen miles east of Barbados.

Ronnie was returned to Rio and didn't give himself up until he voluntarily flew home to London in 2001 . . . straight into the hands of Scotland Yard detectives.

We had a great night listening to his tales. He was a real lovable rogue.

My friendship with Simple Minds dates back to their live debut at Satellite City on 17 January 1978. They were third on the bill of a 'punk rock' gig headlined by reggae band, Steel Pulse, and featuring Rev Volting And The Backstabbers and The Nu-Sonics, soon to become Orange Juice. The disco – all sparkly walls and sticky carpets – was hallowed ground as it was located on the top floor of the Glasgow Apollo.

From the moment the Minds walked on stage there was something about them. The group line-up of Charlie on guitar and violin, Duncan Barnwell on second guitar, Tony Donald on bass and Brian McGee on drums looked a solid unit.

But it was Jim who commanded your attention. He wore a black priest's frock coat – bought from the Briggait flea market – tight jeans, winkle-picker boots and he had a severe pudding-bowl haircut. He didn't look like anybody else I knew or had ever seen in Glasgow.

He also seemed ill at ease, as if he'd rather be anywhere else other than behind the mic in front of 500 music fans. But it was his obvious discomfort that made him so compelling.

It would be too simplistic to say he had the look of a rabbit caught in car headlights, for that would suggest fear. He had NO fear. Instead, Jim had an inner confidence and knew, even then, that Simple Minds had a chance.

They opened their twenty-five-minute set with 'Act Of Love', then powered through 'Wasteland', a cover of The Velvet Underground's 'White Light/White Heat' and 'Pablo Picasso'. Their closing number was an eight-minute-long film theme called 'Pleasantly Disturbed', which saw Charlie switch between his Flying V Gibson guitar and a violin.

I thought they were stunning. After their set, I politely knocked on the dressing-room door and asked Charlie for the name of the band's singer for my review.

Jim vividly recalled that momentous gig when he guested on my BBC Radio Scotland show in January 2022, to promote the release of 'Act Of Love', which the band revisited for their latest album, *Direction Of The Heart*, nearly forty-five years later.

He said: 'I remember how much it meant to us. I mean, did I think we were ready . . . probably not? We walked on to the sound of our own feet. But when Charlie hit that riff for 'Act Of Love' I could feel the energy in me straight away, and before I knew it, we were off.

'Although I say we weren't ready I think we had something about us. You had to have an attitude and a sound. We already had that under our belt from that very first gig. And fortunately, people responded to it.'

Could I have predicted what would follow? Never in a million years. But of the four bands on the bill, it was significant that I focused on them. Even then – after just five songs – I thought they had the potential to make a major impact. When they did, I was fortunate to have an Access All Areas pass to see them become the most successful band in Scottish rock history.

In those early days, I wrote about them in my *Sunday Mail* column and played their songs and interviewed them on Radio Clyde. At times it appeared almost as if our respective careers were running parallel. Jim would drop white labels off at Clyde reception so I got an exclusive first play of their latest track. This was new territory for all of us.

On 14 August 1983, I was with the Minds when they played a massive open-air gig as guests of U2 at Phoenix Park in Dublin . . .

on a dream bill that also included Eurythmics, Big Country, Steel Pulse and Perfect Crime. The day before the show, they sound-checked with a brand-new song that became one of the key tracks on their forthcoming album, *Sparkle in the Rain*. It was the first time anyone had heard the pulsating bass intro to 'Waterfront', now regarded as one of their greatest hits.

When the group opened their set with it the following day it was well received by the 50,000-strong audience. Two months later, I was drafted in to help promote 'Waterfront'.

The band decided to shoot a video for the new single at the Barrowland Ballroom. The Glasgow venue had lain empty since the notorious 'Bible John' murders when three young women were strangled after meeting a man in the East End dancehall between 1968 and 1969.

But promoters Pete Irvine and Barry Wright, of Regular Music, thought the old place had real potential as a concert venue. The Minds needed an audience . . . and fast. I put out an appeal on my Clyde show asking listeners to send a stamped addressed envelope into the station for a ticket ballot. The response was overwhelming. I got sack loads full of mail. It was like the Blue Peter Appeal. After my show, I sat in the Clyde canteen with my colleague Ross King and we dutifully put a pair of tickets into the first 750 envelopes chosen at random. I then went straight to the Head Post Office in George Square at 5 a.m. and stuffed them into the letter box.

On 19 November, the Minds shot some outdoor footage on the old Renfrew Ferry that crossed the River Clyde. The following day they took to the stage at Barrowland and filmed take after take of 'Waterfront' to produce one of their most exciting videos. It was screened all over the world and showed their native Glasgow in a great light.

The video shoot helped reinvent Barrowland and over the next few years artistes such as U2, Radiohead, The Smiths, R.E.M., The Clash, Foo Fighters and The Beastie Boys played there.

In 1986, the band asked for my help again for another slightly more delicate matter. Their rise had been so meteoric that they played three dates at the SECC in February of that year on a world tour to promote their biggest selling album, *Once Upon A Time*. Demand to see the group went through the roof so they also confirmed a show at Ibrox Stadium in Glasgow on 6 June. All 55,000 tickets were snapped up and they added an extra concert the following day.

The rest of the bill was also a bit tasty, for their special guests were Lloyd Cole and the Commotions, The Waterboys, Hipsway and In Tua Nua, with The Cult replacing Lloyd Cole on the second night.

The Minds made a little bit of music history as the first Scottish rock band to headline their own outdoor stadium gig on home soil. Some fans thought Ibrox – home of Rangers F.C. – an odd choice of venue, as it was no secret that Jim and Charlie were diehard fans of Celtic, their most bitter rivals.

I arranged an exclusive interview for the *Daily Record* in the days before the first show. The band lined up for a picture on the pitch with Rangers' star striker Ally McCoist and Maurice Johnston, Celtic's goal machine. Mo, as he was better known, had not yet crossed the great sectarian divide . . . but more on that later.

My story was splashed across the centre spread of the paper. But just twenty-four hours before the first gig, the Minds faced an unforeseen problem. The two shows at Ibrox were part of a European tour that included prestigious dates at Milton Keynes Bowl in England and the San Siro Stadium in Italy, the home ground of Inter and AC Milan. On top of their huge stage structure, the band flew the flags of every country they were visiting – with the standards of England, Scotland, Holland, Germany, Belgium, Switzerland, France and Italy proudly displayed. As they were also playing an outdoor show at Croke Park in Dublin on 28 June, the tricolour – the national flag of Ireland – was also flown overhead.

I received an unexpected phone call from Bruce Findlay, who said: 'Sit at your desk for the next thirty minutes. Don't move. I might need you.'

At that time, Rangers had a tradition, history – call it what you will – of never having signed a high-profile Catholic footballer. Bruce was taken aside by a major figure in the club and told that he needed to remove the flag as it could . . . 'cause a riot'.

'At first, I thought he was joking,' Bruce told me, 'but when I realised he was serious I told him the flag wouldn't cause a problem of any kind. I also informed him that we were also flying a flag with Picasso's white dove, acknowledged as a symbol of peace. I said: "I can assure you, it won't be an issue with anybody attending the gig. I credit our fans with having a little bit more intelligence than that."'

But the club official was not convinced. He wanted it removed from the display. So Bruce called his bluff, saying: 'If you give me the request in writing – on a piece of Rangers F.C. headed notepaper – I'll have the tricolour taken down within ten minutes.'

The written request failed to materialise and the 'problem' miraculously disappeared.

'If I'd have been given a formal letter asking for the Irish flag to be removed I'd have sent it straight over to you by messenger so you could write the story for the paper,' Bruce said.

So the Irish tricolour – plus the flags of eight other countries on the tour itinerary – flew above Ibrox for both shows. It didn't cause any trouble at all. Nobody was outraged. In fact, until now I don't think it's even been mentioned once in the thirty-seven years that followed.

'These were great concerts and historic in that players from Rangers and Celtic – and fans of both teams – sang along as one,' said Bruce. 'It was a united Glasgow. Music can be very powerful stuff.'

Two years later, Mo Johnston came back on to the Simple Minds' radar.

I flew to meet the band in Saint-Tropez, in the South of France, to join them on their 'Street Fighting Years' tour. When I arrived late into Nice airport after my flight had been delayed, I immediately ran into trouble. I got pulled over by a French customs officer who asked to check my luggage . . . a small bag with clothing, and another with miscellaneous items. It was those miscellaneous items that proved of most interest.

Every time I went on the road with the band, I'd bring a 'Red Cross Parcel' of goodies for the dressing room, just to remind them of home. This trip was no exception. The customs guy began to remove the contents of the second bag . . . packets of Tunnock's Caramel Wafers, Caramel Logs and Teacakes, made by Scotland's oldest family bakery firm. There were also boxes of Rowntree's Fruit Pastels and Fruit Gums plus several bags of cinnamon balls and soor plooms.

But it was the main item that piqued the greatest interest. The most valuable part of my cargo was five-dozen potato scones, wrapped in cellophane, six to a pack. He called his mate over and they carefully examined the scones . . . prodding them, holding them up to the light, feeling the weight of each one. I'm sure they thought they'd uncovered a major drug smuggling operation.

Even though most French people speak good English, I had great difficulty explaining the importance of the humble 'tattie scone' as a traditional Scots delicacy. And just why I'd be transporting sixty of them through customs. They shook their heads and pointed me towards the 'Nothing To Declare' exit door.

I joined the band for four gigs in Fréjus, Lyon, Bordeaux and Toulouse. They went down a storm. The show opened with a stirring version of 'Street Fighting Years' – title track of their new album – with Jim crouched down at the top of a zigzag catwalk behind Mel Gaynor's drum kit. As the band played the haunting opening refrain, the singer rose to his full height and began dramatically walking down the ramp, his long coat swaying in the breeze. Jim nicknamed it his *Phantom Of The Opera* moment. An apt description, for he had it timed to perfection to reach the vocal mic to hit the opening lyric.

I was standing in the pit, taking photographs of his entrance, when Jim reached into his coat pocket and threw me down a chunky double chocolate Kit-Kat. A good review was assured.

At the end of the show, tour chef, Ying Ho came into the dressing room with sixty 'tattie scones' fried to perfection as a post-gig treat.

On 2 June, the band were appearing at Stade de la Beaujoire, the home of FC Nantes. Their star player was Mo Johnston, who had signed for the club in 1987, bringing his time at Celtic to a close. He was an instant success, scoring twenty-two goals for the French side, but his contract was coming to an end.

Initially, Mo had said he'd never return to play in Scotland. But he had a change of heart and opened negotiations – via his agent Bill McMurdo – to re-sign with his old club who were being managed by Billy McNeill, a member of the club's Lisbon Lions, the first British team to win the European Cup in 1967. The band urged me to stay out on the tour as Mo and his Nantes teammates were coming to the gig. He'd also organised an after-show party at his house.

Only one problem though, I had to be back in time for my programme on Radio Clyde. I was sorely tempted to take a rare night off and stay on, but when I tried to change my flight ticket it was going to cost an additional £500, so it didn't make sense. I flew back to Glasgow and they headed for Nantes. The gig was a huge success and so was the party. The band stayed up all night and went straight onto the tour bus at 7 a.m. next morning – feeling the worse for wear – to head for their next gig at Forest National in Belgium.

A few days later, I got a call that could have given me one of the biggest scoops of my journalistic career. The band told me Mo had confided that negotiations with Celtic had irretrievably broken down and he wouldn't be returning to the club with whom he'd won league and cup medals and scored seventy-two goals. Instead, he was now planning to sign for Rangers – the other half of the Old Firm – who were going through something of a revolution under new player-manager, Graeme Souness. I couldn't believe what I was hearing. The Celtic fans would never forgive Mo for joining their hated rivals and the Rangers support, who were largely Protestant, would not accept such a high-profile Catholic player. He wouldn't be able to go anywhere without facing the sectarian bile that is such a blight on Scottish society.

But the band revealed all that had been taken into account and that he would live in a house owned by David Murray, the Chairman of Rangers, with twenty-four-hour security. It was the football story of the decade. And I was sworn to secrecy. If the news leaked, the finger of blame would point straight at Simple Minds.

So I kept my mouth shut. I didn't tell a soul. At that moment, I was one of the only people in Glasgow who knew what was going on.

Two weeks later, word was out that the deal to take Mo back to Celtic Park was dead in the water.

Top football writer Allan Herron wrote a piece in the *Sunday Mail* speculating that such a proven goalscorer could be of interest to several UK clubs who were in the market for a striker, including Rangers. Now it was in the public domain. A possible move to Ibrox, of all places, was being talked about.

The following morning, I had a discreet word with the Sports Editor and Chief Football Writer at the *Daily Record* and told them what I knew. But they didn't take me seriously, saying: 'Why would Maurice Johnston go to Rangers? He'd never sign for them. It's all just pub-talk.'

They dismissed my story as complete nonsense.

On Monday, 10 July, I was heading into the office when I saw the bills outside newsagents across the city saying: 'Mo Signs For Gers'.

The *Scottish Sun* had splashed the 'world exclusive' story with the headline: 'Mo Joins Gers: He ends ban on Catholics'.

The paper claimed it was football's biggest-ever scoop and devoted fourteen news pages – plus the entire sports section – to how Rangers had outmanoeuvred their arch-rivals.

When I reached the office, the *Record*'s editorial floor was like a morgue. An inquest was already underway. Why had we not got the story?

I have no regrets. I didn't betray the band's confidence . . . that would have been unthinkable. But, with the benefit of hindsight, I just wish I'd had the foresight to get the bet on Mo Johnston to sign for Rangers. Ladbrokes or William Hill would have needed a mathematician to work out the odds on that one.

I could have made a fucking fortune.

SIDE 3

EVERY PICTURE
TELLS A STORY

Chapter 17
Splish, Splash . . .
I Was Taking a Bath

THERE IS A FRAMED photograph of me – 'with a professional quality finish' – for sale online at the bargain price of £49.99. Why anybody would dream of forking out hard-earned cash to buy it is beyond me. In the picture, I'm trying my best to look cool . . . but failing miserably. By my side is somebody who can achieve that with no effort whatsoever.

Grace Jones is dressed in a green satin peaked cap, an over-sized brown mohair jumper and tiny red shorts with matching fur-trimmed boots. She's also wearing maroon wrap-around shades and long black leather gloves. Grace looks stunning. The photograph was taken as we sipped tea together in the lounge of Blakes Hotel in London.

If I have the appearance of someone gripped by fear, it's perhaps understandable. Grace scares me to death. My first interview with the Jamaican singer, actress and model was an ordeal. Not because Grace was difficult or wouldn't respond to my questions. It was quite the opposite, more that she was so physically intimidating, with a reputation for being cantankerous and totally unpredict-able. As I glanced down at my notes, I was thinking . . . am I one question away from creating a spark which could cause an almighty explosion?

A friend – who was her record plugger – recalled a story where he'd set up a day of TV and radio interviews with Grace in a Manchester hotel. When he repeatedly called her room to make contact there was no reply and the DJs and news presenters – who were all on programme deadlines – began to get a little twitchy. In desperation, after a two-hour delay, he explained the situation to the duty manager who agreed to open her door with a pass key to ensure nothing untoward had happened. Only to discover there was NO Grace. The room was empty. It later transpired that she'd left the hotel, without a word, and caught a flight to Paris.

At the back of my mind was the infamous incident in 1980 for which she is best known. Who can forget when Grace hit the headlines after physically attacking TV host Russell Harty, accusing him of ignoring her – as he chatted to fellow guests, cosmetician Walter Poucher and photographer Patrick Lichfield – during his live BBC1 show? The incident was voted 'the most shocking TV chat show moment of all time'.

In her autobiography, *I'll Never Write My Memoirs*, Grace gave her side of the story. 'I was meant to sit next to Russell Harty and keep still and quiet. I was all dressed up like an Amazonian seductress . . . and treated like the hired help. I thought, this is NO way to treat a guest,' she said. 'We rehearsed the show in some detail. The three of us politely sat all facing each other in a semi-circle. There didn't seem anything to worry about.

'On the live show, it was very different. There was an audience, which immediately changed the atmosphere. Things moved very fast. I wasn't attacking him because I was drunk or stoned. I was lashing out because I felt he was not being proper. I am being sensitive rather than unruly. You can see that if you watch it.

'This is no way to treat a guest. Being stuck there while he ignored me made me feel very uncomfortable. I felt I was provoked.'

Grace was unrepentant and revealed she created such a furore that the BBC wanted to do it all again.

'Pissed off, I poked him in the back. Harty was rude. I wasn't going to put up with that,' she added. 'I lashed out on live television. It takes balls to do that, which could be seen as a little crazy.

'And then they tried to get me back on the show. The ratings soared. I had done him a favour. They wanted a rematch. It was all so tacky.'

When the invite dropped to interview Grace for a second time I almost turned it down. I still hadn't fully recovered from our previous encounter. Would my nerves survive another shredding? But I decided to give it a shot and flew to Milan with her Scots publicist, Murray Chalmers, a wonderful man I affectionately refer to as 'my favourite Dundonian bastard'.

As we checked in at our hotel the omens were not good. The receptionist dropped the bombshell that Grace and her entourage had been out partying the previous night and not rolled home until 6 a.m. She'd hung a 'Do Not Disturb' sign outside her door and issued strict instructions that all telephone calls to her room were to be blocked until further notice.

We went for dinner then spent the next day sightseeing, shopping and hanging around. There was nothing else for it. After waiting patiently for thirty-six hours – with no contact from anybody in her camp – Grace had still not resurfaced. We threw in the towel in frustration. What else could we do?

Just as we'd placed our bags in the taxi to head back to the airport, the receptionist shouted us back saying: 'I've got a call for you.' It was the singer's manager on the line.

Murray picked up the phone and the look on his face was priceless, when he told me: 'Grace is ready for the interview. Now! What do you want to do?'

I didn't want to go home empty-handed so I had a quick word with the driver who said we had only twenty minutes to spare before we'd need to hit the road to catch our flight. At long last we were in 'go' mode.

We were directed to Grace's suite and walked in to face a scene of carnage with empty champagne bottles, half-eaten room service meals spilling off trays and discarded clothes strewn on the floor. There were several people – male and female – in various states of undress lying on the bed or lounging on the sofas. All looked as if they'd had a rough night and appeared oblivious to the fact they suddenly had visitors.

I did a cinematic pan of the room, but there was NO Grace. Were we in the right place? A security man beckoned me over to the toilet door and said: 'Grace is having a bath. If you want to talk to her, you'll need to do it in here.'

I kept waiting for the punchline. But there wasn't one. He was deadly serious. He led me in and introduced me to Ms Jones who was lying in a tub . . . naked as the day she was born.

It all happened so fast I thought I was seeing things. It didn't seem real. But it was, and with the clock ticking, there was no time to waste. I sat on the toilet seat, placed my tape machine on the bidet and pressed 'Record'.

Grace looked exquisite. She covered her modesty beneath lavish suds from a scented bubble bath . . . just like Joan Collins used to do in *Dynasty*. But it didn't last for long. As the bubbles dissolved Grace lay back in all her naked glory.

After keeping me waiting for nearly two days, she was in a real playful mood. Throughout the interview, she talked about herself in the third person, as if Grace Jones was a separate character. I fired questions and she opened up about her new music and acting projects in her distinctive Jamaican drawl.

To Grace, having a conversation with a relative stranger while stark naked seemed like the most natural thing in the world. When I asked if her sensual pop persona came easily or was it part of an act, she told me: 'If Grace is walking down the street and she sees a guy looking at her, she knows exactly what he's thinking. Men desire her. They always want more and more.'

There's not a lot you can say to that. Certainly not while perched on a toilet.

As Murray pointed to his watch, I took the plunge saying:

'Nobody will ever believe I got to interview Grace Jones in her bath. I need proof. So can we do a quick picture?'

I was sure I'd feel her security man's hand on my collar. But she was more than happy to pose for a snap. I sat on the floor and she leaned out of the bath, draping her arms around me covering me in soapsuds.

Walking out of her suite – in a daze – I turned to Murray and said: 'Did I just interview Grace Jones in a bath?'

It was one of the most off-the-wall experiences I've ever had with anyone in the music business. I had to pinch myself just to make sure I wasn't imagining the whole thing.

Spin on a few weeks and I get a late-night phone call from my father who says excitedly: 'You've just been given a mention on the *Dame Edna Experience* on TV. Grace Jones was one of the guests and she was talking about you.'

Unfortunately, I was out at a gig so never got to see the interview and I didn't know anyone who had taped the show so I could watch it later.

Two years on, Grace was playing a series of UK club dates and I travelled down to Birmingham to review her show. I'd only ever seen her on TV in her stylish pop videos. She was fantastic, prowling the stage like a caged tiger performing classic hits such as 'Slave To The Rhythm', 'Pull Up To The Bumper', 'Warm Leatherette' and 'Nipple To The Bottle'. Make no mistake, the singer is a major music talent, something that's often obscured by her crazy antics.

Then, inevitably, things moved up a gear. A number of exuberant fans invaded the stage and began kissing and groping her provocatively. Far from being outraged, Grace welcomed the physical attention and gave as good as she got. She loved every minute of it. As a mass of legs and arms, boobs and bums collapsed on to the stage, the gig was abandoned.

In her dressing room Grace was outraged, but it had nothing to do with being the target of such intimate attention.

She said to me: 'Why did they stop the show? The people were beautiful. I was having so much fun out there.'

It was time to reintroduce myself. I pulled out a glossy print of the picture of Grace hanging out of the bath and hugging me.

'Oh, it's you,' she said, screaming with laughter, 'the guy who turned up when I was in the bath. When word got out everybody wanted to interview me in the bath. But I wouldn't do it . . . you're the only one.'

She grabbed a Sharpie and signed the photograph:

'Splish, splash, taking a bath . . . love, Grace Jones.'

In 2022, Guy Garvey of Elbow was a guest on my BBC Scotland radio show to preview the band's appearance at Edinburgh Castle that summer.

During our interview, I told Guy I wanted his job . . . but NOT as lead singer of his group. Instead, I said I'd much rather take over as the host of his new TV series, *From The Vaults*, screened on Sky Arts. In the programme, Guy has gone back into the vast ITV archive to unearth hidden music gems that have been gathering dust on the shelves for decades. It's been great to see rare or unseen clips of acts like The Sex Pistols, The Clash, Kate Bush, The Smiths, Frankie Goes To Hollywood, Patti Smith, Tom Waits and The Walker Brothers again.

When I sat down to watch episode six in the third series I couldn't have predicted what would come next. In that show, Guy focused on the artistes who'd made a real impact in 1989 such as The Pixies, Sonic Youth, Neneh Cherry and the Happy Mondays. Their archive performances were punctuated by an excerpt from the *Dame Edna Experience* on LWT, when the Aussie housewife-superstar's guests were Hollywood legend, Tony Curtis and Grace Jones.

Guy teed up the clip saying: 'Given her past history with chat show hosts this appearance was refreshingly lovely.'

Dame Edna introduced Grace beautifully when she told viewers: 'My next guest has been called a tigress, but to me she is as friendly as a kitten. She's in the music business and she's just made a fabulous new video . . . in my jacuzzi. Ladies and gentlemen, Ms Grace Jones.'

The statuesque Grace flounced down the studio staircase in a beautiful outfit and headdress, carrying her shoes in her hand.

Dame Edna didn't waste any time in quizzing her about her controversial past. 'You have a reputation for being a quick-tempered little lass,' she said, referring to her infamous encounter with Harty.

Grace replied: 'It depends on if I'm tired, really. I think I was a bit young then. Now I just count to ten . . . and then I hit.'

Dame Edna then asked if it was true she had given interviews in her birthday suit. I immediately sat up in my chair and couldn't believe it when Grace recalled our encounter in 1989 . . . albeit changing the facts ever so slightly.

'I did it recently, actually. I was in the bath and he arrived. I said . . . well, would he mind doing it in the bath?' she told Dame Edna. 'I didn't have any bubbles in this hotel. There was nothing to make the water bubbly. He was quite nervous, but then after he saw that I was very relaxed, he got relaxed.'

Dame Edna quipped: 'He did?' screwing up her face to laughter from the studio audience. Before adding, in the ad-lib to end them all: 'I bet you were relieved to see that, darling.'

At the close of my interview with Guy, I mentioned the Grace Jones moment. I showed him my picture of Grace hanging out of the tub and giving me a hug.

'Is that you with Grace Jones? Oh my goodness . . . that's amazing,' he said, stunned. 'What a claim to fame, man. What an amazing life experience.

'And of course, she would let YOU in . . . you handsome devil. I don't think she'd have let me in the bath with her. I'm gonna add your name across the bottom of the screen for repeats of that programme.'

Just like they do on *Sky News*. Fame at last!

Chapter 18
This Much Talent

THE ADVERT IN *MUSIC WEEK* magazine was straight and to the point: 'Drummer wanted. Must have no immediate family. Please apply to: David St. Hubbins, Nigel Tufnel and Derek Smalls.' The thick black border around the box – similar to a bereavement notice – lent it an added gravitas. I immediately phoned the hotline number.

Spinal Tap – renowned as 'one of England's loudest bands' – were launching their second album, *Break Like The Wind*, in 1992. But they faced an ongoing problem.

The fictional group – immortalised in Rob Reiner's hilarious 1984 'mockumentary' film, *This Is Spinal Tap* – had a tragic history with drummers. In 1966, their original sticks-man, John 'Stumpy' Pepys died in a bizarre gardening accident that police ruled was 'better left unsolved'. In a similar mysterious incident, his successor Eric 'Stumpy Joe' Childs perished after choking on vomit, possibly not his own. The band revealed that fingerprint experts were hampered in their investigation into the death because 'you can't really dust for vomit'. That case also remains unsolved.

Two more drummers – Peter 'James' Bond and Mick Shrimpton – spontaneously combusted on stage midway through gigs. Another, Chris 'Poppa' Cadeau was eaten by his pet snake, a python named Cleopatra. The dangers were obvious. But I felt it was worth the risk . . . the kudos of becoming a part of the musical legacy of Spinal Tap was simply irresistible.

I negotiated with an executive of Island Records, the band's UK record label, and he agreed to submit my name for the final list of applicants. The drum audition was scheduled for The Borderline

Club in Soho in London. I knew the venue well having seen R.E.M. play a secret show there a year earlier – billed as Bingo Hand Job – to launch their album, *Out Of Time*. I was assured my complete inability to play and total lack of musical experience was no impediment to me securing the coveted job on a full-time basis.

A few months earlier, Micky Dolenz of The Monkees and Gina Schock of The Go-Go's had taken part in an open audition in Hollywood. Both were eager to get the gig. Mick Fleetwood of Fleetwood Mac also auditioned while wearing a fireproof body suit. But Tap were still looking for the right man. So I was in with a chance.

The Borderline was packed with 300 fans eager to see their idols up close. I was one of nine names on the audition sheet with Rat Scabies, drummer of The Damned, who was already installed as the bookies' favourite. Set up on the tiny stage was Spinal Tap's instantly recognisable drum kit that had been played by a succession of famous – if rather unfortunate – percussion legends. The first young hopeful, a rocker from a local metal band, took the stage. Let battle commence.

A ninety-second studio mix of Tap's classic hit, 'Big Bottom', was blasted out of the PA system minus the drum track. Each contestant had to play along on the array of floor toms, snares, bass drums and cymbals, displaying all their skills. As I counted off the contestants, panic set in. The only time I'd ever 'played' drums was as a child using my grandmother's knitting needles to pound the leather pouffe as I accompanied a song on the radio. But this was the real deal. Tap meant business.

My name was called and I walked on to a barrage of good-natured abuse . . . but abuse, nevertheless. All three band members – actors Michael McKean, Christopher Guest and Harry Shearer – sat on stools at an elevated judges' podium in full character.

'The stage is all yours,' said guitarist, Nigel Tufnel.

The track boomed out of the speakers – one louder, but of course – as the crowd began singing along. I was swept up in the moment.

I guess if you ask any drummer to quantify the most vital requirement for any kind of successful career, the word coordination would be high on the list. I had none. I could hit the snare and floor tom with my sticks and fire the cymbals and bass drum with my feet . . . but not, for some reason, at the same time. I quickly realised this when the mood in the audience was injected with what I'd term 'unrest'.

I made a snap decision. If I was gonna fuck up, at least fuck up in time. I hit everything around me in some kind of an attempt at a rock rhythm. It was all I could do. The rousing cheer I got at the end of my ninety seconds was a definite sympathy vote.

It was over to the judges' podium for the verdict. Was the job mine? They held up white boards with numbers on them, just like the panel on *Strictly Come Dancing*. I scored minus twelve, which was most encouraging.

Singer David St. Hubbins – who is named after the Patron Saint of Quality Footwear – said, sardonically: 'What we liked about you, Billy, was that you managed to avoid all the old clichés like . . . technique.'

I viewed that as a result. A muted sympathetic cheer from the crowd underlined that.

The eventual winner was a guy from a heavy metal band in North London. His prize was a British Telecom pager that he was instructed to wear on his belt so that the next time a Tap drummer expired in an incident 'better left unsolved' they'd bleep him and he'd immediately join the band.

It is said the real glory of the Olympics is not about the winning but the taking part. I'd climbed a personal Mount Olympus. I played drums for Spinal Tap and have not yet died in a mysterious gardening accident or from spontaneous combustion (at time of writing).

It could be argued that my lack of prowess as a rock drummer is more than compensated for in my expertise as a dancer. But not, I fear, by anybody who's actually seen me strut my stuff. You'll be familiar with the phrase 'he's got two left feet'. I'd settle for that.

My skills on the dance floor were put to the test when I interviewed Diana Ross to preview her show at the SECC in Glasgow in 1997. Ms Ross – as it's said she likes to be addressed – had a reputation for being a pop diva. I was nervous. The location for our chat – the cocktail lounge of Claridge's in London – was intimidating. I felt really self-conscious just walking past the liveried commission-aire stationed at the front door who welcomed VIP guests from all over the world.

My only previous visit to the luxury five-star hotel in Mayfair was when I'd attended a press conference for David Bowie more than a decade earlier.

Ms Ross arrived with her publicist Phil Symes, the UK representa-tive of heavyweight global PR firm, Rogers and Cowan. It didn't get much bigger. I was filming the interview for *Scotland Today*. We had a huge audience. Ms Ross was a global superstar. This was not the time to screw up.

But my fears were unfounded. She was fabulous company . . . warm, chatty and highly amusing. It was a real privilege to hear stories of the early days of Motown Records and how history was made in Hitsville U.S.A. in Detroit.

She was a dream to talk to. We were soon on first-name terms. So I felt bold enough to go for it. I told Ms Ross I was a lifelong fan of The Supremes and loved all of their records . . . apart from one. She gave me a rather puzzled look. I explained that, as an awkward teenager, the part of my school curriculum I hated most was not endless boring periods of maths, physics or geography, but dance practice, where masochistic teachers prepared classes for the annual end-of-term school prom. There was no escape from this traumatic ordeal. I used to really look forward to P.E. classes where we'd go up to Springburn Park nearby and play football – rain, hail or shine.

But as the school dance drew closer, all ball games were binned. For two periods, the boys would line up on one side of the school gymnasium, with the girls on the other. It was like recreating the movie, *West Side Story*, as the Sharks and the Jets faced off . . . but without the sharp clothes or cool New York accents.

'OK, boys, pick a partner.' Those five words provoked blind panic. Who was man enough to get up off the bench and be the first to walk across the no-man's-land to the wall-bars opposite and ask a dame to dance? With the realisation there was NO guarantee she'd say yes.

Comedian Kevin Bridges has an entire routine in his stage act that recreates this ritual in humiliatingly accurate detail. You could be scarred for life.

For two hours we'd be taught the steps for archaic dances such as Strip the Willow or The Dashing White Sergeant, to a soundtrack of accordion music played from a 78rpm disc on an enormous wooden record player. There was no pleasure in this at all.

But, harrowing as it was, it remained a necessary evil. To have any remote chance of meeting, talking to, getting to know, then finally walking a girl home – to perhaps be rewarded with a furtive kiss on the doorstep – there simply was no other way. You HAD to go to the school dance.

In the midst of this torture, there should have been one fleeting point to look forward to . . . the moment we were allowed to dance to a pop record. Now, there was no shortage of choices. My mates would arrive at the gym with albums by The Beatles, The Who, The Faces or The Rolling Stones and advise the teachers which tracks would be most suitable for some movement more rooted in the twentieth century. Their recommendations fell on deaf ears.

For some bizarre reason, the school only owned one solitary seven-inch vinyl single . . . 'Baby Love' by The Supremes, the 1964 No.1 hit performed by Diana, Mary Wilson and Florence Ballard. It's a great record. The song was a fitting soundtrack for the music and cultural revolution created by Berry Gordy after he'd launched his Motown label with the assistance of an $800 loan from his father.

But 'Baby Love' soon lost its appeal.

I explained to Ms Ross that the teachers gleefully taught us a dance called the Bunny Hop, built around a series of jump steps, 360-degree twirls and handclap routines. They claimed it was perfect for this slice of Motown magic. It was impossible to retain any dignity while bunny hopping towards the girl of your dreams. In fairness, I think the lassies were equally as horrified. They didn't want to be there either.

'Can you still remember the steps?' asked Ms Ross.

'I wish I could forget them,' I replied. 'I've even considered electroshock therapy to erase them from my mind.'

I told her how every time 'Baby Love' comes on the radio – even all these years on – I find my left leg almost instinctively sidestepping to start the dance.

'Why don't you show me,' she countered.

On that day, if you were one of the people enjoying afternoon tea and smoked salmon sandwiches in the lounge of Claridge's . . . congratulations.

Diana Ross sang an a cappella version of 'Baby Love' as I danced the Bunny Hop one final time, with choreography that was simply stunning in places. You witnessed a rare moment in music history. But one never to be repeated.

Chapter 19
Opening Night

I COULD SEE BRUCE SPRINGSTEEN walking towards me out of the corner of my eye. I gulped for air. A few minutes earlier, he'd read my review of the opening night of his European tour in Glasgow. What if he didn't like what I'd written or disagreed with a couple of bits of what I felt was constructive criticism of his performance?

I'd gatecrashed a private after-show party at the exclusive Devonshire Hotel following Springsteen's sell-out date at the SECC on 31 March 1993. In addition to the usual first night nerves, The Boss had not played with his band in more than three months. So reputations were on the line.

I'd dictated the copy for my review from a payphone in the foyer then bolted after the last song straight back to the offices of the *Daily Record* to catch the first edition coming hot off the presses. It was always an exciting moment to see something you've written in the heat of battle make it into cold, hard newsprint. When it went well, the feeling of job satisfaction was enormous.

I was pleased with what I'd written, so I thought I'd chance my luck. I arrived at the Dev with a bundle of papers and tried to sweet-talk my way past two burly security guards barring the door. They were having none of it. I managed to catch the eye of the concert's promoter, the legendary Harvey Goldsmith, over their shoulders. He waved me in and said: 'Let's see what you've written then.'

Harvey dished out copies to fellow guests and the chatter was briefly silenced as each began to read the review. It was like the opening night of a new show on Broadway. I could see Springsteen across the room – newspaper in hand – carefully reading my words. I tried to gauge his reaction. But his expression gave nothing away. A few minutes later, he was heading in my direction.

My fears were unfounded. Springsteen approved and shook my hand warmly. He said: 'Hey, buddy, it was good to meet with you yesterday. Thanks for your very kind words. They mean a lot to me. I'm glad you enjoyed the show. Hope I see you again sometime and good luck in the future.'

I'd received the endorsement of 'The Boss'. I tried to stay cool . . . but it took an enormous effort not to slide down the wall and collapse in a heap. His publicist, Jo Donnelly, said: 'You're part of the gang now. If Bruce had not liked what you'd said about him . . . he'd have told you, believe me. He calls it as he sees it. Always has done.'

Thanks to her, I'd met Springsteen for the first time just twenty-four hours earlier in the most unusual circumstances. Two months previously, it had been announced he was to play a surprise gig in Glasgow as a warm-up for the tour. In reality, it was a glorified production rehearsal for a string of twenty-six dates snaking their way across Europe. But Springsteen is so committed that no live appearance could ever be dismissed as a mere rehearsal. He'd built his reputation as an artiste who always gave one hundred per cent at every gig.

I'd put in a request to Jo at Columbia Records asking if I could talk to him. 'Springsteen has never done an interview specifically for Scotland . . . it would be good to put that right,' I told her. Jo said: 'I'll pass your request on to management but don't get your hopes built up. You know he doesn't do much, if anything, in the way of promo.'

Springsteen didn't have to. Tickets for his gigs went on sale and were instantly snapped up by his dedicated fans. What was there to promote? But, Jo went in batting on my behalf and it paid off. Word came through . . . the interview was ON.

Springsteen invited me to watch him soundcheck the day before the gig. There were no seats in the SECC as it was a hastily arranged 12,000 capacity all-standing show in the huge arena.

Following the simultaneous release of his albums, *Human Touch* and *Lucky Town* some months earlier, he was performing with what fans had dubbed 'The Other Band'. It was the first of only four tours when he didn't have the legendary E Street Band by his side. They hadn't played together since December so he was feeling a little rusty.

By their very nature, soundchecks are mundane affairs with endless stop-starts, tedious drum workouts and numerous technical issues needing to be solved. Not with Springsteen. He walked on stage at 4 p.m. precisely and played . . . and played . . . and played. For the next six and a half HOURS.

During songs, he danced the tango with his guitar or lay back on top of the piano playing a solo. As he punched the air to really drive his lyrics home, you'd have sworn you were in Wembley Stadium and there were 70,000 adoring fans around you. But when the singer looked out from the stage into the empty floor of Hall 4 all he could see was a lone figure. I was treated to what was virtually a private gig as he powered through classics like 'Born In The USA', 'Atlantic City', 'Badlands', 'The River', and 'Born To Run'. Each song was delivered with the passion, power and venom we've come to expect from one of rock's greatest live performers.

Within minutes, I had the intro for my story, writing: 'Last night, Bruce Springsteen played a surprise gig to an audience of one . . . me.'

At the close of the soundcheck, he walked off stage at 10.40 p.m. and said: 'Let's find a quiet room backstage where we can talk.'

I'd been promised just five minutes with the great man. Not a lot of time . . . even so, I was confident I could get something from him. But Springsteen had decided to reward me for my patience. As we walked into a tiny production room he turned to his assistant and said: 'See you in twenty.' He closed the door, sat down and gave me his full attention. I switched on my tape recorder.

The Boss immediately looked back to when he made his live debut in Scotland with two memorable shows at The Playhouse in Edinburgh on 16 and 17 May 1981 to launch his classic album, *The River*. He was even a little apologetic it had taken him twelve long years to come back again.

'I loved playing in Edinburgh, the audience were great. I've never forgotten the welcome I got on my first visit to the capital,' he told me. 'We drove into Scotland in the early morning and I was amazed at the scenery. It was really misty and the countryside was a beautiful deep green colour. I've never forgotten that. Friends told me to come to Glasgow this time. They said it was a hard rock 'n' roll town. I'm sorry for not getting here sooner. I've NO excuses.'

Springsteen revealed he was looking forward to playing in the city for the very first time and planned to treat fans to his usual marathon set. 'I'm used to being on stage for three hours. I'm not sure how it ended up that way . . . it kinda crept up on me,' he said. 'When I used to play in bars I did five fifty-five-minute sets every night. But it wasn't so intense. The more songs you write the more the fans want to hear them. I didn't intentionally set out to play until I dropped.'

As we chatted, he asked me if I had a favourite song from his vast catalogue. I told him it was his masterpiece, 'Thunder Road', especially the stripped-down version that appears on the *Live 1975–85* triple album box set.

'Well, we might just play that tomorrow night. You never know,' said Bruce, tantalisingly. And he delivered, for 'Thunder Road' was included in his six-song encore.

Just before the interview came to a close, the singer also gave me an insight into his family life with wife, Patti Scialfa. At that time, the couple had two children, son Evan, two, and one-year-old daughter Jessica Rae. The proud dad said: 'Being a parent does change the way you look at things. Kids learn what you do. So you have to think about how you're behaving. I have a lot of ideals on how I want to live my life and I've got to put them into practice now.'

I glanced at my watch. My twenty minutes was nearly up. But there was just time for me to mark the occasion. Springsteen knew I was a fan. It was obvious. So I asked if it would be possible to get a picture with him as a souvenir of the interview.

A quick snap would also look great in the *Record* and be firm evidence I'd beaten all the other papers in landing the big stories yet again. But his management aide suddenly reappeared and was intent on dragging him away. I thought the moment had gone, until Springsteen took charge.

He grabbed my camera and walked over to a security guard posted on the stage door and said: 'Hey fella, can you take a picture of me and my buddy, Billy?'

Click. I had another great shot for my collection.

Chapter 20
What About ABBA?

LET ME GET THIS RIGHT. You want me to phone Björn, Benny, Agnetha and Frida and ask them to get back together again – for one night only – and do it for a fee of just £250?

'I think they'd be brilliant. It would be the perfect way to close the show after "The Bells",' said executive producer Tommo, bursting with enthusiasm. 'They love Glasgow. Why don't you call them and see what they say?'

The boss was right. ABBA did love the city. They'd namechecked it in their smash hit 'Super Trouper', their ninth – and final – UK No.1 single.

I loved working alongside Tommo, as he was affectionately known. He was an award-winning journalist and broadcaster, highly respected in media circles as a 'good operator'. He was also the ultimate vibe-up merchant whose affable manner always encouraged you to run that extra mile. But on this occasion, I was very close to strangling him.

He led the team on *Late Edition*, a weekly light-entertainment show hosted by Kirsty Young and Jim White on Scottish Television. In 1995, the station's hierarchy decided a *Late Edition* Hogmanay Special – a mix of music and chat – would be beamed live from the studios to bring in the New Year. We'd be up against BBC Scotland who played it safe with a show of more traditional music, which included a link to the massive street party in the shadow of Edinburgh Castle. They usually won the annual 'Battle of The Bells' for TV ratings. So doing anything that deviated from that format was risky, to say the least.

In 1994, I'd taken voluntary redundancy from the *Daily Record* after eleven successful years as the paper's music writer. It felt like the right time to move on. Tommo brought me into the world of television and quickly showed me the ropes. It was completely new territory for me. He hired me as a celebrity booker and wanted access to my vast contacts book to sprinkle some star names across STV's output.

I'd organised the acts for *Late Edition* and scored a pretty good hit rate. Our guests included actress Liz Dawn, better known as Vera Duckworth, landlady of The Rover's Return in *Coronation Street*, world champion boxer 'Prince' Naseem Hamed and Noddy Holder, lead singer of Slade. I'd also signed up music acts such as Status Quo, Midge Ure, Ocean Colour Scene, Squeeze, Kula Shaker, Joan Armatrading, Sparks, Marc Almond and Del Amitri to play on the show.

I was told to pull out all the stops for our Hogmanay special. But this was easier said than done because my budget was best described as minimal. I was given £250 per act for 'expenses'. That barely covered the cost of a London-Glasgow return flight ticket.

Luckily the major record labels viewed a slot on the programme as valuable TV promotion. So they were happy to cover travel costs. But my biggest problem was the date . . . 31 December. Nobody wanted to work on New Year's Eve unless you were prepared to pay big bucks.

The going rate for a headline act playing Princes Street Gardens was £50,000 and counting. Most artistes preferred to spend time with their families unless you crossed their palm with some serious silver. So I decided to stay close to home. I booked my mates GUN to play a couple of their hits including their recent single, 'Word Up', a cover of the song by US funk group, Cameo. The Glasgow band's new, rockier version had peaked at No.8 giving them their biggest-ever chart success. It also won the prize for Best Cover at the MTV Europe Awards in Berlin, beating off opposition from 'Love Is All Around' by Wet Wet Wet and 'Go West' by the Pet Shop Boys.

I also secured The Silencers to perform their latest single, 'Wild Mountain Thyme'. We filmed them in an outdoor set lit by flaming torches at Stirling Castle the previous week. It looked amazing and the sentiment behind the song was absolutely perfect for the programme. But I was struggling to confirm a third music act and the clock was ticking.

'What about ABBA?' said Tommo.

I waited for him to start laughing. When he didn't, I realised he was deadly serious, or maybe just confused. Was he talking about Björn Again, the ABBA tribute act from Australia, who sold out concert venues around the UK? At that time, the girl who portrayed Agnetha was a singer from Paisley, so there was a strong local connection.

But no, he was indeed referring to the 1974 Eurovision Song Contest winners from Stockholm. I explained politely, but firmly, that ABBA had not worked together since 1982 and in the years that followed had turned down colossal sums of cash to stage a one-off reunion.

An hour later, he was back on the line. 'Why don't we try for Billy Joel?'

I'm a great believer in asking. If you don't ask . . . you don't get. But there comes a point where you have to take a reality pill.

'We'd need to fly Billy Joel, his girlfriend, manager, musical director and security man first class from New York to Glasgow,' I told him, in exasperation. 'We'd need to book four suites at the Hilton Hotel and have a limousine on standby. And that's not all . . . we'd also need to pick up the tab for all food and drinks during their stay. Are you prepared to do that?'

You can guess the answer. He was not to be deterred, however. He phoned back later that afternoon saying: 'Neil Sedaka. We could try for him.'

The boss was nothing if not optimistic. In the end, I booked Hue and Cry who performed their hit song, 'Looking For Linda'.

I also paired the duo – brothers Pat and Greg Kane – with Scottish jazz singer Carol Kidd to collaborate on a beautiful duet of 'Get Here', a cover of the 1991 Oleta Adams hit. It was a highlight of the show and it only cost me an extra tenner for a taxi.

Pat had insisted that he was back home before midnight so he could bring in the New Year with his wife and family. So we pre-recorded the duet and slotted it in 'as live' later in the running order. Viewers were none the wiser and I had a cab waiting outside to whisk him straight back to his flat in the West End of Glasgow the second he finished the track.

The show went without a hitch – thanks largely to Kirsty and Jim who were a good team – and the boss was delighted. We had a good laugh about his ambitious plan to re-form ABBA.

Four years later, the group were offered $1 billion – yes billion, you read that correctly – by an American-British business consortium to reunite for a concert tour.

'It's a hell of a lot of money to say no to but we decided it wasn't for us,' Benny Andersson told a Swedish newspaper. Maybe they should have got Tommo involved in the negotiations.

Television was a real step into the unknown for me. In the early eighties – thanks to my profile in the *Daily Record* and Radio Clyde – I was invited to audition for a music magazine show at Granada Television in Manchester. I had to interview Tony Wilson on camera and it was a real privilege to talk to the founder of seminal indie label Factory Records who had discovered bands such as Joy Division, The Happy Mondays and A Certain Ratio.

But I came a cropper when doing links from the autocue. I was reading the text so fast the operator was forced to spin it around like the barrels of a slot machine. I got a rejection letter the following week.

I fared a little better on the BBC.

In 1984, I was asked by Mike Appleton, the producer of *Whistle Test* to take part in *Rock Around the Clock*, an ambitious twelve -hour music marathon being screened live from 3 p.m. to 3 a.m. on BBC2. It was anchored by the show's regular presenters David Hepworth, Mark Ellen and Andy Kershaw who introduced a menu of live concerts from venues across the UK, archive studio sessions, video clips and interviews.

I was the host of two gigs at the Barrowland Ballroom in Glasgow by Aztec Camera and The Cure. It felt strange introducing Roddy Frame and his group – who had just released their second album, *Knife* – to a capacity audience at four o'clock in the afternoon, with the bustling Barras market going full throttle just outside. It was real seat-of-the-pants stuff for me but thankfully the gig went without a hitch.

But I ran into a problem before The Cure took to the stage a few hours later. As we were due to go live, a member of the band's crew requested bottles of mineral water for lead vocalist, Robert Smith.

'He can't do the gig without them. He needs it for his voice,' he told me.

Barrowland did not stock mineral water. Perrier was pretty much still an unknown quantity outside of a few trendy wine bars in the West End of the city.

'What about the local pubs? They must sell mineral water,' he said.

In my earpiece, I could hear the director in London saying: 'We're going live to Glasgow in five,' as his studio P.A. began the countdown.

I told The Cure's roadie: 'I can take you around some of the bars near here and buy you a side of beef, a bag of dope, a leather jacket, 500 cigarettes or a Ford Fiesta . . . all at a knock-down price. But you're in the East End of Glasgow. If the people here knew you could make money by selling bottles of water . . . the River Clyde would be drained dry.'

So Robert Smith never got his mineral water. I'm not sure what, if anything, he used as a substitute. But I can confirm he was in fine voice from first song until last.

The following week, I received a handwritten letter from legendary Scots comedian, Chic Murray. He was starring in the stage musical, *You'll Never Walk Alone* on Merseyside – portraying Bill Shankly, boss of Liverpool FC – when he caught my appearance on *Whistle Test*.

His note read: 'Billy, Saw you on TV on Saturday. You were on before I could reach the switch. Yours, Chic.'

Appleton was pleased with my rookie performance. Later that year, he asked me to host a concert by Big Country at Edinburgh Playhouse on Hogmanay that was screened live as part of the New Year celebrations on BBC2. When Stuart Adamson and his band welcomed-in 1985, I toasted them at the side of the stage with a bottle of Lucozade.

The following year, I returned to Barrowland to present another Hogmanay concert headlined by King as part of the channel's marathon *Whistle Test* special.

Working for Scottish Television was a real steep learning curve. Tommo had first drafted me into the team behind Kirsty, a twice-weekly teatime chat show presented by Kirsty Young, who was rising fast up through the ranks. Until then, the programme had been very issue led with topics of interest to a largely female audience. But he wanted to introduce a more showbiz element to the programme to give it a bit of extra colour. The show had a great time slot – leading into the main *ITV Evening News* at 6 p.m. – so we always had a big audience.

Kirsty was great to work with. Even at that very early stage of her screen career she was the consummate professional and had a great sense of humour. We quickly became good friends.

I booked a diverse line-up of chat guests including singer Elvis Costello, ice skating legends Torvill and Dean, comedians Hale and Pace and even the cast of Aussie TV drama, *Prisoner: Cell Block H*, which had a huge following in Scotland. I also signed up actor Bill Tarmey – better known as Jack Duckworth in *Coronation Street* – an accomplished singer who'd just released his new album, *After Hours* on EMI Records.

Before the show, I took Bill for lunch at a local Chinese restaurant, and he was great company. At the end of the meal, I told him I'd organise a taxi to take us back to the STV studio. But he said: 'It's a lovely day. The sun is shining. The studio is not far away . . . so why don't we walk back?'

And that's exactly what we did. As we strolled down Sauchiehall Street the actor caused an absolute sensation. Crowds of shoppers gathered around him, some shouting: 'Hey Jack, there's a guy in the Savoy Centre who'll fix your watch for a fiver' . . . a reference to his character's ongoing problems with his timepiece. Or 'Specsavers can make you up a new pair of glasses in an hour' . . . which would have solved the problem of Jack's own pair which were held together by sticky tape.

When I booked US country music superstar, Garth Brooks, it quickly became a major production. The boss wasn't familiar with the singer or his music, but I put his mind at ease saying: 'Trust me. This guy is currently one of the biggest stars in the business.'

I got a message from Garth's camp that he was keen to get to know Kirsty before taking part in the show. So on 5 October 1994 – just two days before the interview – Kirsty and I were flown out to Berlin to see his concert at the 10,000-capacity Deutschlandhalle arena.

The next day, we travelled back on the same flight as Garth and his entourage. I'd arranged for two limousines to pick them up at Glasgow Airport, to transport them to their hotel in style. But the singer from Tulsa, Oklahoma, had a reputation for being very down-to-earth. He completely body swerved the luxury cars and told his band to pile into a minibus I'd also laid on to carry their luggage. They all ended up sitting on top of each other.

When Garth arrived for the show the following day his every move was shadowed by a US film crew making a fly-on-the-wall documentary of the tour. I had a magic moment when I sat with him alone in the dressing room as he worked on a new song he was writing . . . singing unfinished lyrics scribbled in a battered old notebook.

When we went on air, Garth really warmed to Kirsty. His insistence that they met in advance paid off and the interview was outstanding. He played his first major Scottish arena gig at Aberdeen Exhibition Centre twenty-four hours later.

By coincidence, the following week a film of his 1993 concert at Houston Astrodome in Texas was screened on BBC2. During the gig – in front of 68,000 fans – Garth pulled out all the stops . . . smashing guitars, performing in a ring of fire and 'flying' out over the audience on a piano wire. It was incredible.

The next day Tommo called me into his office and said: 'Sloany, did you see Garth Brooks on TV last night? Wasn't it amazing? Was that who we had on Kirsty?' I don't think he could believe we'd had such a huge star as a guest on the show.

Then things really accelerated for me. I heard that *Scotland Today* – the station's flagship daily news programme – was looking for a music and entertainment correspondent. So I approached Scott Ferguson – the Head of News – and threw my hat into the ring. Scott – the older brother of comedian and actor, Craig Ferguson, who shot to fame hosting *The Late Late Show* in America – was very encouraging and gave me the job. Suddenly, I was the programme's on-screen showbiz reporter appearing at lunchtime with great presenters such as Angus Simpson, John MacKay, Sarah Heaney and Andrea Brymer, who were all a pleasure to work with.

On a Monday, I'd preview the latest storylines in TV soaps like *Coronation Street* and STV's own, *Take The High Road*. And on a Friday, I'd interview the UK's top pop stars to publicise their latest album releases or tour dates.

I was able to attract artistes of the stature of U2, David Bowie, Mick Jagger, Rod Stewart, Elton John, Roxy Music, Tom Jones, Kylie Minogue, The Spice Girls, Bryan Adams and Tony Bennett to appear on the programme. *Scotland Today* had never had such a star-studded line-up and we got a positive response from viewers.

The adrenalin rush of live television proved addictive. Anything could happen . . . and it often did. I fixed up an interview with Richard Fairbrass, lead singer of Right Said Fred, who was visiting Glasgow on a promo tour. I persuaded the producer to have him appear on the programme live rather than in a shorter, pre-recorded film package.

Richard – and his brother Fred – had cracked the charts with the singles, 'I'm Too Sexy' and 'Deeply Dippy'. He was a real larger-than-life, colourful character and the women loved him. So I knew he would be good value on the Friday music slot.

On the day of the show, Richard and his publicist visited Radio Clyde in Clydebank to record an interview before heading to STV. I phoned Clyde reception and was assured they'd just jumped into a taxi and were en route. But as we got closer to the start of the programme there was no sign of them. I repeatedly called the publicist's mobile, but it was switched off.

When *Scotland Today* went on air at 1 p.m., presenter Angus Simpson flagged up the appearance of the star who sang 'I'm too sexy for my shirt'.

I called reception and the security guards at the back gate and told them that if a big, bald, fake-tanned, muscle-bound guy arrived not to waste time making up visitors' passes . . . just to rush him straight to the main studio.

But Richard didn't show up.

On my recommendation, we had twelve-minutes of programme time devoted to an interview with a pop star who had gone AWOL. What could we do? Angus introduced part two by jokingly saying: 'If anybody sees the lead singer of Right Said Fred bring him to the studio immediately.' I sat on the opposite stool bullshitting my way through facts and figures about the group's pop career. It was the longest, most uncomfortable twelve minutes of my life. And, I've never seen – or spoken to – Richard Fairbrass to this day. I've still no idea why he didn't turn up.

In the summer of 1995, I was Associate Producer on STV's coverage of T in the Park staged at Strathclyde Park, on the outskirts of Glasgow. The festival – then in its second year – was an ambitious attempt by local concert promoter Stuart Clumpas to establish a weekend music and camping event north of the border. It really captured the imagination of music fans and we made two highlights programmes featuring a bill that included Paul Weller, The Charlatans, M People, Kylie Minogue and The Prodigy.

The following year, as the festival grew arms and legs, so did STV's coverage. Scott Ferguson called me into his office and said: 'Good news. I've got a producer for this year's T in the Park . . . YOU! Are you up for it?'

Suddenly, I was in charge of a team of directors, cameramen, sound engineers, riggers, film editors and in control of a budget of £95,000. I didn't have a clue where to start and felt way out of my depth.

When I chose Fiona Mckenzie, who worked in the newsroom, as my No.2 it raised a few eyebrows in the building. She had no previous experience of working on music events. But Fiona got things done and that's exactly what I needed. Our team was completed by two youngsters . . . gofers who ran errands on other programmes.

I hit an immediate problem. Radiohead – who were the headline band on the Main Stage – refused point-blank to be filmed.

Dealing with American acts such as Foo Fighters, Beck, Frank Black, No Doubt and Canadian acts Alanis Morissette and Barenaked Ladies also proved tricky because they went through every line of STV's basic contract with a fine-tooth comb. We'd receive our legal documents by return fax and they had so much information blacked out it looked more like a redacted FBI file from the archives of the Kennedy assassination.

But one US band who were a breeze to work with were a totally unknown outfit called Dogstar. They'd been given a plum spot on the NME Stage thanks to the reputation of their bass player, Keanu Reeves, star of blockbuster movies such as *Speed*, *The Matrix* and *John Wick*. The band's UK record label flew me out to Hollywood to interview Keanu at the famous A&M Studios on Sunset Strip, once owned by screen legend, Charlie Chaplin.

He was a nice guy and very passionate about music. When he began talking about the British punk-rock explosion I thought he was going to namecheck The Sex Pistols, The Damned or The Clash. But he took me by surprise when he said: 'My biggest inspiration was The Exploited, a punk rock band from Edinburgh. I bought a lot of their records on import in the early eighties and they sounded incredible. Their lead singer Wattie Buchan was an amazing frontman. I'm a big fan of the group.'

I nearly fell off my seat.

When Dogstar played at T in the Park, Keanu shunned the big star treatment. He arrived at the site on a shuttle bus from Buchanan Street Station to the amazement of fans also heading to the event. One by one, we managed to get most bands on the bill – including Pulp, The Prodigy, Black Grape, the Manic Street Preachers and Teenage Fanclub – to agree to be filmed.

At the eleventh hour, Radiohead finally came on board and gave me the thumbs up to shoot three songs, 'Fake Plastic Trees', 'High and Dry' and 'Street Spirit (Fade Out)'.

But we almost came a cropper before anybody had played a single note of music. I was asked if I wanted to hire a portacabin in the backstage Media Village to use as our studio base for the duration of the festival. But my budget was so tight I couldn't afford the £150 hire fee.

'Don't worry about it . . . I'll sort something out,' said Fiona. I didn't give it a second thought.

I arrived on site to be confronted by a battered old Portakabin she'd rented from a local building site – for just £50 – with the name of the construction firm Bovis, emblazoned on the front. When promoter Stuart Clumpas saw it he went potty and got his crew to re-route the wire fence straight across the front door so we couldn't get into it. It was a couple of hours before he'd cooled down enough to order the guys to dismantle the fence and give us access.

But it proved a master stroke because when record pluggers brought their artistes into the Media Village to do interviews we were easy to find. Our Bovis H.Q. shone like a beacon.

In the end, I made six one-hour shows – featuring all the top acts on the Main Stage, NME Stage and King Tut's Tent – plus another couple of 'best of' compilations. Fiona played an absolute blinder guiding me through a post-event minefield of film edits and sound dubs. She was crucial in delivering the programmes on time. I couldn't have done it without her.

As T in the Park got bigger the event simply outgrew its location at Strathclyde Park and was moved to Balado, about a ninety-minute drive from Glasgow. Where on earth was Balado? Nobody wanted to go there. But I was completely wrong. A former disused airfield in Kinross, it was a more rural site and the perfect home for Scotland's No.1 annual rock event.

I was part of STV's production team for the next two festivals before the BBC came in with a big money offer and won the broadcast rights. But I covered T in the Park for the next sixteen years, reporting on the festival for the *Sunday Mail* and hosting my Radio Clyde show live from backstage.

The bigger it got, the crazier it became. I still bear the scars. I'd fought the punk rock wars and had now survived the trenches at T in the Park.

I should have been awarded a medal for valour.

Chapter 21
Hang The DJ

'IT'S 350 QUID, CASH in hand. And you get to play the SECC. How many people can say that?'

Kay Wilson had made me an offer I couldn't refuse. She booked the acts who appeared at Scotland's number one arena venue. Her contacts book was crammed full of hotline numbers for agents representing The Rolling Stones, Paul McCartney, Bruce Springsteen, Tom Jones, Tina Turner, Neil Diamond, U2 and some of the biggest stars in the music business. But Kay had a major problem so, for one night only, she was prepared to set her sights considerably lower.

'Status Quo are playing tonight. It's completely sold out. But I'm in deep shit. Be a pal and help me,' said Kay, the desperation in her voice was tangible.

In 1998, the veteran rock band were driving up from Manchester to play an annual Christmas gig at the SECC, minus their tour support act, T'Pau. The previous night, Carol Decker, the group's lead singer, had struggled to get through the gig suffering from flu and laryngitis. Now, she'd lost her voice. She couldn't sing. Doctor's orders.

'Get me a band to open the show,' pleaded Kay. 'Who do you know? Phone somebody.'

Only one problem, for a country with a strong rock tradition, Scotland didn't have too many gigging rock bands. So options were limited.

As we weren't spoiled for choice, I suggested getting a DJ instead. You wouldn't have to faff around hiring vans, humping gear or dealing with dopey roadies. Why not call big Tom Russell, of *The Friday Night Rock Show* on Radio Clyde? He'd be perfect. He'd turn up with his box of Iron Maiden, Whitesnake, Deep Purple, Motorhead and Metallica albums, vibe up the crowd and problem solved. I gave Kay his number.

She called me back ten minutes later. The desperation in her voice had been racked up considerably. Tom had a booking in a lounge bar in Kilwinning and wasn't available.

'Why don't you do it?' said Kay. 'You've done a bit of DJ-ing.'

Kay was right. I had done a bit of club DJ-ing in my early days on Radio Clyde. Sadly, my C.V. didn't make impressive reading. I'd once hosted a disastrous DJ set at a rough punk rock gig at Glasgow College of Technology using only one broken turntable and had been lucky to escape with my life.

On another occasion, I'd been hired to play a Sunday afternoon 'alternative disco' in the Tamdhu in Bannockburn. After plugging the gig non-stop on my show, I felt totally deflated when only one guy turned up. His £3 admission didn't even cover the cost of turning the power on in the venue.

As I watched BBC1's *Football Focus* with the sound turned down, Kay was growing ever more desperate at the end of the telephone. 'Do it for me. Please. Pretty please. As a favour. It's 350 quid. Cash. I'll get the promoter to put it in an envelope for you,' she said, displaying the negotiating skills which had previously secured the services of Mick Jagger and Paul McCartney.

Now, you can buy a lot of chicken chow mein for £350. Even so, I was torn. My mind flashed back to those vintage *Oor Wullie* comic strips where the spiky-haired, dungaree-wearing tearaway faced some mischievous dilemma. Suddenly, on one shoulder I saw a prim well-groomed angelic Wullie saying: 'No, Billy, don't do it. It's wrong.' While on the other, a devilish Wullie was saying: 'Fuckin' go for it. What you worried about? You'll kill 'em.'

Verbally, Kay had beaten me into submission.

'I'll do it,' I said, 'but keep it well low-key. Low-key . . . do you hear me?'

No sooner had the words left my lips when I knew I'd regret it.

Was I nervous? Let's put it this way, a doner kebab I'd eaten in 1984 suddenly made rumbling noises in my lower intestine and began heading south.

I was suffering from stage fright eight hours before I'd even reached the venue. At 7.30 p.m., I reported for duty at the stage door of the SECC's cavernous Hall 4 clutching my trusty box of CDs, and was quickly escorted into the Status Quo production office. The brief was simple. I'd go on at 8 p.m., play some rock tracks for forty minutes to vibe up the audience, collect my 350 quid – envelope optional – and, job done, was more than welcome to hang around to groove with rock legends Francis Rossi and Rick Parfitt.

I headed for the stage . . . and blind panic.

On peeking through the thick black drapes I suddenly realised Kay's idea of 'low-key' differed greatly from mine. Normally, the DJ console would be tucked in at the side of the stage – next to the sound monitor mixer – just out of sight of the baying hordes better known as the audience. Not this time. The decks were strategically placed centre stage on the exact spot of the front vocal mic.

The house lights dimmed. The 8,500-strong, inebriated, largely male audience let out a roar of what I'd like to think was expectancy but with hindsight was probably closer to the ferocious growl of a lion marking its territory.

A spotlight picked out a lone figure as I walked on the empty stage to be met with a cry of: 'Is that no' that c*** from the *Sunday Mail*?'

I swiftly grabbed the DJ mic.

'How you doin'?' I said. In the growing aural swell of what can only be described as a potent mix of blind hate and total indifference I could pick out shouts of 'Fuckin' shite' and 'Get to fuck, ya prick'.

It was time to get this show on the road. I cued up my first CD – 'Now I'm Here' by Queen – and the group's 1975 classic hit boomed out of the speakers. Some punters were singing along. A few others began playing air guitar. What was I worried about? The devilish Oor Wullie had been right all along . . . this was a piece of piss. Or was it?

Modern hi-fi technology is a wonderful thing. To load a CD couldn't be simpler. You press a button, a little drawer slides out, you drop in your compact disc, cue up the track and press 'Play'. And, you can do all of this in, say, eight seconds. Tops.

Therein lies the problem. 'Now I'm Here' has a duration of four minutes twelve seconds. After I'd taken my allotted eight seconds to select the next CD that left more than four minutes of, well, nothing. Ten thousand pairs of piercing eyes fixed on me with the accuracy of Exocet missiles and the groundswell of feeling coming in waves from audience to stage seemed to be saying: 'Dae something'.

In those early, pioneering days at Radio Clyde I should have been schooled by masters. My mate, 'Tiger' Tim, created hysteria on the Clyde Disco Roadshows as he worked the crowds dressed in his trademark tiger-striped jumpsuits and staged endless wet T-shirt contests or kissing marathons. That was his act and the punters loved it.

But my 'act' consisted of filing through dozens of CDs pretending to be earnestly making my next selection. It wasn't quite the visual extravaganza of sheer abandonment that would help propel superstar DJs like Fatboy Slim or Tiësto to captivate 50,000-strong audiences many years later.

'Now I'm Here' thundered to a climax and I fired the next track, 'The Boys Are Back in Town' by Thin Lizzy. Well, not quite. In the semi-darkness, did I press the wrong button? Push the wrong fader? Hell knows. There was a dull, electric thud and the power on the mic and decks fused.

The audience went wild, though not in appreciation.

'Ya fuckin' wanker' and 'Put another shilling in the meter' were two of the barbs of wit which flew my way, as a roadie, wearing a headband with a miner's lamp affixed, crawled underneath the DJ console furiously trying to restore power. He got the decks re-juiced and I quickly played another couple of rock anthems but could sense the best adjective to describe the heightened atmosphere would be . . . mutinous.

As a missile – a sweaty training shoe – just missed me I realised my life was at stake. Now, and don't ask me why, I decided to improvise. I stuck a finger in my ear and pretended I was being given a radio message via an in-ear monitor.

'Great news guys . . . I've just been told the Quo are in the building.' This fake 'bulletin' earned a smattering of grudging applause largely drowned out sadly by shouts of: 'Who gives a fuck?' Within seconds, the abuse from the audience threatened to engulf my latest hot pick . . . 'Won't Get Fooled Again' by The Who. I was sinking fast.

Cries of 'Sumo . . . sumo' sparked off spontaneous laughter, which – albeit for a split second – softened the mood on the audience's 'Hate-o-Meter'.

It was time for action from the file marked 'Drastic'. I did the old radio message trick again and shouted into the mic: 'We're just ten minutes from Quo time.' Ten minutes from Quo time? What the fuck was I on about? It was like a line from a bad Dave Lee Travis voice-over.

Quo time? I can only surmise I'd now fused the power supply from my brain to mouth. So I copped out. I grabbed the mic and shouted manfully: 'It's been great playing for you. Enjoy the Quo. And I'll leave you with one of the all-time classics . . . 'Bat Out Of Hell' By Meat Loaf.'

Epic song. It sounded amazing blasting out of the huge PA system. But chosen solely because its nine minute forty-seven-seconds duration took me past my allotted forty-minute set time. As the mighty Meat stood like a sinner before the gates of Heaven for the next nine minutes I hid beneath the DJ deck pretending to be refiling my CDs in the box. The audience sussed it and treated me to a bizarre greatest hits abuse compilation of chants. Another missile bounced off the apron of the stage. When the song ended, a spotlight once more picked out the lone figure as I walked off to the sound of my own footsteps.

'You did well,' said the promoter backstage as I signed a chit to receive my 350 quid. He was wise to limit his conversation to those three short words after seeing the traumatised look on my face.

The scars still cut deep. Even now, twenty-five years later, every time I hear Phil Lynott sing 'The Boys Are Back In Town', that same dull, electric thud punches my brain. Senses fused temporarily.

But, if you're a music fan it doesn't get much better. On 5 December 1998 I supported the legendary Status Quo at the SECC in Glasgow on the 'It's Good To Tour' string of sixteen sold-out UK dates. It's there in black and white. Listed in the venue's star-studded record books. I've got 8,500 witnesses.

Kay Wilson was dead right. I DID get to play the SECC. How many people can say that?

Chapter 22
Take That . . . and That

I'M COMPLETELY STARK NAKED. It's a sight most definitely not for the squeamish. Mark Owen of Take That says hello. The towel wrapped around his waist is the only thing protecting his modesty. Don't race ahead of me. I've got a perfectly logical explanation.

It was 21 July 1993, and the group – Mark, Gary Barlow, Robbie Williams, Howard Donald and Jason Orange – were preparing to take the stage at the SECC in Glasgow. All 8,500 tickets for the gig had been snapped up months ago.

I'd been assigned to review the show for the *Daily Record*, but it was proving problematic. Take That's publicist was being – what's the best way to put it – totally uncooperative. There were no review tickets. All my requests for an interview with any of the band members had been ignored. She even refused to supply a couple of stock quotes from the guys – however innocuous – that I could have woven into a story. Scotland's national newspaper was being stonewalled.

But then events gathered a sudden momentum. Take That were holed up in The Moat House Hotel, which is part of the vast SECC complex. The place was under siege, surrounded by hundreds of teenage female fans trying to get a glimpse of their idols. Security at the entrance to the hotel was tight.

I discovered the group were relaxing in the health club. The screaming girls had their noses pressed hard against the windows of the swimming pool. Through the tinted glass you could just make out the shadowy figure of Robbie Williams jumping into the water.

I spotted a colleague from the *Record* heading for the gym for his usual lunchtime workout. As a health club member, he was permitted to sign in two guests and agreed to help photographer John Gunion and myself get into the building. I paid my £5 admission fee, wrote my name in the visitor's book and ten minutes later, I was getting undressed in the male changing room alongside Mark Owen.

The singer went into the sauna and I joined him after a few moments. We had the suite to ourselves so I made some idle chit-chat.

'What's all the commotion outside? There are hundreds of girls going crazy. What's going on?' I asked him.

As we baked in the heat, Mark told me – almost apologetically – that he was partly to blame. He was member of a group called Take That, he said. They were playing later tonight at the SECC next door. This happened everywhere they went. The girls didn't mean any harm. They just got a bit overexcited. We baked a little more before Mark headed off to cool down in the pool. A nicer guy you couldn't meet.

I went to my locker and scribbled down everything he said in my notebook. He didn't say anything particularly earth shattering – or remotely incriminating – but at least I now had three or four paragraphs of live quotes. A real Take That exclusive.

Please believe me, I would never normally employ such an underhand approach, but the band's publicist had proven so unhelpful and obstructive, she had really pissed me off. It was time for some guerrilla-style tactics.

As it turned out, Mark's comments would get binned. We didn't print a single line of what he said. There was a much bigger story on the horizon.

John spotted Robbie, Gary and Howard larking about in the water. We swung into action.

'I had a sports bag so it looked like I was going to the gym, but I had two cameras stashed inside,' John recalled. 'The changing room had a door which led straight into the swimming pool area. Robbie was in the water directly opposite and he spotted my camera right away. I only managed to shoot off two frames when he alerted his security guys and shouted to his band mates to duck under the water.

'The two minders grabbed me and dragged me out into reception. They took both cameras, ripped the film out of them, told me to fuck off and threw me out of the hotel.'

Half time score: *Daily Record* – 0, Take That – 1. It was all to play for.

Spin on to showtime. As the audience arrived at the SECC, John and I spent time getting vox pops from excited fans and photographing them posing with their Take That banners. There was a real feel-good atmosphere in the venue. It wouldn't last for long.

We still had no access to the concert so all we heard was the sound of Take That performing through the wall in Hall 4 and the girls' piercing screams. As the gig came to a close, the main concourse was packed full of parents waiting to pick up their kids to take them home safely. Then, I got a tip-off on how Take That planned to make their escape at the end of the show.

An SECC security staffer discreetly told me they were going to open the service doors behind the stage and run the band across the concourse and into an empty Hall 5. They'd come straight out the other side and into the service elevator of the Moat House Hotel. It sounded ingenious. But how were they going to get them safely across such a crowded concourse?

'Watch this,' he told me.

A few minutes later, he walked up to the area adjacent to Hall 4 and shouted: 'Could I please have your attention? In a few moments time the concert will be over and we will be opening these doors. In order not to create a bottleneck – when the audience start leaving – would you please move back so we can keep this area clear.' The mums and dads dutifully parted like the Red Sea. It was amazing.

John and I had been sent a reinforcement – *Record* photographer, Charlie Donnelly. I briefed him on what was going to happen in a few moments' time. I also spotted a mate – who could really handle himself – and asked him to keep an eye on John and Charlie if the going got rough.

The doors of Hall 4 burst open and Gary, Mark, Robbie, Howard and Jason – wrapped in towels and dressing gowns – began running across the 60ft-wide PUBLIC passageway flanked by a team of burly security guards. The parents waiting for their kids couldn't believe their eyes.

John and Charlie started snapping. I had one of the spare cameras and fired off a few shots too. Then, it all turned really nasty. I saw John being thrown to the ground and set upon. He did NOT retaliate. He couldn't . . . he was trying to protect himself.

'As they were sprinting past us one of the security guys shouted: "Look, it's him from this afternoon,"' John recalled. 'Then three of them piled on to me and started choking me with my camera strap and punching me in the face. They pulled me into Hall 5 and I thought . . . that's it, I'm really going to get a hiding now. But it was actually the security guys from the SECC who saved me. They pulled the bouncers off. I think they would have kept on beating me if they had not stepped in. I was very badly injured.'

It was chaos. John was taken into a First Aid room for treatment. Some youngsters were screaming . . . but not in adoration. They were terrified.

I'd covered concerts by several pop bands – including Bros, Wham, Culture Club and New Kids On The Block – and never witnessed such disgraceful scenes.

Until that moment, the youngsters attending the gig had been having the time of their lives. There had been no ill feeling.

Once we made sure John was in safe hands, Charlie and I legged it back to the office – just a few blocks away – to hand over our camera film.

'Sit down and start writing,' said the night editor, as soon as I told him what had happened.

When he got the pictures back from the darkroom he was jubilant. 'I've got a GREAT photograph which shows John being attacked. I'm going to splash it on page one,' he said.

He was right. The shot was stunning. It appeared to show John being beaten, and a guy flying through the air – fist clenched – just inches away from landing another brutal blow to his face.

'We can't use that picture,' I told him.

'Why the fuck not? It perfectly shows these animals assaulting our photographer on a public highway. I'm going big on it,' he said, forcibly.

I grabbed the print from him and delivered the bad news.

'That guy isn't trying to punch John Gunion,' I said. 'He's a mate of mine. He's not attacking John . . . he's having a go at Take That's minders. He is one of our gang.'

Luckily, we had several other graphic shots that illustrated what had taken place.

Our banner headline read: 'Take That! Snaps They Tried to Ban' . . . followed by a story where I wrote: 'These are the pictures Take That DIDN'T want *Record* readers to see'.

We also received a massive boost when a number of parents turned up at the office voluntarily to say they'd witnessed the assault on John and were prepared to make a statement to the police on his behalf.

One dad told me: 'I felt like getting involved but I had my own two children with me. Instead, I drove straight to Cranstonhill police station and told them what I had seen.'

Another mum – who was at the SECC with her two daughters – was also disgusted by what had taken place.

She said: 'We went round to the service entrance as the kids were hoping to get autographs from Take That. Suddenly everyone, including the children, started screaming. I saw the photographer on the ground being kicked and punched.

'He got up and I shouted: "What's going on?" He was trying to run away from them. He's not a big lad and it was obvious he only wanted to take a picture. It was absolutely shocking.'

Later, police sent a full report on the incident to the Procurator Fiscal, whose spokesman said: 'We will consider it carefully when it arrives.'

The story – splashed across page one and an inside double spread – was an unfortunate climax to what, for most pop fans, had been a thoroughly enjoyable evening.

John recovered and lived to fight – or should that be photograph – another day.

'In one of the pictures we used in the paper you can see my eye is bruised,' he told me. 'Another shows the minders hitting me. In the background there are families looking at this in absolute horror.

'Some mums and dads complained the bouncers were far too heavy-handed and there was no need for them to act like that.'

Several months later, a member of Take That's security team stood trial in the Sheriff Court in Glasgow on charges relating to the incident.

'I remember standing outside waiting to get a photograph of him if he was found guilty,' recalled John. 'But he got off and the charges were dropped. When he walked out he shouted "Freedom" and punched the air in triumph. At least, this time he wasn't punching me.

'For months after that, when I was covering big football matches on a Saturday, guys in the crowd would shout . . . "Hey, it's the Take That snapper". So I was famous . . . for all the wrong reasons.'

In the interests of balance, I should point out that in the years that followed I was fortunate to interview Gary Barlow, Mark Owen and Robbie Williams on several occasions. I can confirm that all three were perfect gentlemen and it was a pleasure to talk to them about their various solo projects. Indeed, a real highlight of my career was my encounter with Robbie when he was one of the headline artistes on the Main Stage at the T in the Park festival in 1998.

I was covering the event for Scottish Television and we asked several big acts if we could film them as they walked to the stage . . . like shadowing a boxer entering the ring. I got the cold shoulder from everyone except the singer, who was promoting his debut album, *Life Thru A Lens*.

I met Robbie at his dressing-room door and my camera team filmed a convoy of people – with us at the centre – moving towards the concert arena. Robbie was psyched up and it was fascinating to get an insight into how an artiste feels just minutes before facing their audience . . . in his case 45,000 devoted fans in a field at Balado, near Kinross, on a lovely sun-kissed afternoon.

When I asked if he got nervous, he jokingly began making beeps and whirring noises – like a computer going into meltdown. Then, tongue firmly planted in his cheek, Robbie told me:

'It feels great. Absolutely amazing. And I think it's going to be the biggest, up-for-it-crowd I've ever had. Right now, I'm up on a mountain in India really enjoying myself and taking in the vibe.

'I sort of go deep within myself and find the inner me. It's lovely, but I will resume consciousness and carry on to do my gig.'

Then, being serious for a moment, he added: 'Just the fact that I can come to a festival and people give me respect and enjoy what I do is for me the biggest confidence boost because it's winning over a different audience.'

When we reached the ramp leading up to the stage, I told Robbie that his audience awaited and wished him well. But he wasn't finished quite yet. I was strictly forbidden from being in that area, but the singer beckoned me – and my crew – to join him.

As his intro tape – Frank Sinatra singing his 1966 hit, 'That's Life' – boomed out over the PA system, Robbie began performing just for our cameras. He sang along with the track and did a little dance routine.

He was dating Nicole Appleton of All Saints at the time and kissed and embraced her. He also played straight to the camera by saying: 'You looking at me . . . you looking at me' – copying the famous line of dialogue by Robert De Niro in the movie, *Taxi Driver*. By coincidence, Robbie had his hair styled in a Mohican cut so it made his homage to the film's anti-hero, Travis Bickle, even more convincing.

When the band took the stage to kick-start the opening song, 'Let Me Entertain You', I was just three feet from Robbie when he went 'into the zone'.

He danced on the spot with his eyes focused on the crowd visible through a gap in the stage drapes . . . completely oblivious to everyone around him. As the intro played, the singer knew exactly when to make his move. In the sheer excitement, I broke another rule and told my cameraman: 'We're going with him.'

We followed Robbie out on to the stage and he punched the air triumphantly before the massive crowd. The director beautifully cut a sequence in black and white – mixing into full colour as he reached the vocal mic – and we used it as the opening montage of our first T in the Park highlights show.

It was a brilliant and unscripted moment never to be repeated.

Chapter 23
Phone Some of Your Pop Star Pals

IT WAS A PHONE call I'll never forget . . . and it came at a very dark moment when it felt like the walls were closing in.

'Billy, it's Stuart – what can I do to help you?'

Such selfless generosity was typical of Stuart Adamson. He had the heart of a lion. The lead singer and guitarist of Big Country was on the line from his home in Nashville, Tennessee, to offer his full support. I'd been handed the task of organising Scotland For Kosovo: A Concert For The Refugees – to aid victims of the conflict in the war-torn region. But I knew nothing about staging a charity rock concert. The last few weeks had been a turbulent period and we'd reached a crisis point.

I needed a break – and fast – or else we'd regretfully have to pull the plug on the show set for 31 May 1999, at the SECC in Glasgow. It would be a painful humiliation for the *Sunday Mail* who had launched the event. The possibility of the editor tendering his resignation was now a stark reality.

'What do you need?' said Stuart. 'Can we come and play the gig?'

While grateful for his kind gesture it seemed totally impractical. The singer who grew up in Dunfermline was now 4,000 miles away across the Atlantic.

'So what? I'll go to the airport, jump on a flight and be with you in nine hours,' he said, insistently. 'We've also just made an album with Eddi Reader . . . we'll bring her along to do a couple of numbers too. Stick us on the bill.'

Thanks to that unsolicited phone call – which came completely out of the blue – Big Country were confirmed as our headline act. When I relayed the news to Jim Kerr of Simple Minds he said: 'They're a great band so put them on last . . . they can close the show. There's no way we're following them.'

Rewind six weeks earlier to when I'd received another phone call, this one from the editor's secretary.

'Where are you? Get your backside in here. Jim wants to talk to you right away!' she said.

I had a good relationship with Jim Cassidy. He was a great guy who called a spade a spade and was fiercely loyal to his staff.

When Jim got the bit between his teeth with a good idea there was no stopping him. This was one such occasion. He went into full motormouth mode. The paper was planning to stage a concert to aid the plight of refugees in the Balkans. The aim was to raise £200,000, money that would go to Direct Aid, the Edinburgh-based charity who were one of the main agencies working for victims of the war in Kosovo.

As luck would have it, the BBC had organised 'Music Live', a six-day celebration of music in venues across Glasgow, including the SECC. Jim had negotiated a deal with the venue management where the PA, lights and staging would be left in place for an additional forty-eight-hour period. The team there – box office staff, security men and road crew – had pledged to give their services for free.

The date was set for 31 May – a Bank Holiday Monday – and the BBC would broadcast the concert as the finale of 'Music Live'. It sounded fantastic. Who's playing?

'That's what I wanted to talk to you about,' said Jim, rather sheepishly. 'I need you to phone some of your pop star pals.'

I nearly fainted. I told him that the SECC was Scotland's number one arena with a capacity of 8,500, and while some of the biggest names in music had appeared there, many had not quite managed to sell it out. Any concert is only as good as the stars who are playing it, irrespective of the cause.

'See what you can do. We'll announce it in next week's paper,' he said.

I walked out of his office in a daze. This was some 'ask'.

There was only one place to start. I put a call in to Jim Kerr, who as you know is one of my closest friends, and outlined the plans. He was receptive to the idea and said he'd get back to me.

I then called Jools Gizzi, guitarist of Glasgow rock band GUN, another good mate. This was a much more tricky conversation. GUN had split two years earlier, bowing out with an emotional farewell gig at Barrowland. I asked Jools if the band members would even consider reforming for one night only – to support the cause – before going their separate ways all over again.

Next, I touched base with a promo guy who was plugging 'Safe', the latest single by ex-Bronski Beat and Communards' star Jimmy Somerville. Of all the Scottish artistes I'd interviewed over the years the singer had somehow slipped through the net. I'd never met or even spoken to him. Would Jimmy be up for taking part in the show?

I also contacted Paul Buchanan, the musical genius behind The Blue Nile – one of Scotland's most influential groups – to see if he'd lend his support.

Jim Kerr got back to me within a couple of days and said: 'Count us in.' This was great news because when he committed to a project he always gave one hundred per cent.

I couldn't believe it when GUN agreed to get together for a final whirl and play their string of hits one last time.

Then word came through that Jimmy Somerville would also appear, performing three of his most popular songs accompanied by two dancers. And, at this point Paul Buchanan was still very much part of the equation. The bill was shaping up well, but I still didn't think it was strong enough . . . we needed a little more to make a real impact.

For all of Jim Cassidy's many qualities, patience was not one of them. He was the kind of guy who always wanted something done yesterday.

'Give me another week. The bill will look much better if we've got a few more big names,' I told him.

But he wouldn't hear of it, he was champing at the bit to go to print. We splashed the gig on page one of the *Sunday Mail* on 2 May saying: 'Scotland is ready to rock for Kosovo. Some of the biggest names on the Scottish pop scene will join forces in a spectacular gala concert.' I revealed that there was even more to come. I'd contacted every other major Scottish pop act and asked them to appear.

Mike Closier, Chief Executive of the SECC, was delighted to give us the use of Hall 4, the main arena, for free.

He told me: 'The SECC has been host to many marvellous concerts by most of the rock world's major artistes. But this one is special.'

Promoters, DF Concerts – the team behind T in the Park – pledged their support to organise the production of the show.

I told how every single penny from ticket sales and donations would go straight into the pot. The Bank of Scotland agreed to sponsor the event with a huge cash sum. In an interview, Peter Burt, Group Chief Executive told me: 'We are delighted to be associated with such a worthy cause.

'The harrowing sight of the Kosovar refugees on our screens every night affects us all. The bank supports the efforts of the *Sunday Mail* and the young people of Scotland to ease the suffering of these war victims.'

Suddenly, it was all systems go. The box office staff at the SECC came in specially that Sunday – their day off – to man the telephone lines. Tickets went on sale at 10 a.m. just hours after the paper hit newsagents and shops around the country. But the stampede we'd expected by fans failed to materialise. It was baffling. We only sold around 2,000 tickets . . . not even a quarter of the capacity of the venue.

As a first day sale, it was a disaster. We had work to do. I hit the phones again and was soon able to confirm Teenage Fanclub, who had a real cult following amongst indie music fans. They were a valuable addition to the line-up.

Jackie Bird, news anchor of *Reporting Scotland* on BBC Television and comedian Jonathan Watson also came on board to host the show.

To give things a bit of extra-added spice, Jonathan agreed to appear in the guise of ex-Celtic star Frank McAvennie, who he'd immortalised on the football TV comedy show, *Only An Excuse*.

Funnyman Fred MacAulay and singer Mary Kiani said they'd also help out, introducing some of the bands.

The tickets were selling – but in fits and starts – so we needed something to really boost some activity at the box office.

I was working around the clock in the *Sunday Mail* office with a multitude of tasks including trying to compile a running order and designing a brochure to be sold at the event.

I'd spoken directly to several star names on the Scottish music scene, but they all ran for cover. Some – who were more than happy to use the paper to promote their new records – didn't even have the courtesy to return my calls. It was very disappointing.

One said: 'We don't want to be involved in war and all that stuff.' But they'd completely missed the point. We were simply trying to raise cash to buy medical supplies for the victims of that war . . . people who badly needed our help.

We tried to drum up more publicity to get our message across. But all the other Scottish newspapers and radio stations ignored the concert as it was seen to be an exclusive *Sunday Mail* project.

Jim called a few of his fellow editors and persuaded them to give the event a bit of coverage. We had to get the message across to as wide an audience as possible.

I was sitting at my desk one Saturday night when he said: 'Phone Midge Ure. It would be great to have him on the bill.' He stood over me as I made the call. Midge was getting his daughters ready for bed and promised to ring back in twenty minutes.

When he did I told him what we were planning.

'I'm not sure what I've got in the diary. Let me check with my manager on Monday and I'll get back to you,' he said.

Midge was as good as his word. He called me to say the date was clear and he'd be delighted to take part. The Scots musician who had helped organise Live Aid in 1985 – the most star-studded pop char-ity concert of all time – was now on the bill.

I also added Ricky Ross and his wife, Lorraine McIntosh of Deacon Blue, who agreed to perform a special piano-vocal set of the band's hits including 'Raintown' and 'Dignity'.

As the gig got closer the ticket sales got a real boost with the addition of Big Country and Eddi Reader. We carried interviews with several of the artistes who were passionate about the cause.

Jim Kerr told me: 'This kind of concert has never been done before in Scotland and it's ironic that it has taken the Kosovo tragedy to pull it together. The brilliant thing is that ALL proceeds will go to help the innocent victims. We have been inspired by how the Scottish public has responded to get aid to the refugees. Simple Minds will give heart and soul to this event.'

And Midge Ure said: 'Only a year ago, I played a gig in Belgrade. Now there is mayhem and destruction. The plight of the refugees has touched everyone. I'm delighted to be part of what I'm sure will be a real night to remember.'

In the days before the show, we also got support from the political arena. Prime Minister, Tony Blair, and Scotland's First Minister, Donald Dewar, both heaped praise on the paper for all our efforts to aid the refugees.

'The Scots have responded with characteristic generosity to the paper's appeal. This concert will show once more that the decent people of Scotland are determined to do their bit to help,' said the PM.

While First Minister, Dewar, added: 'We all have a duty to do what we can to relieve the suffering. I'm sure the concert will be a great success.' He also confirmed he would attend the event in a further show of support.

But on the day of the gig, we hit a problem. Our production manager, Dougie Souness, took me aside and told me that Strathclyde Police had received a bomb threat. We quickly organised a search of the concert arena and backstage area but thankfully found nothing to cause any alarm.

The paper had also invited eighty Kosovar refugees to be our guests. They had fled the conflict in their homeland and relocated to Scotland. We laid on coaches to transport them from the Red Road flats in Glasgow where they were now living to the SECC, to meet the artistes before the show.

When Teenage Fanclub kicked things off – with a five-song set that included their hit, 'Sparky's Dream' – they played to a near capacity audience. We'd sold almost 8,000 tickets – at £20 a time – which was a real result. At times it had felt like we'd scrapped for every single sale.

The atmosphere was electric. The audience got behind all the acts and there was a lot of goodwill in the venue.

A hilarious moment came when the real Frank McAvennie arrived backstage to be met by comic Jonathan Watson portraying him – with fake teeth, wig and his catchphrase 'Wherz the burdz?'

The Frankie-boy loved it. You couldn't tell them apart.

GUN, Jimmy Somerville and Ricky Ross and Lorraine McIntosh of Deacon Blue played their hits and really had the crowd on their side. Then Simple Minds nearly took the roof off with 'Waterfront', 'Someone Somewhere (In Summertime)' 'Alive and Kicking' and 'Don't You (Forget About Me)'.

Next up it was Midge Ure whose solo set included 'Breathe' and a great version of the Ultravox hit, 'Dancing With Tears In My Eyes', whose poignant lyrics were perfect for the occasion.

All that was left was for Big Country to close the show. Stuart Adamson had made the trip across the Atlantic – at his own expense – to nail his colours to the mast. They were incredible, performing classics like 'In A Big Country' and 'Fields Of Fire'. Their special guest Eddi Reader joined them on vocals for new single, 'Fragile Thing', a song from their latest album, *Driving To Damascus*.

Stuart and the band brought the show to a triumphant close with a blistering 'Rockin' In The Free World', a cover of the Neil Young song.

They dragged me on stage to take a bow. I was choked with emotion . . . it had been a long and difficult journey to get there.

The singer told me: 'I've been appalled by what's going on in Kosovo. You feel almost totally helpless about coming to the aid of the refugees. So that's why this gig is so important. We're all responsible – either directly or indirectly – for the welfare of these people. We should do something to try to help them, no matter how small an act.'

The show was broadcast live on BBC Radio Scotland and excerpts from the gig were aired on Radio 1. We also got great coverage on *Sky News* and across several local radio channels.

In the days that followed – when the dust settled – the bean counters did their stuff and confirmed that the gig had raised a total of £225,000.

Denis Rutovitz of Direct Aid said: 'The really marvellous thing is that this will enable us to help the very great number of people from Kosovo who have been either driven out of their homes or have fled in terror from what's happening there. The money raised by the *Sunday Mail* concert will go to help people rebuild their lives.'

Did our £225,000 make any difference? I honestly don't know. I hope so. But at least we had a go.

The story didn't end there. A few months later, I was invited to travel to Kosovo with Big Country. The band were asked to take part in The Return, a three-day festival of dance, music and theatre being staged in Pristina. Again, they were more than happy to give their talent – and time – free of charge.

The event was organised by Oscar winning actress, Dame Vanessa Redgrave, in her role as the United Nations Children's Fund Special Representative for the Performing Arts. The diverse line-up also featured American composer and pianist, Philip Glass, actor Angus Macfadyen and singer Lulu.

We flew to Macedonia and were transported over the border in a military convoy, flanked by a British army peacekeeping force, into the capital city of Kosovo. The devastation was horrendous. Everywhere you looked buildings lay in ruins after the bombing raids.

The local people were very welcoming and were anxious to show us the results of the attacks they had been forced to endure. Some of their stories were harrowing.

On the first night, Philip Glass gave a piano recital in a theatre that had not been damaged. The following day, the main event of the festival was staged in a sports centre that had also escaped the bombing.

The place was packed, I think more out of curiosity than anything else. Dame Vanessa Redgrave gave a poetry reading and Angus

Macfadyen delivered a literary monologue. What the locals made of it, I'm not sure. If nothing else, it provided a little bit of respite – however brief – from what they'd endured in recent months.

When Lulu took to the stage she was sensational, performing her hits including her signature song, 'Shout', to a taped backing track. The audience loved her. She later visited the barracks of the British soldiers – posing for photographs and signing autographs.

Before Big Country played, I took Stuart Adamson aside for a quick interview. But I could see he was very troubled. 'I'm glad we came to Pristina to see first-hand what's been going on here. We'll do anything to help these people,' he told me. 'But somehow, this just doesn't seem right. We're more than happy to play for them . . . but tomorrow we'll get on a plane and go back home. We're leaving them in the middle of all this chaos. Their lives will never be the same again. What's going to happen to them?'

I tried to reassure Stuart that he'd done everything he possibly could to help and for all the right reasons.

Big Country were incredible in Pristina that night, with Stuart's mood giving his performance even more fire and passion than usual. They played using primitive sound equipment to an audience who'd probably never seen a top-flight rock band before, and didn't know any of their songs. But it didn't matter because they knew Big Country were the real deal. They really made a connection.

When the trip was over, we flew back to the UK. At Heathrow, I said farewell to Stuart before he caught his connecting flight home to Nashville. I didn't know it would be the last time I'd ever see him. This story, sadly, does not have a happy ending.

I later discovered that Stuart had been having problems related to alcohol addiction and had begun drinking again after being sober for ten years. In 2001, I spoke with Ian Grant, the manager of Big Country, who'd been in contact with him. He told me that Stuart was keen to speak to me. For what reason, I don't know. I was given his home number in Nashville and called several times but nobody answered.

Then one night I rang him again and was surprised when Stuart picked up the phone. He sounded fine and said: 'Yes, I do want to speak to you . . . but not right now. I'll call you in a couple of days.'

That was the last time I heard his voice.

On 26 November Stuart was reported missing by his second wife, Melanie. The couple had been experiencing marital difficulties and she had filed for a divorce on the day he disappeared. On Monday, 17 December I arrived at STV for my usual slot on lunchtime *Scotland Today* where I'd preview the week's TV soaps. Ten minutes before we went on air, I rang my number at the *Sunday Mail* to check for any phone messages. There was one new voicemail which said, bluntly: 'This is Ian Grant . . . call me.'

I knew from the tone of his voice something was very wrong. I rang Ian straight away and was stunned when he told me that Stuart was dead. He'd been found the previous night in a hotel room in Honolulu, Hawaii, after taking his own life. Details were scant, but Ian understandably sounded completely shell-shocked. I couldn't believe what I was hearing.

In an instant, a flood of memories flashed into my mind. I'd been in Stuart's company on numerous occasions. He was a dear friend. I'd only ever experienced great times with him. He was one of life's 'good guys' with so much to live for both as an individual and a musician.

Why had he chosen to end it all . . . and at the age of just forty-three? It didn't make any sense. How could it?

I told Ian that *Scotland Today* was going live in a few minutes time: what did he want me to do?

'I'd rather the story came from you,' he said, in a voice cracking with emotion.

I quickly briefed the news editor who told me to sit in position opposite the live fixed camera in the newsroom, and he immediately called the studio gallery. Seconds later, the opening titles of the programme were running and I heard anchor John MacKay say: 'We start this lunchtime with a breaking news story. I'll hand you over to our Music Correspondent, Billy Sloan, live in the *Scotland Today* newsroom.'

From memory, I think I described it as 'the story I didn't ever want to have to deliver'. I still don't really know what I said or how I got the words out. I was numb . . . and fighting back the tears.

Above: Scotland's musicians rocked for Kosovo raising £225,000 to buy medical supplies to aid victims in the war-torn region.

I join Bruce Watson and Stuart Adamson of Big Country on a trip to the bomb ravaged city of Pristina.

Right: In 2022, Rod made his first trip to the Barrowland to receive a top award from the music biz charity, Nordoff Robbins (Scotland).

Below: A furious Rod didn't hold back when he called me from his home in Beverly Hills. The result was one of my biggest ever stories.

I line-up for Rod's football team to face a German side in Stuttgart. We beat them 5-2 with the singer grabbing a hat-trick.

Keith introduces me to his bandmates Charlie Watts and Ronnie Wood
backstage at the SECC.

One of my favourite rock star
snaps. I pose with Keith at the Stage
Door of Glasgow Apollo
in 1973.

There's only one Mick Jagger.
I'm given Access All Areas on
The Rolling Stones' 'Bigger Bang'
tour in Portugal.

The place where the Motown magic was made . . . Hitsville U.S.A at 2648 West Grand Boulevard in Detroit.

It was a real privilege to hear how Smokey Robinson – and Berry Gordy – launched Motown Records in 1959.

A valiant effort . . . but it's impossible to look cool when you're sitting alongside Bryan Ferry of Roxy Music.

In the presence of a true musical genius . . . Stevie Wonder plays my all-time favourite love song at the Savoy.

Top of the Scots . . .
I join Lulu to present
Annie Lennox with her
prestigious Tartan Clef
award.

Hitching a helicopter ride
with Simon Le Bon of
Duran Duran to a Radio 1
Roadshow in Dorset.

Clare Grogan receives her Tartan
Clef award. My interview with the
Altered Images star was very special
and emotional.

I caught up with Paolo Nutini in
Washington D.C. Little did I know
we'd end up blagging our way into
The White House.

Paul McCartney headlined Green's Playhouse in 1973 with his new band Wings ... one of his first major gigs since his split from The Beatles.

I visit Macca's H.Q. in London for an interview to preview his spectacular show at Hampden Park in 2010.

On the hallowed ground of Studio 2 in Abbey Road with the 'Fifth Beatle' ... Sir George Martin.

I join the staff at the SECC to present U2 with special awards for their surprise shows at the venue in 2001.

The official poster from the two best gigs it's ever been my pleasure to attend.

I've always been welcomed into the U2 camp . . . this time meeting the band at a TV show in their native Dublin.

From Las Vegas to T in the Park . . . with Tom Jones before he takes the stage at Scotland's No. 1 pop festival.

Above: Cher got in touch with me to offer her support to help save a Glasgow hospital from closure.

Left: Tony Bennett may have left his heart in San Francisco but when we met he left his footprints on a hotel bed in Glasgow.

When Tina Turner invited me to a party in Paris . . . it was an offer I couldn't refuse.

Coldplay, left, will headline the fund-raising concert

Plea to help farm

SOME OF the biggest names in
pop, including U2 and Robbie
Williams, have declined to play
at the giant benefit planned by

BY LOUISE JURY
Media Correspondent

which will take place from

Thanks to *The Independent*
I become the lead singer of
Coldplay . . . for 24 hours.

Following in the footsteps
of Elvis Presley at the
historic Sun Studio in
Memphis.

Midge Ure and I are
presented with Tartan
Clef awards by Nordoff
Robbins (Scotland)
in 2005.

Hello Dolly . . . I'll never
forget my first interview
with the 'Queen of
Country', Dolly Parton.

I then went straight to the studio to prepare for my regular TV soaps slot. In fairness, the news editor asked if I wanted to bail out . . . but that would have thrown the programme into total chaos. At such short notice, they'd have nothing to fill the twelve-minute time slot.

I went live with Andrea Brymer and introduced clips from that week's episodes of *Coronation Street* and *Take The High Road*, bringing viewers up to date with the latest storylines. Andrea helped me through what was the toughest live broadcast of my career. I'm forever grateful to her.

At the end of the programme, I was summoned to main reception to meet a number of newspaper and radio reporters asking if I had any more information. All I could do was repeat what Ian had told me and give them a bit of background into Stuart's life. It was one of the biggest stories of my journalistic career. And one of the worst.

Stuart Adamson was only too willing to help anyone. He'd do it without hesitation. That's the kind of man he was. But at the end he must have felt so alone. Whatever problems he faced, his many friends could have helped him conquer his demons.

Sadly, we never got the chance. I miss him.

SIDE 4

IT'S ONLY ROCK 'N' ROLL
(BUT I LIKE IT)

Chapter 24
Rod's Revenge

'BILL, CAN I CALL you back in two minutes from another part of the house?' Rod Stewart was on the line from his mansion in Beverly Hills, California. My guess is that he wanted to switch phones and talk to me well out of earshot of his girlfriend, Penny Lancaster.

Rod was furious. But you'd never have guessed it from the measured tone of his voice. The singer has lived all of his adult life in the glare of the world's press. He fully understood the value of a well-placed newspaper headline and knew exactly how to sink a harpoon. Rod wanted revenge. So he called me at the *Sunday Mail*.

The previous year, 2003, Penny had been signed up – in a fanfare of publicity – by Scots fashion entrepreneur, Michelle Mone, to be 'the face' of her female underwear brand, Ultimo. Rod accompanied his girlfriend to the glittering launch of the new Ultimo range at the Clyde Auditorium in Glasgow. The star-studded party was the hottest ticket in town.

She took the catwalk by storm and he paid her a glowing tribute when he told *Hello!* magazine: 'I am really proud of Penny. She is a very independent and bright lady in her own right and – as everyone saw last night – she is also visually stunning. I don't know what others think but I never tire of looking at her. But as much as I love her looks there is so much more to Penny. She is as lovely inside as she appears on the outside.'

Penny soon discovered that her success would be short-lived. After just twelve months in the spotlight, she was dropped by Mone. What made an already difficult situation even more raw was that the Ultimo boss then hired Rachel Hunter, the New Zealand-born supermodel, who was also Rod's wife. Rod married her in 1986, just two years after he'd split from his first wife, Alana. Rod and Rachel had two children together, but their marriage hit the rocks after thirteen years, with the couple blaming 'irreconcilable differences' for the collapse of their relationship.

When the story that Mone had recruited Rachel as the new 'face' of Ultimo hit the papers I remember thinking that was a little bit naughty. But maybe it's imperative that to run a money-spinning lingerie empire you've got to possess a ruthless streak. Business is business.

To make matters worse, at a photocall for her new range, Mone told reporters that she'd only hired Penny, for a fee of £200,000, because she was 'cheap' . . . as at the time she couldn't afford Rachel's £1 million price tag.

As if to rub salt into the wound, when asked to sum up the qualities of both models, Mone compared Rachel to Brazilian World Cup star Ronaldo and Penny to a player with lowly Falkirk FC.

Rod was livid. And he didn't hold back. Careful to keep his temper in check, he told me: 'I think Michelle Mone is a nasty piece of work . . . I really do. She is a manipulative cow. She really needs to be put in her place and if this is revenge, so be it. I'm sticking up for my old lady. Penny doesn't want to admit it, but she's been hurt by all of this. She's been in tears.

'Penny is a beautiful girl. I love her and hate to see her get hurt in this way. She did nothing wrong.

'Put yourself in her place. How do you think it feels to be told you're being replaced by Rod's wife?'

I couldn't believe what I was hearing. He was furious and had no hesitation in jumping to Penny's defence. But the most surprising thing was that Rod delivered his attack with the calm of a guy phoning in his order for a Chinese takeaway. He didn't shout and scream. Much as he would have been entitled to. Instead, he let his well-chosen words make a noise.

I barely asked him a single question. Rod knew precisely what he wanted to say. He began dating Penny in 1999 and she became his third wife eight years later.

He revealed that when Penny was first approached by Mone he sought the advice of several close friends who were major figures in the business community in Scotland. They all said the same thing . . . don't touch her with a barge pole.

'I was warned about her by a few people I know in Scotland,' revealed Rod. 'I was told Michelle was a devious, conniving, publicity-seeking son-of-a-bitch. They all said she was a user. I was so wary I said to Penny: "Keep your distance, keep your distance." But Penny, being an outgoing girl, did her best for Ultimo and worked very, very hard.

'She got on well with Michelle. They became sort of friends. Michelle got so much media coverage you could never have bought it. I thought the way Penny handled it was brilliant.

'If business has come to an end, it's finished. That's it and everyone should remain friends. To get kicked in the teeth like this is horrible. Michelle was determined to rub Penny's nose in it. I thought that was really unfair. What an ungracious way to treat my girlfriend. It's really fucking annoying.'

Rod and Penny were befriended by Mone and her husband Michael after a concert at the SECC in Glasgow in 2002. The superstar claims Mone 'begged' Penny to promote Ultimo products, but then pleaded poverty saying she could only afford a fee of £200,000. He reckoned that was well below the going rate for such a high-profile assignment.

That same year, Mone's company MJM International had come within fifteen minutes of bankruptcy and was only saved by loans from friends.

Rod told me: 'Michelle was on her knees to Penny to promote Ultimo. She was pleading poverty saying they were such a small company and even promised her shares in the firm.

'So Penny took a very slim payment for the job. I'm not going to tell you exactly how much because to some people it will be a lot of money. But in that business it wasn't a huge amount.

'I was also keen to help this small Scottish firm so I went up to Glasgow in 2003 and attended the Ultimo launch. I was backing Penny and backing the company. But Michelle has treated Penny horribly since then.'

I could see the editor hovering at the news desk. He was the only other person in the office who had been told the identity of the caller on the other end of my phone line. I gave him a thumbs-up to let him know the interview was going well. It would get even better.

When Mone unveiled Rachel Hunter as her new signing for Ultimo the news hit all the papers, as you'd expect. But for some inexplicable reason, the bra boss really stuck the knife in when she said: 'I only hired Penny because she was affordable. Rachel was always my first choice. We had Rachel in mind from the beginning but couldn't afford her.

'That's why we hooked up with Penny . . . she was cheaper.'

Her comments really hit a raw nerve with Rod.

'It's disgusting to call my girlfriend cheap,' said Rod, now struggling to contain his fury. 'I think Penny has taken such a bashing over this whole Michelle Mone thing. I feel it's time to stick up for her because she's not going to stick up for herself.'

But there was worse to come. Aside from women and music, Rod's other big passion in life is football. As a teenager, he played for Middlesex Schoolboys and later – spurred on by his father Bob – had trials at Brentford FC, then a Third Division side.

'It would have been great to be a professional footballer like my heroes Denis Law and Jimmy Johnstone,' he once told me. 'I don't think I'd have had the real discipline for it though. The whole fitness thing wouldn't have been a problem because I've always kept myself in shape. But I liked to get drunk and make music too much. And anyway, my career would have been all over by the time I'd hit my thirties. With music I can go on for as long as I like.'

I can vouch for Rod's abilities as a player. On a trip to interview him in Stuttgart, he buttonholed me in the foyer of the hotel the moment I arrived saying: 'I heard you were coming, so I've put you in the squad for tomorrow. We're playing against the German promoters, who are a very good side. I hope you've brought your boots.'

Rod was right. The Germans were a good side, but we beat them 5-2 and he scored a hat-trick.

So, of all the hurtful remarks made by Mone, there was one that really cut to the bone. 'What did you think of her football comment?' I asked him.

Rod replied: 'What football comment?'

He had not heard the line where Mone had compared Rachel to Ronaldo and Penny to a Falkirk player.

He went quiet for a few seconds, then sighed and said: 'That makes me even more angry. Penny worked her bloody arse off for Michelle. So to get that sort of statement is very unfair. That's REALLY pissed me off.'

During our twenty-five-minute-long conversation it was clear Rod was absolutely disgusted by the way Penny had been treated. He had no hesitation in jumping to her defence. But there was one moment that underlined just how angry, and hurt, he felt personally.

'I don't think Penny has got a single bad bone in her body. But Michelle's entire skeleton reeks of self-interest.'

I nearly dropped the phone. That was my headline. It's not the kind of statement you make off the top of your head. The way Mone had treated his girlfriend had clearly been eating away at him, even 5,000 miles away beneath the shadow of the Hollywood Hills.

The singer could have approached any of his contacts in Fleet Street, but he called me instead. He knew by putting his side of the story across in the pages of the biggest Sunday newspaper in Scotland it would have maximum impact.

'Penny has been treated terribly shabbily and I want Michelle to lay off. I still like her husband Michael – he's a great guy and a big Celtic fan. I don't want this to get in the way of our friendship,' said Rod. 'But I've had it with Michelle. I'm absolutely sick of her. Penny and Ultimo were a lovely combination for a while. It should have ended amicably instead of stirring up shit and kicking mud in her face.'

This was a page one story. I had it all on tape. It was one of the biggest scoops of my journalistic career.

'Okay, Bill, do you think you've got enough?' asked Rod, in what's got to be one of the biggest understatements of his career. 'And, anyway, I can't stand her Ultimo stuff. I prefer the underwear in Victoria's Secret.'

Now, the real hard work began. I played excerpts of the interview for the editor and his deputy. No matter where I stopped the tape, every quote from Rod was dynamite. We agreed it was important to keep a very tight lid on the story and this extended to not informing one executive on the paper who was friendly with Mone. We didn't want any leaks.

My exclusive would be splashed across page one, with the full interview appearing on a colour spread inside the paper.

The plan was to run a substitute story on those three pages for the first edition, then ditch it and replace it with Rod's broadside against Mone in all the editions that followed. This was a tactic intended to thwart any of our rivals – like the *News Of The World* or *Mail on Sunday* – from nicking our material.

I was due to attend a wedding on the Friday when the article would be laid out and edited. The timing was unfortunate because it's always preferable to be on the editorial floor in case of any unforeseen last-minute problems. During a break at the reception, I gave the editor a quick call to see if everything was okay, only to discover he suddenly had an issue with the story.

A local comedian, Des McLean – who co-hosted the Breakfast Show with George Bowie on Radio Clyde – had built a reputation for making prank phone calls. Des was a brilliant mimic who did great impersonations of stars such as Sean Connery or Billy Connolly. He had chatted to scores of listeners on air and fooled them into thinking they were having a conversation with a famous celebrity.

'Are you a hundred per cent certain it was Rod Stewart you were talking to the other night?' said the editor. 'Is there a chance it could have been Des McLean at the wind-up?'

What on earth was he on about? I'd interviewed Rod on numerous occasions in the past. We knew each other well. His voice was unmistakable. Wasn't it?

Even though I was certain I had spoken to Rod in Beverly Hills, the editor had now planted a niggling seed of doubt – however miniscule – in my head.

Des was a mate and a colleague at Clyde. Surely he wouldn't sacrifice my reputation on the altar of the Breakfast Show, just to get a few laughs at my expense?

I ducked out of the wedding and put a call in to Moira Bellas – Rod's UK publicist – who had contacted me initially to say the singer wanted to talk about 'a matter that was troubling him'. Moira must have thought I'd gone loopy when I quizzed her about the 'true identity' of the person who'd speared Mone so skilfully.

'I can assure you it WAS Rod Stewart you were talking to on the phone,' said a bewildered Ms Bellas. The following night, as the second edition of the *Sunday Mail* thundered off the presses at 1 a.m., the splash headline said it all:

'Rod's Revenge'.

Then the final piece of the jigsaw was put into place. Our Chief Reporter, Marion Scott, contacted Mone and informed her of the story we were running to give her the opportunity of a right-to-reply. The Ultimo boss claimed she was stunned by Rod's remarks.

'Some of the comments I made concerning Rachel and Penny were twisted,' she said. 'A journalist asked for a comparison and I compared them to footballers. It wasn't meant as a criticism. Rachel is known as an international model and has been since she was just seventeen years old. Penny was only known as Rod's girlfriend and a model in the UK.

'There were comments that I'd said Penny was cheap. What I actually said was we did first approach Rachel but found her too expensive. All during her time with us, Penny did a fantastic job.'

Then, Mone added, in what almost sounded like a veiled threat: 'I'm stunned Rod has made these comments when I have only ever been protective of Penny. In fact, I know things about her that would really shock the world. But I would never open my mouth about that.'

When the *Sunday Mail* hit the streets, we sent six copies by Federal Express courier straight to Rod and his manager in California. On Monday, the story was followed-up by newspapers and radio phone-in shows around the country.

I'd gone to London on another assignment, which was a bit of luck because my exclusive was also being covered on *Good Morning Britain* and *Lorraine* on ITV. I was picked up from my hotel at 5 a.m. and driven to the studios to be interviewed first by John Stapleton and Eamonn Holmes, and then by Lorraine Kelly.

I sat on the sofa holding up a copy of the *Sunday Mail*. The 'Rod's Revenge' headline had real impact and it was great publicity for us.

I later got word that the singer had seen the paper and was delighted with our coverage.

But his spat with Mone would get a second wind.

In 2006, I received a request from the BBC asking if I would take part in a new documentary series called, '*You Can't Fire Me, I'm Famous*', presented by Piers Morgan. As the title suggests, the show focused on a number of high-profile fallouts between stars and their employers. The producers wanted to tell the inside story of the bust-up between Penny and Rod and the boss of Ultimo. They'd also lined up programmes on Naomi Campbell, Martine McCutcheon, Louis Walsh, Abi Titmuss and Richard Bacon. A camera crew filmed me at my desk – proudly holding a 'Rod's Revenge' front page – and I relayed the story one final time.

Rod married Penny a year later and the couple have two children.

The next time I met him was backstage at the SECC in Glasgow when he introduced me to his new wife saying: 'Penny, this is Billy . . . he's the guy who wrote that nice story about us in the paper a little while back.'

Mone split from her husband Michael in 2011. She is now better known as Baroness Mone, OBE, a Conservative life peer with a seat in the House of Lords . . . a title given to her by former Prime Minister, David Cameron, in 2015.

Mone married the billionaire Scots businessman, Doug Barrowman five years later.

She is currently on a leave of absence from the Lords – 'to clear her name' – after claims she was linked to a controversial multi-million-pound PPE deal during the COVID pandemic.

Chapter 25
Rolling with The Stones

KEITH RICHARDS WAS ON the warpath. He was prowling up and down his dressing room in the SECC in Glasgow like a caged animal. The heavy Jamaican dub-reggae being pumped out of a giant ghetto blaster at ear shattering volume added further menace to the situation.

I'd been summoned to a meeting with Keith at just thirty minutes' notice. There wasn't time to get nervous. A scurrilous story had appeared in a Scottish newspaper saying The Rolling Stones had invested in two defibrillators – machines used to give an electric shock to restore a heartbeat – to get through the tour. It claimed the devices were on standby in case any of the band members – Keith, Mick Jagger, Ronnie Wood and Charlie Watts, whose combined ages at the time was 237 – needed revived if their hearts pegged out during a show.

Keith was livid. He wanted to set the record straight . . . and more.

'Do you know the cat who wrote that story?' he hissed. 'Tell him I'll meet him in an alley late at night. Anywhere he wants. Just him and me, nobody else around, and we'll sort this out. It won't be pretty.'

Keith wasn't kidding.

But despite his anger, there was some truth in the article. Michael Cohl, the Stones' tour director had bought the defibrillators after the shock death of crew chief, 'Chuch' Magee, who'd worked with the band for thirty years. He suffered a heart attack, aged fifty-four, during rehearsals for the tour in Toronto, Canada, in 2002.

Cohl figured that with more than 200 people travelling with the band – and a further 200 recruited locally in each city – it was perhaps inevitable somebody would require medical attention if any such emergencies occurred in the future. So it was a very wise move. Of course, the hope was the defibrillators would never need to be taken out of their metal flight-cases.

The story had badly affected Keith who was still grieving for his friend. He was furious with the journalist and spat his words out with real venom.

'That asshole. Is that all you've got to say? What an angle. Such a trite, banal, crappy, inaccurate story,' he said. 'I've read enough crap about myself, right? The headline said . . . Start Me Up. Thanks a lot pal. I was gonna invite him here but I didn't know if he'd have the balls to come. He'd have left naked and crying for his mummy.

'It's not often I get mad but when I read the report saying these machines were for me in case I conked out, it made me angry. This really got to me.'

In a career spanning forty years – full of headline hitting controversies and drug busts – I'd have thought the guitarist would not have been fussed any more about what the press said about the group. He'd surely read it all before. But it was quite the reverse.

In 1990, my brother was hired as part of a press team to go on the road with 'the greatest rock 'n' roll band in the world' on their Urban Jungle tour of the UK and Europe. He travelled with the Stones' massive entourage, liaising with local journalists and photographers so they got access to the shows.

As the tour moved from city to city one of his main tasks was to buy every newspaper that had reviewed the gig and get their reports translated into English. He'd then write a summary – attaching photocopies of the clippings – and compile two identical folders with all the information. One would be slipped under Keith's hotel-room door and the other delivered to Mick. And there was all hell to pay if they didn't receive them.

In Spain, the photocopying machine in the band's hotel was on the blink so he got the reviews duplicated in a local Internet cafe at a cost of seventy euros. When he rather nervously presented the receipt to the band's accountant for authorisation, he was told: 'This is The Rolling Stones. The highest grossing tour in music history. Do not annoy me for seventy-fucking-euros. Stick it on your expenses . . . and get out of my fucking office.'

Over the years, I've interviewed every member of the Stones, with the exception of Brian Jones who died in 1969. As you can imagine, talking to Keith one-to-one was a major box ticked.

The band played the SECC on 1 and 3 September 2003 in what were arguably the greatest shows ever staged at the venue. During our chat he spoke with real affection for their piano player turned road manager Ian 'Stu' Stewart, who was born in Pittenweem in Fife. He was a founder member of the Stones with Jones in 1962.

Keith took me by surprise when he talked up the band's little-known Scots heritage.

'The Stones are a Scottish band. We'd have been nothing without Stu,' he said, with real affection. 'He started the group and he's one of your lot. We're very proud of that fact. Me, Mick, Ronnie and Charlie wouldn't be here if it wasn't for him.'

Stewart was removed from the band line-up in 1963 by manager Andrew Loog Oldham, who felt he looked 'too normal' and did not fit their bad-boy pop image. He became their road manager and also continued as their pianist until his death in 1985.

Keith revealed: 'When I hear a Scots accent, I look at Charlie and he looks at me . . . and it reminds us of him. Stu is up there looking down on us'.

'I talk to Stu every day. Charlie and I miss him immensely. We both know we STILL work for him. Every time I play a show I think . . . this one's for Stu.

'I'll never forget the first time we crossed the border on tour. Stu rolled down the van window and said to some passer-by: "Can you tell us the way to the Odeon in Glasgow?"

'The local people were looking at us as if we were mad. But Stu was Scottish all the way and that has always stayed with us. He used to claim he was the rightful Laird of Pittenweem. I wouldn't argue with that.'

'Why didn't anybody in Scotland claim us?'

We did, finally. In 2017, I organised a posthumous award for Stu on behalf of music industry charity Nordoff Robbins (Scotland).

I've been a member of the fund-raising committee for more than twenty years.

We presented his widow, Cynthia, and son, Giles, with a Tartan Clef in recognition of his immense contribution to the Stones' music over the years. It was the first award ever given to the late Scots musician.

Mick, Keith, Ronnie and Charlie were so delighted their friend was being recognised by his peers they recorded heartfelt video messages that were played at the event.

Keith's tribute was priceless. He claimed Stu – who was a golf nut – was a great piano player but a terrible road manager. He'd book the Stones into a hotel in the countryside, which had a golf course, and play a round of eighteen holes every morning before they got up out of bed.

It kept them well away from any screaming girl fans.

Keith said: 'We're fifteen miles out of town and we're ready to rock and roll. "What the hell are we doing here, Stu?" He'd say . . . "It's the best place for you away from the crowds". Meanwhile, you find out it's because he'd got a golf course.'

I first rubbed shoulders with the Stones when they headlined Glasgow Apollo – on 16 September 1973 – to showcase their eleventh album, *Goats Head Soup*. When the band's trucks rolled up outside the theatre at the crack of dawn that morning, I was waiting outside the stage door and volunteered to help the roadies unload the gear. It was mutually beneficial because they always welcomed an extra pair of hands and in return gave me an Access All Areas crew pass that got me into the gig.

There is nothing like the razzmatazz created when the Stones' rock 'n' roll circus comes to town, even in those early, pre-stadium days. The buzz backstage was electric.

To be just inches away from Mick Jagger as he prepared to go on – glammed up in glitter and mascara and wearing a star-studded jumpsuit – was absolutely incredible. The excitement was so palpable he appeared to be physically levitating off the floor. I was hooked and never missed a performance by the band in Scotland from that day on.

They returned to play a three-night engagement at the Apollo on 10, 11 and 12 May, 1976. The third show coincided with the European Cup Final between Bayern Munich and Saint Étienne that was being played at Hampden Park. For twenty-four hours, Glasgow was the party capital of Europe as thousands of German and French fans invaded the city. And in a rare move, the council agreed to grant all pubs a late license until 3 a.m., which gave the place a real carnival atmosphere. Mick was photographed hanging out with Bayern legends, Franz Beckenbauer and Gerd Müller at the Central Hotel as they celebrated their 1-0 victory.

When the Stones rolled into town again to play Glasgow Apollo in 1982 they created more hysteria. I got a whisper that the band would be announcing their UK tour dates in a rather furtive fashion. At a number of venues around the country – including the Apollo – a handwritten notice simply stating: 'The Rolling Stones in concert . . . tickets on sale now' was taped to the front doors at twelve-noon precisely. It was followed up with an announcement on local radio news bulletins. Me and my mates were in position outside the Apollo and amongst the first people to snap up prime seats for the show.

The box office was besieged as fans arrived from all over the country. Within fifteen minutes there was a queue around the block and the tickets, priced £6.50, sold out. A week later they were fetching £100 on the black market.

I got another insight into The Rolling Stones' world on their 'Urban Jungle' tour. The band had a reputation for cherry-picking great acts to support them. The star-studded list of artistes who have opened for them over the years includes Ike & Tina Turner, Prince, Foo Fighters, Bon Jovi, Sheryl Crow, Guns N' Roses and Lenny Kravitz. Playing with the Stones is not just considered a rare privilege but also a real badge of honour. Particularly for new, fast-rising acts.

I was delighted when my mates GUN, the Scottish rock band, were chosen – ahead of some very big names – to support them on twenty-six dates on the European leg of the tour. They were handpicked by Mick and Keith who were knocked out by the band's 1989 debut album, *Taking On The World*, and thought they'd be a perfect opening act.

The tour kicked off at De Kuip – home of Feyenoord football club in Rotterdam, Holland – in front of a capacity 64,000-strong audience on 18 May.

'We were on the road in America when the news came through we'd got the Stones' tour. And it was all down to the fact that Mick and Keith LOVED our record. We couldn't believe it,' recalled Jools Gizzi, guitarist of GUN. 'We still had two dates to play at the famous Whisky a Go Go in Hollywood . . . one for our fans and the other, a really important show, for the media and radio DJs.

'A decision was quickly made to play both on the same day and we flew overnight from Los Angeles to Rotterdam to join the Stones.

'Our dressing room was a Portakabin behind the stage and minutes before we were due on I looked out of the window and saw our manager Rab walking towards us with Mick Jagger. He came in and wished us all the best for the tour saying: "If there's anything you need . . . please don't hesitate to ask."

'He made us feel real welcome.'

I was reporting on the show for the paper and it was a very proud moment to see my pals win over the staunch Stones' audience with a powerful set that included their Top 40 hits 'Better Days' and 'Shame On You'.

But it was a real baptism of fire for the emerging Glasgow band and would take a bit of getting used to. 'We were performing on a stage that was absolutely massive . . . it was bigger than some of the club venues we've played,' Jools told me later in the tour. 'It was a great experience for us. If you can win over a Rolling Stones' audience you can do anything. And as a bonus we got to watch them every night.'

But after just a week on the tour, GUN thought they'd blotted their copybook when they were summoned by Jim Callaghan, the band's head of security. He lined them up and demanded they hand over their AAA laminate tour passes.

'Callaghan wasn't happy. Our first thoughts were . . . what have we done? We've blown it,' admitted Jools.

It was quite the reverse. Callaghan took the passes and affixed an additional sticker – the Stones' tongue logo – to each one. This granted them immediate access to the band's exclusive inner sanctum backstage, nicknamed Camp X-Ray, after the infamous US detention facility at Guantanamo Bay in Cuba.

'Callaghan told us, quite firmly, that we were on this tour as special guests of The Rolling Stones,' revealed Jools. 'He said: "The band want you to come and hang out . . . so don't hide yourselves away. They want to see you."

'Up until that point, we'd deliberately kept a low profile because we didn't want to intrude. But they welcomed us in night after night for a game of pool or a quick jam session before we went on stage. They couldn't have been more hospitable.'

GUN rose to the challenge and played a real blinder on the tour. I caught a few other shows including a memorable night in Madrid. As I was sitting with the band in the dressing room before the gig, Charlie Watts wandered in, sat down and began chatting. He recommended a few places to check out in the city and told us about a great little cafe he'd discovered where he'd gone for lunch with his wife, Shirley. He couldn't have been more friendly and was genuinely interested in the boys.

When I was travelling back to London, I spotted Charlie at the airport escorting Shirley – who was booked on the same flight – to the departure gate. It was just the two of them. The superstar drummer didn't surround himself with minders or flunkeys from the Stones' entourage. With the minimum of fuss he kissed her goodbye and waved her off just like a regular guy.

I was there too when GUN played their final show on home soil at Hampden Park on 9 July. The Stones were waiting in the wings with bottles of champagne to say 'thank you'. As both bands posed for a photograph to mark the occasion, Keith and Ronnie produced two Fender guitars as props for the picture.

'I was holding Ronnie's limited-edition custom-built Fender Stratocaster and our other guitarist Baby Stafford had Keith's Fender Telecaster,' Jools told me. 'But when we went to hand them back they said: "Keep them . . . they're yours." It was amazing.

'You couldn't buy these guitars. Fender only made around 150 copies but they were never put up for sale.

'The company presented them to people like Jimmy Page, Eric Clapton, Jeff Beck, Slash and other iconic guitar players. My guitar probably cost around £10,000. I asked Ronnie to sign it so it's probably worth even more now.

'I use it when I'm writing songs and have played it in the studio on every GUN album we've made since then. I'd never part with it . . . I value it too much.'

The GUN boys gave me an exclusive on the picture and I splashed it across my column in the *Daily Record*.

It would be another nine years before I got the opportunity to interview the Stones for the first time. In 1998, their Bridges To Babylon stadium tour ground to a halt when shows in Edinburgh, Sheffield and London were hastily cancelled in protest against the new Labour government's changes to UK tax laws. The band claimed the rules would cost them £10 million, putting the European shows in jeopardy.

Mick was quoted in *The Times* saying: 'If we did the UK shows it would have meant the entire European tour ran at a loss . . . and we couldn't have that. We are sorry for the changes foisted on us and the inconvenience caused. Personally, it has been a very difficult decision to make.

'A Rolling Stones tour is a two-year project and there are over 200 people involved. We would have played for charity but the Inland Revenue couldn't bend the rules. I understand that, but it is a shame.'

The gigs were rescheduled on the back of the release of *No Security*, a live album recorded in Europe, the US and South America.

The band confirmed a new date at Murrayfield Stadium in Edinburgh on 4 June 1999. To whip up a bit of publicity for the UK shows I was flown to Miami – with a select number of journalists – to see the band perform at the National Car Rental Center in Sunrise, Florida. I was granted a thirty-minute interview with Mick. However, when I arrived at their luxurious five-star beachfront hotel all was not well.

Keith, who tends to keep unconventional hours, had been out with friends the previous night and didn't get to bed until 5 a.m.

But his beauty sleep was disturbed just a few hours later when work started on a building site next door. The guitarist was woken by the sound of a pneumatic hammer pounding huge metal struts into the foundations. He wasn't happy and dispatched a member of the crew to offer the builders $25,000 if they'd put a stop to the almighty racket . . . at least until much later in the day so he wasn't disturbed. The deal was politely turned down.

Mick is the total opposite. He is accompanied on tour by a personal trainer who oversees a rigorous daily fitness programme to keep him in shape for the shows. I was nervous about meeting him. As rock stars go, they don't come much bigger.

I'd hired a local TV crew to film the interview and we set up in a private suite. My only instruction from Tony King, the band's tour publicist, was: 'Lose the lava lamp . . . I don't like it'. He also told us to use more subdued lighting to make the room a little more atmospheric.

Hotel porters wheeled in trolleys laden with every drink imaginable from the finest champagne to chilled bottles of Guinness, a favourite tipple of Ronnie Wood. But my fears were unfounded. When Mick arrived he cut an impressive figure, looking more like a Wall Street broker than a rock singer.

What struck me was just how incredibly professional he was. When I asked a question, he'd mull it over for a few seconds, before replying with a comprehensive answer. There was lots of eye contact.

My main problem though was actually reading the questions as the 'subdued' lighting in the room was now so dim I struggled to see them and had to pull up my notes to within inches of my eyes. I am sure Mick must have thought he was being interviewed by Mr Magoo.

But he was in good form throughout our chat, especially when the conversation turned to Oasis, the new bad boys of British pop. Did he see any of the Stones' early rebelliousness during the 1960s in the brothers Gallagher?

'Oh yeah, you see yourself all the time . . . the constant boozing and when you lash out at everyone,' said Mick. 'I can remember being drunk and threatening families in their motor cars on Sunday drives and thinking, why did I do that? Why was I being so menacing? I dunno, it was just me being young and mad and drunk.'

A few months previously, Liam Gallagher had publicly challenged each of the Stones to a 'square go' in Primrose Hill during a music press interview.

'That was a great laugh. Before that we'd been friendly and everything. I don't really know where that came from,' said Mick. 'Then some guys who were fans of ours went round to his house wearing Mick Jagger masks and challenged him to come out. He wouldn't open the door. It was really quite an amusing picture. But I'm not really interested in getting into a fight with him.'

In 2005, the Stones hit the road for another massive world tour in support of their twenty-second album, *A Bigger Bang*. The earnings generated by an exhaustive string of 146 shows – spread over a two-year period – topped $560 million making it then the highest grossing rock tour of all time.

On 5 February 2006, they performed 'Start Me Up', 'Rough Justice' and '(I Can't Get No) Satisfaction' at the half-time show at Superbowl XL in Detroit.

A fortnight later, they played to an estimated audience of more than two million people on Copacabana Beach in Rio de Janeiro in Brazil.

The band also performed their first-ever gig in China – appearing at Shanghai Grand Stage on 8 April – but under strict conditions. The Chinese authorities insisted they should not play classic hits like 'Brown Sugar', 'Honky Tonk Women', 'Beast Of Burden' and 'Let's Spend the Night Together' because the lyrics were 'too suggestive'.

But then, during a month-long summer break, disaster struck. Keith and his wife Patti went on holiday to Fiji and were joined on the trip by Ronnie and his missus, Jo.

During the vacation, Keith slipped while climbing on the branch of a tree and suffered serious head injuries. He was rushed to hospital in New Zealand and had brain surgery to remove a blood clot. As a result, the band were forced to cancel six shows – at a cost of

£1 million each – and some media commentators predicted it could be their last ever tour. A claim firmly denied by Mick.

When Keith recovered he apologised to fans for 'falling off my perch' but it was clear he'd been traumatised by the experience.

I was invited to interview Mick, Keith, Ronnie and Charlie to preview their gig at Hampden Park on 25 August. It was a dream assignment.

I flew out to Estádio do Dragão in Portugal – home of FC Porto – to meet the band. Charlie was back on his drum stool for the first time since being diagnosed with throat cancer. I had planned to ask him about his illness – once we were well into our interview – but he caught me off guard when he began talking about it from the outset. His honesty about fighting the disease stopped me in my tracks.

'I suppose for me personally it's good to be here, if you know what I mean. I was quite ill before. When we started the tour in America I thought . . . it's amazing I'm still here doing this,' he admitted. 'When the doctor said: "You have cancer of the throat" it was like hitting a brick wall really. I didn't feel ill or anything. I'd had an operation to remove a lump and that was it.

'The doctors in the Royal Marsden Hospital were fantastic. There were people in there in a much worst state than me. I'd see young guys in a pretty bad way – maybe eighteen or nineteen years old – really suffering. It didn't seem right. I'd lived a life. But they might never get the chance. It was really very sobering . . . especially in the world I live in. It makes it look really silly.'

I was totally absorbed as Charlie revealed – in his typical laid-back manner – how he'd stared death in the face. 'I sat for the whole nine months wondering if I'd ever be fit enough to play again,' he told me. 'I was at Ronnie Scott's playing with this jazz thing that I had and the following week was in hospital getting an operation. Then it was diagnosed as cancer. So I went from Ronnie Scott's to thinking . . . I'm gonna die.

'As soon as you hear the C-word, that's what comes into your head. Not because I felt ill but because I thought that's what happened when you got cancer.

'Why did I keep on playing with the band? It's all I know. What else was I going to do? Mick would ring each week to see how I was getting on and say: 'Whenever you're ready, give us a call.'

'Eventually I said: "I'll come next week." Then it was a worry to see if I could do it. I didn't know if I could still play.

'I didn't want to retire. I always think you get a bit older when you retire, not that I'm old now.'

When Ronnie took his seat for our interview, Keith's accident was still very much on his mind. 'I was there. I witnessed it. He dropped right behind me and I thought, what the fuck was that? Boom, boom . . . a double smack on the ground,' recalled Ronnie. 'It wasn't a palm tree, folks, but an old branch he was casually climbing about, then he thought he was Tarzan for a second and lost his grip.

'It was quite frightening. Over the next few days I could see him getting a bit depressed with headaches. I started to get worried and that's when he had to be airlifted to get proper medical attention.

'I knew he'd come through it all right – which he has – but you never know. Lots of people have died from simple concussion like that.'

Mick was also very concerned about his band mate. He told me: 'This is the tour of the moment for us and it's been a pretty good experience apart from a slight bump in the Keith department. The last time when he fell off a ladder at home, I kept thinking . . . he should never go up anything without a parachute.

'It can be quite a laugh because it's got this comedy side to it. But it's also got this other more serious side. I was worried about him. But while the recovery rate is very high, I'm sure for Keith it wasn't very funny at all.

'Now, we get people out in the audience waving blow up palm trees at him. So you've got to take it with a sense of humour, I suppose.'

Ronnie also opened up about going into rehab in a bid to conquer his ongoing battle with alcoholism. It was a success and, when we talked, he'd been sober for three years and said he'd never felt better.

'I think it's taught us all a lesson. Especially Keith, with a near death experience, and with Charlie and all that. And my rehab. You only live once and you've gotta look after yourself.

'It reflects in the music. We're happy to still be here and people keep showing up in their droves and having a great time. That's what really turns us on. But it's hard after a great show not to sort of celebrate. Now I get back to my hotel room and whip on a *CSI* or a good movie – a mystery or a thriller – as fast as possible, and just indulge to take my mind off it. I get coffee-ed out a lot these days.'

But it was when I posed the question of whether the Stones could have continued without Keith – drafting in a substitute guitarist – that I received the most poignant answer. Mick dismissed the idea out of hand. 'It wasn't something we ever had to really consider,' he said.

But I was taken aback by Charlie's take on it. Could the Stones have hit the road without their guitar-playing talisman? 'I wouldn't have done. You can't tour without Mick and Keith. It wouldn't be The Rolling Stones,' Charlie told me. 'But I think they could tour without me . . . but not without them. They ARE the Stones.'

His words were strangely prophetic. After the cancer returned, Charlie sadly passed away in 2021, aged eighty. And, just as he'd predicted, the Stones kept on rolling.

I caught up with Mick once more in Chicago in 2018 to preview the band's show at Murrayfield Stadium in Edinburgh on their No Filter tour. Yet again, several music critics speculated that, finally, this WOULD be the last time.

When I put the question to Mick – who was now seventy-four years old – he said: 'Someone asked me the other day was it hard playing shows at your age. But I haven't really thought about this being our last tour, to be honest. There will come a point where we aren't gonna do it any more. Or we can't do it any more. But I'm not thinking about that this summer.

'When the time comes I think you'd have to be honest enough to walk away if you weren't enjoying it. If it was just too much of an 'ask' physically, to do it with the energy that you really require. Then you'd have to seriously consider it, yeah. But I haven't reached that point yet.'

The singer's continuing strict fitness regime – where he runs and works out every day – keeps him fully match fit.

He told me: 'It's quite a long show – over two hours – so you've got to conserve some sort of energy. It's like playing any kind of sport. You don't go full at it all the time. It may appear that you do . . . but you don't.

'At the end you feel okay. You're not gonna lie flat on your back. That would not be a good ending.

'Ten minutes after a show I'm usually in a car going back to the hotel. I'm pretty tired sometimes. But after an hour I feel all right. I sometimes make the mistake of going out dancing which is not a good idea. On the last tour I did make one or two errors like that.

'Getting a bit over exuberant in the after-show dance side of things. That's no good. But I don't usually feel that bad.'

Last summer, I travelled down to Anfield Stadium in Liverpool to see the opening night of the UK leg of the band's SIXTY tour celebrating their musical achievements over six incredible decades.

I went to the gig with Jools Gizzi of GUN and Raymond Meade who plays with Ocean Colour Scene. Both, like me, are Stones fanatics. It was the band's first-ever tour without Charlie behind the drum kit and they paid a lovely tribute to their dear friend on the giant video screens.

When the Stones hit the stage and launched into 'Street Fighting Man', I simultaneously got goosebumps then found myself getting very emotional. Suddenly the thought occurred that maybe this COULD be the last time I'd ever see them on stage. I may not get another opportunity.

They were astounding. Mick, seventy-nine, really led from the front as they powered through a stunning nineteen-song set that included 'Tumbling Dice', 'Sympathy For The Devil', 'Jumpin' Jack Flash' and an epic 'Midnight Rambler'. They also dusted off some live rarities from their back catalogue like '19th Nervous Breakdown', 'Get Off Of My Cloud', 'Out Of Time' and 'Paint It Black'.

The chemistry – and affection – between Mick, Keith and Ronnie was self-evident. This was a band at the very top of their game.

On the long drive back to Glasgow I compared notes with Jools and Raymond and discovered they too had felt very emotional.

'I turned away because I didn't want you to see my eyes filling up,' admitted Jools.

Two days later, Raymond sent me a review from the *Washington Post* that perfectly summed up how each of us felt. The headline read: 'This isn't a band of survivors re-enacting their once greatness. This is the greatness.'

Chapter 26
Music to Soothe the Soul

THE TEARS WELL UP in my eyes as Stevie Wonder starts to sing my favourite love song. This version of 'Knocks Me Off My Feet' will stay in my heart forever because the Motown legend is playing it just for me.

I have seen him perform live on several occasions, but this is no concert venue. I'm sitting one-on-one with Stevie in a suite at The Savoy Hotel in London. As his fingers dance across the keys of a little electric piano, he repeats the soulful refrain of the classic hit from his 1976 masterpiece, *Songs In The Key Of Life*.

It has never sounded better. I have to pinch myself to make sure what's happening is real.

For the previous thirty minutes – in a wide-ranging interview – this musical genius of a man had shared his thoughts about his family, his phenomenal career and his continuing quest for civil rights, justice and equality. Stevie was visiting the UK in 2005 to launch *A Time To Love*, his first album in more than a decade. Earlier, in the grand ballroom of The Savoy, he had hosted a press conference for the UK and European media, playfully answering a series of questions by often adopting an exaggerated accent of a London city gent. But I'd been granted the only face-to-face interview for my radio show. It was a once in a lifetime opportunity.

As I was being shown into his suite, Keith Harris – a record industry executive who has represented Stevie since the 1970s – took me aside and said quietly: 'Ask him about the suit.'

Interviewing Stevie Wonder is a unique experience. He has a real aura. You realise immediately that you're in the presence of greatness.

His exceptional catalogue of songs like 'Living For The City', 'Higher Ground', 'Superstition', 'Uptight (Everything's Alright)', 'I Was Made To Love Her', 'For Once In My Life' and 'Happy Birthday' – in his case the list truly is endless – have broken down barriers and made history.

A Time To Love – his twenty-third studio album – was a worthy addition and one of his most personal works. A key song, 'Positivity', featured his daughter Aisha Morris on vocals.

It was almost thirty years since we'd heard her voice for the first time on the 1976 single, 'Isn't She Lovely', when proud father Stevie recorded her cries in the hospital delivery room just minutes after she was born. 'It's been really wonderful working with Aisha. We knew at a very young age – when she was maybe seven or eight years old – that she had a desire to sing,' Stevie told me.

'Over the years she would hear me play certain songs and sing them to me. I'd say, wow you sound really good. So I thought, why don't we use her to sing a part on 'Positivity'. She sounded sincere, very warm and had the right kind of spirit.'

Stevie punctuated our conversation by playing his keyboard to illustrate his answers. I got the first taste of it when I asked if he had a favourite song from the countless hits he'd composed.

'I always say when I'm asked that question – using a quote by Duke Ellington – that I haven't written it yet,' he said. 'For different reasons, I have different favourite songs. I have "Living For The City" days, "True Love" days and "My Cherie Amour" days.

'*Songs In The Key Of Life* is, I would say definitely – covering the spectrums that it does – one of my most favourites. But there are also things on *Innervisions* I remember doing, or stuff on *Fulfillingness' First Finale* I also enjoy. Or, *Hotter Than July*.

'Different emotions come into my heart.'

The first of several magic moments during our chat came when he reminisced about his classic 1969 hit single, 'My Cherie Amour'. The song, which he wrote in one hour, was inspired by a girlfriend he'd met at the Michigan School for the Blind.

'I wrote it in the back of the Fox Theatre in Detroit on an old reel-to-reel tape,' he revealed. 'It was originally titled 'Oh, My Marsha' because it was about a girl I used to go out with. But fortunately, Sylvia Moy worked on it with me and she came up with 'My Cherie Amour', which sounded a whole lot better.

'We cut it and it was put on the B-side of a song called, 'I Don't Know Why I Love You'. But a DJ in Chicago actually started playing the flip side of the record and that's how it became popular.'

I was then treated to a snippet of how the song first sounded back in 1966 when Stevie sang the earliest lyrics of 'Oh, My Marsha'.

He did the same when I asked if there were any songs by other artistes that he really admired. Stevie began to sing 'Michelle' by The Beatles and told me: 'I love "Michelle" very much. It's a very pretty song.'

Our conversation settled on the now historic period in 1965 when Stevie visited the UK for the first time as part of the Motortown Revue. The Motown sound had been championed on this side of the Atlantic by The Beatles and Dusty Springfield in the early 1960s. But few music fans in this country were familiar with the acts signed to owner Berry Gordy's artiste roster in Detroit.

The revue – starring The Supremes, Martha and the Vandellas, Smokey Robinson and the Miracles, the Earl Van Dyke Six and Little Stevie Wonder, as he was then known – kicked off their first British tour at Finsbury Park Astoria in London on 20 March. During a twenty-four-day trip they performed two shows a night in twenty-one different theatres, often to very sparse audiences. While the tour was a critical success it proved a commercial disaster because most record buyers were not yet familiar with the ground-breaking Motown releases.

Georgie Fame and the Blue Flames – who'd hit No.1 with the single, 'Yeh, Yeh' – were quickly added to the bill in a bid to boost ticket sales.

Stevie, then aged just fourteen, was the youngest person on the fifty-two-seater coach that travelled the length and breadth of the country. 'It was a tough life. When I was on the road with the Motortown Revue everyone over the age of fourteen or fifteen were my parents,' he said. 'I had two dollars and fifty cents a week – that's the equivalent of £1 – so it was like crazy for me out there.

'If I wanted candy, they wouldn't let me have any. I was definitely being chaperoned. There was no messing around or being silly.

'Looking back on it, I think it was great because it allowed me to really understand the value of having the pleasures of discipline which was necessary and it was appropriate as well.

'The musicians were so good it was like taking giant steps. I'd hear them and think . . . how did they do that? So I was challenged to get better and do the best that I could.'

I could see Keith out of the corner of my eye prompting me. It was time to 'Ask him about the suit'.

On 1 April the Motortown Revue rolled into Glasgow for two performances – a matinee at 6.40 p.m. and an evening show at 9 p.m. – at the Odeon Cinema in Renfield Street. Stevie had just scored his first US No.1 hit with 'Fingertips', a two-part single recorded live at the Regal Theatre in Chicago and released on the Motown imprint label, Tamla. Marvin Gaye played drums on the track before he became a big star in his own right.

After doing his spot at the matinee, Stevie was taking a break in his dressing room when there was a knock on the door. A guy – who said he was a member of staff at the Odeon – asked if he'd like his stage suit cleaned to freshen it up for the second show. He claimed he was taking a batch of laundry to the dry cleaners just around the corner.

'It's true. This guy – he was like a cleaner's man from Glasgow – said he could get my suit steam-cleaned and pressed in time for the second show,' recalled Stevie.

'It was a nice, nice suit and we said: "Do you think you can get it cleaned?" He replied: "Of course I can get it cleaned . . . give it to me." So we handed the suit over and he said: "I'll get it right back for you." I said: "Are you sure?" And he said: "Yep." He sounded so sincere and so real.

'When the next show came we never saw him again. I still don't know what happened to it. So where is my suit, baby?'

This became a running gag during the rest of our chat. Every time we heard a police siren in the main road outside The Savoy, Stevie would joke: 'Call the cops . . . maybe they've found my suit.'

On a more serious note, I then asked Stevie if he could record a message for the Cash For Kids appeal on Radio Clyde that raised money annually to help underprivileged children in Scotland. He had no hesitation. Straight off the bat he recorded the most sincere message saying: 'Cash For Kids is your commitment to helping those less fortunate than you. Cash For Kids secures and guarantees that every single child that is within the sound of my voice will have a happy holiday season with food, clothing or equipment for school that they need. Cash For Kids is not just for those children – but for you – for your heart and the best part of you giving to a worthy cause.'

It was very significant – not to mention incredibly professional – that Stevie pointedly started each part of his message with the name of the charity. He knew that even if his words were edited into a soundbite or on-air sting, he'd still be hammering the cause home.

At the close of the interview, Stevie promised he would return to Scotland to play live. He was a man on a mission.

'I will definitely be in Glasgow. I'll make sure they hook me up there . . . and you and I will find the guy who stole my suit,' he said, laughing.

But there was one final piece of Stevie Wonder magic to come. I took the plunge and politely asked if he would play 'Knocks Me Off My Feet' to take us out of the programme. He was happy to oblige. The version he performed just for me was totally unique as he sang:

'Glasgow, I don't want to bore you with it/give me my suit back.'

I was mesmerised.

We said our goodbyes and minutes later I was in a taxi heading to Heathrow Airport to catch a flight home, the tape of our interview clutched tightly in my hand. In reality, I probably didn't need a cab at all. I was on such a high I could easily have floated on air all the way from The Savoy to Terminal 5.

The following year, I was privileged to interview another Motown giant when invited to meet Smokey Robinson at The Dorchester hotel in London. He was in the capital to promote his 2006 album, *Timeless Love*, and also receive an Outstanding Contribution to Music honour at the prestigious *Q Magazine* awards.

Just meeting Smokey – who was born plain William Robinson in Detroit in 1940 – was another almighty adrenalin rush. As I walked along the corridor to his suite I could hear his instantly recognis-able – almost feminine sounding – voice, as he chatted to a member of his entourage. My heart started racing and when we sat down on the sofa to kick off our chat, I was again so overwhelmed it was difficult to get the first question out.

The singer recalled how he'd helped to form the label with Berry Gordy – who got an $800 loan from his father – to launch the com-pany in Detroit in 1958. Listening to him was like turning the pages of a pop history book and he too gave me a unique insight into the magic made at Hitsville U.S.A. – the recording studio built in Gordy's former family home – located at 2648 West Grand Boulevard.

One of my first questions was so obvious it almost asked itself. How did he get the name, Smokey?

'When I was about three years old, my favourite uncle used to take me to the movies to see cowboy films,' he said. 'I was a big fan of cowboys, especially the ones who sang like Gene Autry and Roy Rogers. So he had a cowboy name for me, which was Smokey Joe.

'At that age, whenever anybody asked me what my name was – being a little boy – I'd say: Smokey Joe. That name stuck with me and when I got to around twelve years old I dropped the Joe off. Since then, very few people in my life – including my school teachers – have ever called me anything other than Smokey.'

It was fascinating to hear him retrace his first steps as Vice Presi-dent of the labels that were incorporated under the Motown brand.

'Berry said: "We are NOT gonna make black music. We're gonna make music for the world. We're gonna have songs with great beats and great stories,"' he told me.

'That's what we set out to do, and my gosh we did way beyond our wildest dreams. You could not have told any of us – including Berry Gordy – that it would have grown to what it has become worldwide.

'But it was tough. There was a lot of discrimination going on. If you were black and made a record you were automatically catego-rised as having a rhythm and blues sound. So, at first, you had to be a success on black radio stations before you could cross over. You were only able to do that if your record was big enough.

'I think Motown broke down a lot of those barriers because it got to the point where white radio stations were clamouring for our songs even before the black stations. They wanted to have them first.'

In 1999, I'd visited Detroit on an assignment to interview Liam and Noel Gallagher of Oasis. But the highlight of my trip was undoubtedly making the pilgrimage to Hitsville U.S.A. The building is now a museum that attracts visitors from all over the world. It also has been given the status of a national heritage site and place of historical interest.

I paid my $20 admission fee and stepped over the threshold, walking in the footsteps of The Supremes, Marvin Gaye, The Jackson Five, The Temptations, Martha and the Vandellas, and many more. I can say without fear of contradiction, it was one of THE most awe-inspiring moments in my career. So, when Smokey reminisced about those early days, I could visualise everything he told me.

'Berry bought this house which had a garage attached. We tore the kitchen out and made it into the control room,' Smokey recalled. 'We put a big glass window between that and the garage and it became Studio A. We called it Hitsville U.S.A. and that's where it really all began.

'It was a wonderful place to be. We all sang or did hand claps or foot stomps or finger snaps on each other's records. It was like the competitiveness that goes on in a family . . . but there was love. We were the Motown family. That is not a myth.'

Smokey spoke with real affection about some of the artistes he made records with.

'When Michael Jackson was ten years old he was more like forty. He sang and acted like it . . . he was never really a kid until he grew up,' revealed Smokey. 'He was very, very talented. We knew The Jackson 5 were gonna be big because they were so unique.

'Marvin Gaye was suave . . . very cool. He never wanted to be a rhythm and blues singer. When he first came over to Motown, he wanted to be the Nat King Cole of the label. The first release we had with him was 'Mr Sandman'. But Mickey Stevenson – who was our

A&R director – convinced Marvin that if he really wanted to get some hits he should sing rhythm and blues.

'He and Mickey wrote this number called 'Stubborn Kind Of Fellow' – it was about Marvin – and when it was a huge hit it turned his life around.

'Marvin was a wonderful man. We spent so much time together and were very close.'

During my tour of Hitsville U.S.A. the museum guide pointed out a small red leather sofa upstairs. It was where Marvin Gaye used to curl up and sleep if it was too late to go home after an all-night recording session.

He also pointed out an air conditioning vent that doubled as the area where handclaps were recorded on a track, as they echoed beautifully in the metal duct overhead.

In the hallway, was an old Hershey vending machine with bars of chocolate still in the slots, all now inedible of course.

As soon as Berry made some money, he moved his family out of the house so the label could utilise every available space. They upped and went and didn't take anything with them. His wife's entire wardrobe still hangs in the closet – as she left it – to this day. Hitsville U.S.A. has been frozen in time.

But to step into the hallowed ground of Studio A, an area dominated by the original Motown piano – an 1877 Steinway Model D – literally took my breath away. In recent years, the instrument had fallen into disrepair. Paul McCartney helped finance its restoration.

This was the exact spot where The Funk Brothers – the resident band of session musicians led by Joe Hunter, Earl Van Dyke and James Jamerson – played on classic hits like 'The Tears of a Clown', 'My Girl', 'I Heard It Through The Grapevine', 'Papa Was A Rolling Stone' and 'Ain't No Mountain High Enough'.

Smokey recalled the moment Stevie Wonder arrived.

'Stevie was just a kid. He was discovered by Ron White who was one of The Miracles. He heard him sing and brought him over to Motown,' he said. 'He was very energetic. Stevie is blind but he's NOT handicapped . . . he's never been handicapped. Once he's familiar with the surroundings, he gets around just like he can see.

'He's a phenomenal person who has written and performed some of the greatest music in history.'

Those sentiments were echoed by Martha Reeves, who was also blown away by his talent and personality.

When I sat down with her – backstage at The Arches in Glasgow in 2010 – she vividly recalled the moment she joined the Motown family.

Martha was singing in a local club when she was spotted by Stevenson. He gave her his business card and invited her to come in for an audition.

'I turned up first thing the following morning. I didn't realise Mickey meant for me to call up and book an appointment,' she told me. 'He said: "What are you doing here?" And I said: "Don't you remember giving me a card and inviting me here?"'

'Mickey replied: "But you make an appointment for auditions that are held every third Thursday . . . this is only the first of the month."'

'I was gonna cry when he looked at me and said: "Answer this phone." They only had one line in the A&R department but it was ringing off the hook at the time.

'He said: "I'll be right back". But he was gone for three hours. There were people constantly coming in and out.

'When Mickey returned I had taken messages and notes, regulated the piano, got the musicians their pay and had taken over as the A&R secretary. He knew I was indispensable.

'Through time, I'd even type up my own contract.'

I discovered Martha also had a vivid recollection of the first time she met Stevie.

'Ronnie White of The Miracles had watched him directing a Pentecostal choir in church and said to Berry: "You ought to see this kid."

'He came in the door alone and I said: "Hello, how are you? What's your name?" He told me it was Stevie.

'I told him I was Martha and he came directly to me and said: "I want to see what you look like," and put his little fingers all over my face trying to determine if I was as nice a person as I sounded, I guess.

'He stumbled over a waste-basket so he took it and dumped it on the floor and started beating the bongos on the bottom of it.

'I said: "Wait a minute." So I grabbed the basket and picked up the waste paper and put it back in.

'By the time I'd sorted that out he'd reached the telephone that had digital tones and was playing a tune on the keypad. I thought: Oh my God, he could call Russia.

'I took the phone from him and before I could turn my head he was at the typewriter and was playing rhythms on the keys.

'He finally discovered a piano and played the theme of the TV cartoon, *Mighty Mouse*.

'Ronnie came in the door and said: "Okay Stevie, it's time for your audition." So they took him a few steps into Studio A and he found the baby grand and he began to play it like a concert pianist.

'He goes on to the full set of drums and he plays them, then he went to the xylophone and played a tune on that too.

'Just as this audition was about to end he reached in his pocket and pulled out this tiny harmonica and played it.

'At that moment, Berry Gordy said: "This kid is a wonder." And that's what his name became . . . Little Stevie Wonder.'

My conversation with Martha was less of an interview and more like listening to an eye-witness account of a period in musical and cultural history that will never be repeated. Her achievements with records such as 'Heat Wave' 'Dancing In The Street', 'Nowhere To Run' and 'Jimmy Mack' have influenced a generation of performers.

It was fascinating to hear Martha relive how she saw first hand how Berry Gordy realised his dream of creating a musical assembly line of the highest quality, modelled on his time working at the Lincoln-Mercury car plant in 1955.

'There was no such thing as a typical day in Hitsville U.S.A. There was always people coming and going,' she recalled. 'I remember when Freddie Gorman came in and he popped his mailbag down on the floor. He had helped to write the song, 'Please Mr Postman' while he was actually still a postman himself who sang with The Originals.

'I saw producers with hit records questioning if they'd pass the test when they took them up to the Quality Control department.

'Berry would say to the different writers and secretaries – people he'd gathered around him for their opinion – "Would you buy this record . . . or would you buy a hot dog?"

'They would help choose the records that would go out to the public. The producers were in awe of Berry and they listened to him. He's the reason for all the great songs that came out of Hitsville U.S.A.

'He was a taskmaster who insisted that things be done right. I've seen him mix songs at the board himself that he either wrote or other producers needed a hand with. He would record as many as 150 takes as a master until he got it the way he wanted.

'Or else he'd go back to the first two or three and listen to them again. He knew the sound he was looking for. And it was the Sound of Young America, which became the company slogan.

'The Funk Brothers also deserve fifty per cent of the credit for the success of Motown's music. They would determine who the record was for and they'd play in a certain way. So even though they were the same group of people, their music for The Supremes or Stevie Wonder or The Temptations or The Four Tops or The Vandellas never sounded alike. It was always different and suited to each group.'

But I discovered that what Martha was most proud of was that Motown helped break down racial barriers, not just in America, but around the world.

'Berry was smart enough to have five or six different labels with the Motown sound – including Tamla, Rare Earth and Gordy,' she said. 'But in the beginning, in order for us to get our music played we wouldn't have our pictures on the record covers in case some of the white DJs saw that we were actually not white singers as they first thought. He wanted them to judge the music by the artiste.

'We'd go to places – especially in the deep south of America – where we would play for audiences where the white people were upstairs and the black people were downstairs.

'I remember Smokey standing on stage and asking the guys who had the clubs – who were on either side – to move back and not hit another person in the head.

'Whoever got up – whether they were white, black or whatever – they would hit them. They didn't want integration. They knew they were in control as long as they stood with those clubs. But Smokey asked them to stand down.

'When we started the finale which was 'Mickey's Monkey' – Smokey's big hit at the time – people got up and started dancing and mixing with one another.

'We saw people who wouldn't even speak to each other before the concert actually embracing and dancing together. They were laughing and having a good time as our music was intended for them to do.

'And when the music stopped nobody could remember where they had been sitting before which was great. On the next couple of dates that we did there was no more segregation. I know we had a lot to do with that.

'After we'd been going for about a year or so we'd go back to those places and they would be sitting together and having a good time.

'It's a thrill following in the footsteps of greats like Billie Holiday, Satchmo Armstrong and Sammy Davis Jr. who were breaking down racial barriers.

'Music was invented to soothe the soul. I'm glad that was a part of my career.'

'So Motown music broke down a lot of barriers which had existed prior to that time. It was done through music and I think music is love . . . so it was done through love.'

Chapter 27
A Life Filled with Love

CLARE GROGAN HAD JUST come off stage at a charity concert in Glasgow when she said: 'Billy, I'd like you to meet someone . . . this is Elle.'

When she introduced me to her beautiful fourteen-year-old daughter in 2018, it was a very emotional moment. For this was actually the second time we had met. Elle would not have remembered the first . . . but I will never forget it.

As a baby, she was the focus of the most heartwarming story I've ever written in my career as a journalist. Clare and her husband, record producer Stephen Lironi, had adopted the child when she was just eight months old. It brought to an end twelve traumatic years of trying to start a family. I still feel privileged that Clare took me into her confidence and allowed me to share in what was such a deeply private period in her life.

My friendship with the singer who shot to fame with pop group, Altered Images, dates back to 1979. Clare was a 'face' on the local music scene and I'd run into her at venues like the Hellfire Club rehearsal room or trendy city nightclub, Maestro's.

She always looked amazing with a unique style that really made her stand out. I thought she was a star before I'd heard her sing. Clare formed the band – with bass player Johnny McElhone – and within eighteen months, they were on *Top of the Pops* with the hit singles 'Happy Birthday' and 'I Could Be Happy', and were touring with Siouxsie And The Banshees and U2.

It was while appearing on the BBC's No.1 pop show that she also caught the eye of Gary Kemp of Spandau Ballet. She became the inspiration for his greatest song, 'True'.

'I was infatuated with Clare Grogan. At one point, I travelled up to Scotland to have tea with her mum and dad,' Gary told *The Guardian*. 'Although my feelings were unrequited and the relationship was platonic, it was enough to trigger a song, 'True'.

'It's about how difficult it is to be honest when you're trying to write a love song to someone. Hence: "Why do I find it hard to write the next line?" The lyrics are full of coded messages to Clare.

'I was twenty-two and she was eighteen. "True" was really a song about me and my idea of love.'

I was well placed as Clare shot to stardom. I interviewed her on numerous occasions documenting her meteoric rise both as a singer and an accomplished actress. Then in 2006, I wrote a story about her for the *Sunday Mail* that eclipsed everything that had gone before. Clare and husband Stephen had tried to start a family but were unsuccessful. During that difficult time, she suffered recurring miscarriages and, after a series of IVF treatments failed, the couple had almost given up hope of ever becoming parents.

But in 2003 she bumped into an old friend who had adopted a child. Her happiness inspired the singer to explore the possibility of giving an unwanted infant a loving home. As you can imagine, it was a life-changing moment for the couple. But the singer's success and high profile created problems.

Clare was approached by several newspapers who wanted to tell her story. But she was wary about talking to a journalist she didn't know and had no previous relationship with. She was also very careful when taking Elle out in her pram for fear of photographers trying to snatch a picture of her daughter.

In a bid to defuse the situation, I approached Clare and asked if she was prepared to talk to me, somebody she could trust and feel more comfortable with. She had a vivid memory of me asking her, during one of our earliest chats, if she had dreams of becoming a mum.

'I can remember you interviewing me twenty years ago and asking if I wanted children,' she recalled. 'I said: "I'd like five kids." And I meant it. So it was really hard to suddenly realise you can't have them. When we decided to start a family we were just very unlucky. I suffered recurring miscarriages. Doctors could not pinpoint a specific reason.'

After talking things over with Stephen – who she married in Glasgow in 1994 – she agreed to speak to me. It was a bold step because she'd been very guarded about her private affairs in the past. This was moving into a much more sensitive area.

The couple's life with their new baby daughter changed overnight, but at that early stage they did not know what lay ahead. They explained that they'd decided to go public about the adoption in the hope that by telling their incredible story it could encourage other childless couples to follow the same path.

When I visited Clare at home in London I didn't know what to expect. This was new territory for me too.

As soon as I walked in, I immediately saw the difference the baby girl – then known as Lucia – had made to their lives.

'Lucia is Elle's middle name. I wanted to protect her at that time. I always will . . . but Elle is her name,' she explained, more recently.

Clare and I sat down on the sofa – as her daughter played with her toys on the carpet – and the singer spoke in the most moving way about how it felt to become a mother.

'Lucia has taken away all the pain, grief, despair and heartache we've been carrying around for the last twelve years,' Clare told me. 'She has made total sense of everything. It was a very difficult time but it's much easier to talk about it now because we've got our happy ending.'

I felt totally out of my depth. In terms of the subject matter, it was arguably the most difficult interview I've been a part of. I'm sure a female journalist would have had a greater understanding and approached the story from a completely different perspective. But I think Clare sensed that and carefully steered me through the emotional minefield she and Stephen had encountered.

I barely asked her a question. Clare was so erudite and articulate and knew exactly how she wanted to tell her story.

She poured her heart out.

'I'd gone through a period of not being able to conceive and began to get anxious – because of my age – so we decided to try the

IVF route to speed things up,' she recalled. 'That didn't work for me either. It was pretty tough to take because you're continually on a cycle of hope and despair. I had four IVF treatments. They say if it doesn't work after three attempts that's it. I decided to try one more for luck.

'I used to find it incredibly comforting to read about the experiences of other women who were in a similar position. I was like a magnet to the subject. I'd also read so much hoo-ha about it. It was as if any woman could decide she wanted a baby, have IVF and get pregnant automatically. But it doesn't work like that.'

It was then that the couple contacted an adoption agency and underwent a meticulous programme of parenting groups, social-work visits and police and medical checks. It was their original plan, after reading how many babies had been abandoned in China, to give a loving home to a child from that part of the world.

'But I couldn't help thinking there were children in this country who needed help,' said Clare. 'I was aware that by adopting a child, my happiness was perhaps the result of somebody else's family tragedy. I just wanted to give a child the opportunity to have a loving life.'

A crucial moment in the story came when Clare's mind was on other things. She was on the road in a 1980s package tour – sharing a bill with Toyah, Nick Heyward of Haircut 100 and Ben Volpeliere-Pierrot of Curiosity Killed the Cat – playing to packed theatres across the UK.

On 20 October 2004, Clare was appearing at The Playhouse in Edinburgh and it was perhaps fitting that when she received the news that put an end to all of her heartache, it was delivered on home soil.

'I was about to go on stage when I got a phone call saying we'd been accepted. I was overwhelmed with tears of joy,' she said. 'The hardest thing was NOT to tell the 2,500 people in the audience I was going to be a mum.'

The following year, the adoption agency informed Clare and Stephen they had a beautiful baby girl they thought would be suitable. But they still had to clear one final hurdle. The couple were asked to attend a Matching Panel to be assessed by fourteen people who had to decide on their suitability as parents.

Clare said: 'It was incredibly nerve-wracking. We had to tell them what we had to offer this wee person. All we had to give was unconditional love. They said they'd tell us the following day.

'When that came they asked us to leave the room before making their decision. The chairman called us back and said: "We think you'll make fantastic parents."'

As she spoke, I could only imagine the overwhelming happiness she and Stephen had felt.

But there was more to come. As Lucia played at our feet, Clare recalled when they visited their daughter – who had been with foster parents – for the very first time.

With tears of happiness running down her face, she said: 'We were told what time to arrive and set off really early. We practically camped outside the front door.

'When we walked into the house, Lucia was sitting with her toys on the floor. She looked up at us and it was as if she knew. It was extraordinary. We spent a couple of hours with her, then visited her every day for a week so she got used to us.'

Clare stopped talking. She was in floods of tears. I held her hand in mine as tears began running down my face too. We both sat quietly and took a moment. It was absolutely magical to see Lucia looking up at her mother with such contentment. I'll never forget it.

When they finally took the child home, Clare said that all the pain they had experienced over the previous twelve years evaporated.

'Everybody else was crying buckets. I was so happy I hardly cried at all . . . I'd had all my crying years,' she recalled. 'It was hard work. As soon as we got her – at eight months old – Lucia weighed 20lbs, so even carrying her around was tough. She's a strapping girl. But it was a real joy. My feet haven't touched the ground since.

'Stephen and I feel everything we've been through – all the pain, grief and raw emotion – was for a good reason. Just look at Lucia. She's not hard to completely open your heart to.'

I knew I had a major exclusive. This was the first time Clare had spoken about becoming a mother and she'd done so in the most moving way imaginable.

'I've never talked about my private life . . . ever,' she said. 'My motivation in agreeing to do this interview is simple. If I can use my public profile to help, I'm happy to do it because there's such a shortage of adoptive parents in Britain. If somebody who reads this then decides to pick up the phone and make that call it will be worth it.'

At this point, Stephen arrived so my photographer could shoot a family portrait. But while the couple were only too happy to show off their beautiful baby daughter, there was one stipulation.

Clare insisted that we did not fully identify Lucia in the pages of the *Sunday Mail* out of respect for the feelings of her birth mother.

We took a series of pictures – being careful to only show her in profile – and asked them to choose the ones they were comfortable with.

In the months that followed, Clare stepped back from her career in music and television to be a full-time mum. 'I've waited a long time for my maternity leave so I plan to enjoy it,' she told me. 'I'm having such fun with Lucia. We go to the singing group together. She loves singing and dancing.

'Our favourites are "The Wheels on the Bus" and "Twinkle Twinkle Little Star". I've not played her any Altered Images records yet, but I have been known to tie a bow in her hair.'

Clare revealed there was one photograph with Lucia she couldn't wait to show off.

'My mum used to have pictures of both of my sister's kids on the sideboard . . . and an empty frame for my first child,' she said. 'She used to say to me . . . Clare, I'm NOT giving up. Talk about putting Stephen and I under pressure. Now, happily, she's got a lovely picture of Lucia alongside the others.'

Clare still keeps a clipping of my story. I don't know if she's ever shown it to Elle.

The 'red-top' tabloids at times come in for criticism, often justifiably so. It's virtually impossible these days to pick up a newspaper and it not to be full of doom and gloom.

Sadly, it's the world we live in.

I still feel very humbled that Clare Grogan chose to share the story of the most pivotal moment of her life with me . . . so I could in turn share it with our two million readers.

I thank her for that. It was an uplifting experience and in all my years in journalism it's the interview I'm most proud of.

Chapter 28
Who Were The Beatles?

PAUL MCCARTNEY HAS A book on a shelf at home titled, *Who Were The Beatles?* Of all the many hundreds of tomes written about the group this one really stands out. The slim 106-page paperback – published in America in 2006 – was written specifically to teach schoolchildren about the achievements of The Fab Four. For one of music's most successful living performers it's a rather offbeat record of his past life.

'The further you get away from the heyday of The Beatles the more amazing it has become,' Paul told me when I interviewed him in 2010. 'It's grown in stature. At the time we didn't think it would last more than five years.

'Now, it's a bit legendary, which can be a little embarrassing. Somebody said, kids are learning about us in school. Wow. They're doing the history of the twentieth century and you're in the books.'

Who Were The Beatles? is illustrated with caricature drawings of famous moments such as when John, Paul, George and Ringo dressed in their Sgt. Pepper military-style uniforms or walked over the zebra crossing in Abbey Road. It's part of a No.1 *New York Times* best-selling series that also includes *What Is Rock And Roll?* and *What Was Woodstock?*

'It's a funny little book and it's written for children. It's completely wrong, by the way,' he said, laughing. 'But it is funny trying to teach five-year-olds about The Beatles.

'When I also look back at archive film clips of us I do it with a mix of pride and sorrow. But mainly it's just fondness . . . ah, look at us there. It's like seeing your old home movies. There is a feeling of sadness, though, because we've lost John and George.'

There are a few real perks in this job. Top of the list is that on rare occasions you get to meet people who have not just made records but also made rock history. Try to imagine what it's like to sit in a room with Paul McCartney – have his sole attention – and ask him about his life and career. I've been in that position four times and taken up two hours of his precious time. That doesn't sound a lot but it was a valuable opportunity to get an insight into the genius of his chosen craft.

And two hours is way more than it took him to write many of his classic songs.

Is there one single question about The Beatles that he hasn't been asked a thousand times? Probably not, but it's to his enormous credit he answers them all with real enthusiasm. Paul is the consummate professional.

I sat down with him for the first time at Air London in 1986 where he was working on tracks for *Press To Play*, his sixth solo album. Just walking into the studio – situated at 214 Oxford Street in the midst of the capital's bustling West End – was very daunting. The complex – founded by Beatles' producer, George Martin – is where a host of classic albums like *The Kick Inside* by Kate Bush, *For Your Pleasure* by Roxy Music and *Rio* by Duran Duran were all recorded. You could sense the ghosts coming out of the walls. But with Paul McCartney, just where do you start?

It's impossible to put his stature as an artiste to the back of your mind. The songs he wrote with John Lennon were, and remain, the soundtrack to my life. I was so nervous and overawed meeting him that I forgot to switch my tape recorder on for the first couple of questions. Thankfully, another of Paul's skills is how to put you totally at ease. I rectified the problem and the interview went smoothly.

We talked about a variety of subjects including fame and how he dealt with the pressures of being one of the most recognisable musicians on the planet.

'Linda and I decided right from the start that we would try to lead as normal a family life as we possibly could,' he told me. 'We didn't want to go down the nanny route. We'd bring the children up – and look after them – on our own.

'If I'm at home and want a cup of tea, I'd rather just get up and make one myself instead of having to rely on somebody else to do it for me. I don't like all that stuff.

'I remember once in The Beatles I was being driven to an appointment in a big limousine. I was sitting in the back – on my own – and when the chauffeur turned a corner I went bouncing across the seat from one end to the other. I remember thinking . . . this is ridiculous. So I tend not to do things like that if I can avoid it. It doesn't seem real.'

Paul revealed he often travels by train from his home into his office in London, with the minimum of fuss. He'll also use the Tube or public transport to get across the city because it's faster and more convenient. It's a tactic he employs everywhere he goes and it helps him keep reality in check.

'I didn't need grounded when I was growing up in Liverpool. I was trying to get into clubs and they were chucking me out. I got a lot of experience of that,' he recalled. 'But once fame arrived it was decision time. Okay, now what do I do? If I don't like this over-attention then I'm going to have to get out.

'But I decided I liked what I did. I love music too much to NOT do it. I thought, you're going to have to get a strategy for dealing with this life that you're now going to have. So I said to myself, I'm going to go on the bus and see what happens. People would notice you, but it was never as bad as you thought. Nobody would jump on you and go crazy. If I want to go on the Tube or into a shop, I just do it. And it's nearly always fine.'

When you sit and talk to Paul McCartney what strikes you is how remarkably down to earth he is. Despite his superstar status, you could be chatting to some bloke you'd just met in your local pub.

He shared one story that brilliantly underlined his approach.

'I was in New York – which is still a BIG place for The Beatles and me – so I get a lot of shouts on the streets of "Hey Paul, cool man",' he told me on another occasion.

'I was going Uptown and was late so I decided to jump on a bus. I could see that people had noticed me but it was fine. I paid my money to the driver and sat down on my own. There was a black lady looking at me and she said: "Hey, are you Paul McCartney?"

'I said: "Yes I am." She said: "What you doin' on the bus?"'

'I replied: "I'm going Uptown, just like you are. And anyway, don't go shouting across the bus . . . come and sit here." There was a spare seat next to me.

'I could see all the other people with their shoulders going, having a good laugh, but they were keeping their heads down.

'It was great because I treated it like she was just an ordinary person and so was I. So we were just jiving away and I got off at my stop no problem at all. It was a fun bus ride.

'But I've always done that. I hate the idea of success robbing you of your private life. So I always say to people if I get asked for an autograph in the middle of a meal: 'I'm really sorry but I don't do that while I'm eating. I hope you understand. This is my private bit.'

'And most people go, "Oh, I'm sorry." They DO get it. I just have a few little rules and most people respect that.'

I was a little too young to see The Beatles live. But when Paul embarked on the next stage of his incredible career – first with his group, Wings, then as a solo artiste – I soon caught up. I worked as a steward in Green's Playhouse in Glasgow when Wings played the venue on 24 May 1973, with tickets priced just £1.40. It was his first UK headline tour as an ex-Beatle and he was finding his feet again as a performer, after quitting the group three years previously.

I watched his soundcheck where he expertly drilled his band – which included wife Linda, guitarists Denny Laine and Henry McCullough and drummer Denny Seiwell – in the empty theatre. He knew he had it all to prove once more.

But the singer showed he was more than up to the task.

During the show, his loyal Scottish fans were stunned when he refused to play any Beatles numbers as if to underline that Wings were a new band in their own right.

But it was a different story when he returned to the venue, now the Glasgow Apollo, two years later – on a tour to promote the album, *Venus And Mars*.

It was the first time he performed songs such as 'Lady Madonna', 'Blackbird', 'I've Just Seen A Face', 'Yesterday' and 'The Long and Winding Road' in front of a live audience in years, if at all.

After he disbanded Wings in 1981, Paul further embraced his musical past and reacquainted himself with even more songs The Beatles never got the opportunity to play live themselves.

'There are a couple of songs that we do I've never played since we recorded them. Other people have done them but not me,' he said. 'It was always very difficult to do 'Paperback Writer' cause it's got quite complicated harmonies at the beginning and you need four people to sing it.

'With The Beatles, we had Ringo but he couldn't really get in on the harmony thing so it just left the three of us to try and cover it.

'We did it when we first went to Japan but we didn't enjoy it because we didn't do a good job on it. So it went fairly quickly.

'I heard it recently at a party – somebody was playing all this hip, really groovy new modern music and in the middle of it they just banged on 'Paperback Writer' – and it sounded real good. It lived with all this contemporary music and I thought . . . that's a cool track. It just worked. So we started doing it again. With my band now we can cover all those harmonies.

'I wouldn't say this about much stuff. But I think we make a better job of it than The Beatles did.'

Ironically, 'Paperback Writer' was one of the last ever songs the group played at their final paying concert before 25,000 fans at Candlestick Park in San Francisco on 29 August 1966.

As they were being led from the stage, George Harrison said: 'That's it . . . I'm not a Beatle any more.'

When they played on the roof of their Apple Corps HQ in London on 30 January 1969 – to film a sequence for the movie, *Let It Be* – it was the last time they'd ever perform together.

But over the years, there was continued speculation they would reform. In December 1979, Paul helped organise the Concerts for the People of Kampuchea at Hammersmith Odeon in London, to raise funds for the victims of the war in Cambodia. Over four nights,

Queen, Ian Dury And The Blockheads, The Clash, The Who, The Pretenders, Rockpile and The Specials gave their services free for the cause.

I covered two of the gigs including the final night – on 29 December – when Wings performed with their special guests Elvis Costello and Robert Plant of Led Zeppelin. Midway through the gig whispers swept the audience that John Lennon and Yoko Ono had been smuggled in the side door of the venue. Word spread too that George Harrison and Ringo Starr had been spotted backstage. As the lights dimmed, the excitement and expectation levels reached fever pitch. Were we about to see music history in the making? Sadly, the rumours proved false and it was not to be.

Instead, Paul did perform with Rockestra, his own hastily assembled supergroup which featured Pete Townshend of The Who, Ronnie Lane and Kenney Jones of The Faces, Dave Edmunds plus members of Led Zeppelin and The Pretenders.

But when we talked I discovered he was very open to a Beatles reunion. He was adamant it would have happened as the years rolled by. I asked what would it have taken to get John, George and Ringo back into the studio or on stage with him again?

'Loadsa money,' he said, jokingly. 'I don't really know what it would have taken . . . I've no idea. The truth is it could have been a charity thing or it could have been that we'd just all met up and said, let's do it for a laugh.

'You never know. It could have happened. We were asked to do reunion gigs shortly after we broke up. But there wasn't any point. We had just split and by the way, I was doing Wings. We were all busy with other things.

'But it was not to be, so it's all just conjecture.'

When I interviewed him at the SSE Hydro in Glasgow on 14 December 2018, his answer was even more illuminating. He revealed that in his own special way he HAD reformed The Beatles.

'People say . . . what if? I have to stop them and say, that's NOT going to happen,' he told me. 'But if some strange fluke was to happen it would be beautiful.

'Do you know where it does happen? In my dreams. As a musician you often have dreams about being in the studio or on stage, so I'm often with the guys.

'Just the other morning I woke up and said: "I was just with George." And that's very nice. Anyone who has lost people, when you dream about them it's magical, it's like you're with them again just for that second. So that's how I run into them these days. That's how we reform.'

Over the years, I've been lucky to see Paul play live on numerous occasions and he's always delivered.

In 1989, I got a gold-dust ticket for a special 'Rehearsal Concert' in the intimate 300-capacity Playhouse Theatre, behind Charing Cross railway station in London. The show, arranged as a warm-up for a world tour to promote his album, *Flowers In The Dirt* – co-written with Elvis Costello – brought back good memories for the singer. It was the theatre where The Beatles recorded many of their live radio broadcasts for the BBC in the 1960s.

He also confirmed a gig called Get Back to Glasgow at the SECC on 23 June 1990. It was organised as part of the celebrations for Glasgow being named the European City of Culture. Within a wonderful six-week period, McCartney, Luciano Pavarotti, The Rolling Stones and Frank Sinatra all performed in venues across the town.

A decade later, he returned to the city to play Hampden Park on 20 June 2010, with special guests, Texas. The stadium show for an audience of 50,000 people was his biggest-ever concert in Scotland.

Paul invited me to MPL Communications – his London HQ – for a chat to preview the show in the *Daily Record* and for my show on Radio Clyde. My interview was sandwiched between an appointment with a US film crew and a meeting with legendary Beatles producer, George Martin.

As soon as our chat finished, he was dashing off to Abbey Road studios to oversee a mixing session for a new, remastered version of the classic 1973 Wings album, *Band on the Run*.

It was the first time I'd visited his office in Soho Square in the West End. The place was a cosy clutter with bronze Ivor Novello songwriting awards on the shelves and pictures of Rupert the Bear on the walls. He owns the publishing rights to the comic character.

Lying on a chair was a store assistant's apron for B&Q, the DIY warehouse, complete with a 'Paul McCartney' name badge. It was a gift from the company after he'd let slip in an interview that he got asked for an autograph while buying nails at his local store. It was reassuring to know that if writer's block ever set in, Macca was guaranteed a job selling fitted kitchens or cutting plywood to size.

The conversation settled on his increasing appetite for hitting the road and playing his songs. 'I don't know why I enjoy it more now than when I did. I think I find myself a bit more comfortable with the playing live thing,' he admitted. 'It was great then and it's still great now but the difference is you can actually hear what you're doing, and so can the crowd.

'It was like a football match in the old days, particularly if we played big places. We were all just part of some huge celebration.

'But it's nice today with the technical equipment that you can actually sing something and know you're gonna be heard.'

He revealed there were still occasions, though, when things did not quite go to plan and he suffered the ultimate Spinal Tap moment one night during a gig in Pittsburgh, USA.

'I was in America playing these really big baseball stadiums and when you do that instead of going: "Good evening everybody" . . . you've got to go: "GOOD EVENING EVERYBODY."

'Everything has got to be much bigger and you shout more,' he said.

'I had this thing where I would shout out the name of the city like: 'Good evening New York', and it would always get a massive cheer because they all love to hear their name.

'I was in Pittsburgh one night and had some trouble with my voice . . . it had gone during the soundcheck. As we were doing the first number I was thinking is it going to hold out, so I wasn't concentrating at all.

'It got to the bit in the show where I did the big stadium announcement and I shout: "People of Detroit". And it all went . . . *woo-oo-ah*. There was nothing. Normally, you'd get a big cheer. It was like a black hole. I had to think of a way to get out of it.

'Your heart nearly stops but your mind is racing. The computer in your head is going . . . figure it out, figure it out.

'So, this is how it went in real time. I said: "People of Detroit . . . you are not. People of Pittsburgh . . . you are."

'Oh my God! I don't know how I ever got away with that. In a review of the gig the next day it said: "Ah, the old wacky McCartney wit is still there". If only they knew.

'Later, the guys in my crew said . . . we don't know how on earth you came up with that.'

For the gig at the SSE Hydro in 2018, Paul again unearthed some real gems from his glorious back catalogue, to the delight of 13,000 Scots fans.

His superb thirty-nine-song set was loaded with Beatles compositions and included rare live performances of 'Being For The Benefit Of Mr Kite', 'Something', 'Ob-La-Di, Ob-La-Da', 'Birthday', 'Helter Skelter' and 'Golden Slumbers'/'Carry That Weight'/'The End'.

When we talked before the show, his passion for all things Scottish was unabated. Paul recalled the night he made his live debut on Scottish soil playing a now historic gig with The Silver Beetles – as the backing group for Liverpool singer, Johnny Gentle – at Alloa Town Hall on 20 May 1960.

'We'd never really travelled anywhere. In Liverpool, we might have taken a little train trip to Southport or somewhere, half an hour away,' he told me. 'So coming up in the van to Scotland was like travelling to a foreign country. It was primitive. We were playing little village halls, but that was okay because we were primitive too.

'It wasn't like we had any big equipment or anything . . . all we had were guitars and a couple of amps. The audiences didn't know who we were, because nobody did. We were just Johnny Gentle's backing band. And they didn't even know who Johnny Gentle was.

'It was good fun meeting up with the kids. We'd never done this before so we were thrilled that anyone would want to talk to us like we were stars.

'I remember we all changed our names. I was Paul Ramon. He sounded a very exotic character.'

At time of writing, Paul is eighty-one years old and shows no sign of giving up. He is still striving to do more both in the studio and on stage. But has he written his greatest song yet . . . or does that always remain the ultimate goal?

'What is my favourite song? The truth is there is a few of them . . . and for different reasons,' he revealed.

'The most magical was "Yesterday" because I dreamed that. I woke up with the tune in my head and over the next couple of weeks wrote the song. And then it got covered by more than 3,000 people. So how that happened was pure magic.

'But I always want to do better music. It doesn't stop you trying. There's a scenario where I could look at the career of The Beatles and think, wait a minute, we ARE talking 'Eleanor Rigby', 'Let It Be', 'Hey Jude . . . I've probably written my best song. But then you've got to give up and say, right, thank you very much, I'm going off on holiday for the rest of my life.

'I love it too much. So there's always this thought in the back of your mind where you think . . . you never know, I might just come up with something that will be really great. And that keeps you going.'

One thing he was certain about, though, is that there will never be another band like The Beatles. When I put him on the spot and asked if he could envisage a time where a new act came along and changed the face of music and pop culture, he shot straight from the hip.

'My immediate answer is no. Just because of the time, the place and the circumstances. And the talent in The Beatles,' Paul told me. 'That combination of those four guys was pretty interesting. And the work we put in. You look at the time we were together – which wasn't that long – every album was different.

'It was new and successful. So for someone to be able to do that ever again, I kind of doubt it. I'm not sure why because there's loads of great groups around.'

And really warming to the topic, he added: 'See, the nice thing is I DON'T have to be modest about The Beatles any more. I can call them great albums . . . cause it's over. If I was talking about my own records I'd maybe have to be a little bit more modest.

'But for somebody to come out and consistently make album after album, single after single – that just beat the last one and got better and better – I'm not sure that's going to be too easy.

'I wish everyone out there good luck. But I've a feeling there was something very special about The Beatles.'

Chapter 29
The Garage Band . . .
From Garageland

ARRIVING IN TOKYO FOR the first time was an overwhelming experience. From the moment I cleared customs at Narita Airport, it felt like I had stepped into a foreign landscape situated somewhere between the set of the sci-fi movie, *Blade Runner* and a Sega video arcade game. I had most definitely touched down on alien territory.

It was exhilarating . . . I couldn't wait to explore the city.

I'd flown to the Japanese capital to interview Cosmic Rough Riders, who were appearing at Summer Sonic, a rock festival staged in Tokyo and Osaka on 17 and 18 August 2001. The Glasgow band were on a real high having just made their debut on *Top of the Pops* with the hit single, 'Revolution (In The Summertime?)'.

They'd recorded the song at C-Sharp, a community studio located in their local shopping centre, in the sprawling Castlemilk housing estate on the south side of the city. The building was formerly Galloway's the Butchers and lead singer Daniel Wylie recalls taping his vocals adjacent to the refrigerated storeroom where the carcases of meat were hung.

It was the lead track from their album, *Enjoy The Melodic Sunshine* released on Poptones, a new indie label launched by Alan McGee, a fellow Glaswegian best known for discovering Oasis at King Tut's in 1993.

'It was a real big deal for us to be connected with him. He had a reputation for picking winners after signing The Jesus And Mary

Chain, Primal Scream, Teenage Fanclub and of course, Oasis, to his previous label, Creation Records,' said Daniel.

McGee's instinct again proved correct. The album sold more than 100,000 copies and spent seventeen weeks in the UK charts.

Seeing the Cosmics play their first gigs on Japanese soil was a real eye opener. As a virtually unknown UK band, their name was listed in small print at the bottom of the gig poster. Top of the bill were Marilyn Manson, Elbow, Primal Scream, Ocean Colour Scene, Slipknot plus a string of Japanese artistes.

In Tokyo, they were the opening act in a 15,000-capacity arena with a stage time of 11 a.m.

'My first thought was . . . this is pure Spinal Tap. There is going to be nobody there. Who goes to a gig that early?' recalled Daniel. 'When we got to the venue the place was completely empty. There wasn't a single person in the hall.

'But when we walked out on stage, it was rammed. The crowd knew our songs and were singing along with them. We went down an absolute storm. I couldn't believe it.

'The Japanese audience have also got to be THE most polite you can play for. They went crazy during the songs but stood in total silence to listen to what I was saying in between numbers. They were so well mannered. Can you imagine that happening at Barrowland?

'Both gigs in Japan were a real success. We sold another 10,000 albums off the back of them.'

But my trip was about to become even more memorable. When I got back to my hotel room, the red-light message button was flashing on the telephone at my bedside. When I played the voicemail back it said: 'Billy, this is John Giddings. You've done it. We're coming to Glasgow. Call me.'

John is a major player in the UK music industry as the founder of Solo, the agents and promoters for some of the biggest names in rock including The Rolling Stones, David Bowie, Madonna, Genesis, Lady Gaga and Celine Dion. He also represented U2 who several months previously had unveiled details of their 'Elevation' world tour to promote the album, *All That You Can't Leave Behind*. It had kicked off at the National Car Rental Center in Sunrise, Florida, on 24 March, before snaking its way across America.

The European leg – which opened at The Forum in Copenhagen in Denmark on 6 and 7 July – also included gigs in Stockholm, Munich, Paris, Turin, Barcelona plus Slane Castle in Ireland, the NEC in Birmingham and Earl's Court in London. There was one glaring omission, however. There were NO Scottish dates on the tour itinerary . . . U2 had decided not to play in either Glasgow or Edinburgh.

The news went down like a lead balloon with the band's legions of fans in Scotland. It caused an outcry. I wrote an open letter to U2 in my *Sunday Mail* column saying it was unthinkable that they would not be appearing in the one territory outside of their native Ireland that had embraced the band in their very early days.

Scotland was a real U2 stronghold . . . it was a terrible slight. My comments filtered back to the group.

On 26 February I covered the twenty-first Brit Awards at Earl's Court in London where U2 received two of the top prizes. When I met Bono, The Edge, Adam Clayton and Larry Mullen Jr. backstage, there was only one topic of conversation.

'What are they saying about us in Scotland?' asked Bono.

I didn't see any point in soft-soaping him so I said: 'Your name is mud at the moment. The fans just can't believe the band don't want to play in Scotland. It's not gone down well.'

As Bono was being led to the stage, he told me: 'We're working on it. Don't worry . . . we'll sort it out. I promise.'

Minutes later, U2 received the Brit for Best International Group, which was presented by Kylie Minogue and Huey Morgan of Fun Lovin' Criminals. At the climax of the ceremony, they were also given the event's main award for Outstanding Contribution to Music, by Noel Gallagher of Oasis.

Six months later, Bono proved as good as his word.

I called John and he revealed that U2 had slotted in two extra shows at the SECC in Glasgow on 27 and 28 August, little more than a week away. The tickets would go on sale at the venue – first come, first served – just three days earlier. When the news broke it created hysteria as thousands of fans queued out overnight to snap them up.

Dougie Souness, manager of Cosmic Rough Riders lobbied John to get the band the coveted support slot for both shows. They were confirmed at just forty-eight-hours notice. Bosses at the SECC were so overwhelmed by the speed of events they got special plaques made for the fastest selling tickets at the venue to present to the band.

'It was the biggest audience we'd ever faced on home soil,' revealed Daniel. 'After the first night, U2 had a string of limos parked outside our dressing room so they could make a quick getaway.

'I saw Bono running down the ramp from the stage – wearing a hooded boxer's dressing gown – and he said to me: "Hey Daniel, thank you for doing the gig."

'It was our pleasure. We were such huge fans. People talk about Bono and his politics. Some don't like him for that.

'I'd first met the band when they played Tiffany's in Glasgow in the 1980s. I thought they were nice guys then and seeing them again all those years later – when U2 were one of the biggest acts on the planet – I don't think they had changed at all. They were still down-to-earth and very normal.'

On the second night, before U2 made their way to the stage, I joined the SECC's box office staff to present them with their awards. The band were very touched. Their efforts to sort out the confusion surrounding the Scottish dates had not gone unnoticed.

From the opening songs – 'Elevation' and 'Beautiful Day' – they were in superb form and really connected with their loyal Scottish audience. They were on fire as they powered through a set that also included 'Sunday Bloody Sunday', 'Where The Streets Have No Name' and 'Mysterious Ways'. Bono had taken my words at the Brits, all those months earlier, to heart. It led to what was for me the most emotional point in the gig.

During the encore, The Edge began strumming the riff of 'One', as Bono addressed the crowd saying: 'I'd like to thank the Cosmic Rough Riders for opening up the show tonight.'

I was standing at the front of the stage when Bono looked down at me and said: 'And thank Billy Sloan for being the little worm in our ear always saying Glasgow . . . don't forget Glasgow.' I almost passed out with shock as people shook my hand warmly and gave me pats on the back. As a U2 fan, it was a very special moment that I was able to share with 8,500 complete strangers.

But such gestures were not uncommon from U2. As the band got even bigger they felt it important to never lose that personal touch, as I would experience on several occasions.

My forty-year-plus relationship with the Irish supergroup began on the night I interviewed Bono for the first time, backstage at Strathclyde University on 24 January 1981 on the 'Boy' tour. It was one of the main student venues in the city and had a reputation for showcasing up-and-coming acts who went on to bigger things, having promoted early gigs by Pink Floyd, Fleetwood Mac and Elton John.

The double bill of The Ramones and Talking Heads in 1977 – watched by Debbie Harry, who was in the city to play with Blondie at the Apollo – has become part of punk legend in Glasgow.

Another memorable night was when The Jam headlined the venue the following year on a UK tour to promote the album, *All Mod Cons*. I remember being pinned to the wall when they detonated pyrotechnics at the 'A-P-O-C-A-L-Y-P-S-E' climax to hit single, '"A" Bomb In Wardour Street'. The blast almost took the roof off.

I was also fortunate to see the Q Tips play a stormer of a show, fronted by a fast-rising young vocalist named Paul Young in 1981. Within eighteen months, he had gone solo and released *No Parlez*, one of the biggest selling debut albums of the eighties, which included the chart-topping single, 'Wherever I Lay My Hat (That's My Home)', a cover of the 1963 hit by Marvin Gaye.

All gigs at Strathclyde were staged on Level Five, a hall on the fifth floor of the union building. The social committee enforced a strict policy of closing all the bars for thirty minutes when the headline band took the stage to encourage students to go upstairs and check them out. But this courtesy was not extended to support acts who were forced to compete with lager at a mere 40p a pint.

On 9 December 1978, I watched The Police play to just twenty-six people as a support act to the comedy-rock band, Alberto Y Lost Trios Paranoias. Sting on vocals and bass, with guitarist Andy Summers and drummer Stewart Copeland performed an impressive set which featured their singles, 'Roxanne' and 'Can't Stand Losing You', both of which had failed to crack the Top 40.

But nobody wanted to know the band, except me. I'd seen them make their debut on the *Old Grey Whistle Test* two months earlier and thought they were fantastic. I wandered into their dressing room and spent twenty minutes chatting to the group. I've still got the gig flyer they autographed for me, which has become something of a collector's item.

When The Police reissued the singles six months later they enjoyed their first taste of chart success. Superstardom was just around the next bend.

U2 also had their sights set on global success. They were thinking big, straight from the off. I talked to Bono in a vacant gent's toilet on Level Five. It was the only place quiet – and echoey enough – to tape a piece for my show on Radio Clyde.

Their debut album, *Boy*, was a hit in Ireland but had stalled at No.52 in the UK charts. They'd also released an EP, plus four singles, which had not made a dent in the Top 40. But Bono was prepared to play the waiting game. He was brimming with self-assurance.

'This isn't going to happen overnight, so we're in this for the long haul,' he told me. 'We've got the songs to take this thing – whatever it turns out to be – around the world. I think they're good enough. I've no doubt about that.

'We're also building a reputation as a great live band. We want to get out there and play as much as possible.'

In the years that followed, I played U2's records on the show and wrote about them in my newspaper column. It was immensely gratifying to watch the group climb up the ladder, playing venues like Tiffany's, The Playhouse in Edinburgh and Barrowland, then graduating to arenas such as the SECC before moving on to Murrayfield Stadium in Edinburgh and Celtic Park and Hampden Park in Glasgow.

Over those years, U2 also forged a strong friendship with Simple Minds. There was a real mutual respect and affection between both bands, which still exists today. When Bono appeared on *Desert Island Discs* in 2022, he chose 'Someone Somewhere (In Summertime)' by Simple Minds as his final track.

The song opens Simple Minds' 1982 album, *New Gold Dream (81-82-83-84)* that was a huge influence on the Irish band.

Bono told host, Lauren Laverne: 'I remember meeting them when we were in our twenties and thinking wherever they were, wherever they were staying and whatever city they were playing in . . . they were in the moment, fully.

'Very few people get to own a sound and I think in U2 we got to own certain colours of the spectrum or certain feelings that are ours. But some of them are from Simple Minds. We learnt from them.'

In 1984, U2 played two gigs at Barrowland to promote their fourth album, *The Unforgettable Fire*. The Minds decided to show them a little Scots hospitality by hosting a lavish lunch at the Lomond Castle Hotel to celebrate their visit. We all piled onto U2's tour bus and drove to a picturesque setting on the banks of Loch Lomond. The scenery took their breath away.

The trip was captured beautifully in a series of atmospheric shots of Jim Kerr and Bono taken by rock photographer, Anton Corbijn.

It should come as no surprise to learn this self-confessed rock 'n' roll anorak still has a copy of the special lunch menu signed by both bands.

The Minds rolled out the red carpet again as they played three sell-out gigs at Barrowland to kick off the New Year in 1985. On the afternoon of the show on 4 January, I got a call from my dear friend, Jimmy Kerr – Jim's father – from the family home in the south side of Glasgow.

'We've got a couple of visitors. Bono and his wife Ali have just turned up. They're going to spend the next week touring the Scottish Highlands,' he told me.

But first, there was some work to be done.

In an interview with Janice Long on Radio 2, Jim recalled how he discovered that U2's frontman had arrived unexpectedly on his doorstep.

'I got a message saying you've got to call home, your mum's looking for you,' he said. 'I thought that someone had forgot to put a name on the guest list or whatever. I phoned her and she said: 'Bono and Ali are here. They're touring round and found out you're playing and they want to go.

'I said: "Put them on." And she went: "They're upstairs sleeping. I've given them something to eat, and now they're having a wee rest."

'We never saw them before the gig, but as we were playing I could see Bono at the side of the stage just dying to get on. So, of course, we brought him on and did this version of 'New Gold Dream' that seemed to last for about twenty minutes.'

Jim told the Barrowland audience: 'This guy came to my door on Hogmanay and said: 'I want to join the band. I've come all the way from Ireland, and I haven't got a job.'

'So I said: "Can you sing?" And he said: "Yeah, I think so."

'You can be the judge. All the way from Dublin . . . Bono.'

Their epic vocal sparring session – which also contained excerpts of 'Light My Fire' by The Doors and 'Take Me To The River' by Al Green – is featured on the *Silver Box* compilation released in 2004.

There's a well-known phrase that says: 'The bigger they are . . . the nicer they are.' It doesn't always ring true, but in the case of U2 I can vouch for the fact it's one hundred per cent accurate.

In 1993, I saw U2 play the two greatest gigs it's been my pleasure to attend . . . the spectacular Zooropa shows at Celtic Park in Glasgow on 7 and 8 August.

From the opening song, 'Zoo Station' – where Bono danced in silhouette like a marionette in front of the giant video screens – to the closing 'Love Is Blindness' they didn't put a foot wrong. The music, the visuals, the production all worked in tandem and U2 were at the very top of their game. *Q Magazine* later ranked their performance as one of the Best Gigs of All Time.

A real highlight was when Bono spoke via a live video link to a group of people who had sought sanctuary in a bomb shelter in Sarajevo. One mother was able to send a message to her son who managed to escape the fighting. He had made his way to Glasgow and was in the 60,000-strong audience that night. Backstage, U2 took time out to welcome several other fans who had fled to safety.

Billy Mackenzie of The Associates turned up too. The band were thrilled to see him, being such an admirer of his unique voice and musical talents.

I had my son Paul – then aged fifteen – with me and he desperately wanted to meet Bono. The singer could not have been more charming as he chatted to him.

Then, we got a bit of the real Bono magic. As we lined up for a quick photograph, Bono removed his trademark 'Fly' wrap-around shades and put them on Paul for the snap.

When he went to hand the glasses back, Bono said: 'Keep them. They look much better on you than they do on me.'

My son still has them. They'd be worth a fortune if you put them up for auction at Sotheby's or Bonhams. But they are not for sale . . . why would you part with such a personal memento?

Four years later, I headed for Vienna to hook up with U2 on their 'PopMart' tour to film an interview with Bono for Scottish Television. It was organised to preview their gig at Murrayfield Stadium in Edinburgh on 2 September.

The band were headlining Wiener Neustadt, a 65,000-capacity open-air venue, thirty minutes outside the beautiful Austrian city. U2's new stage show – to promote their ninth studio album, *Pop* – was an elaborate production inspired by garish consumerism, supermarkets, pop culture and TV. They performed in front of a 165ft-wide LED screen, beneath a huge McDonald's-style golden arch and a giant olive speared by a 100ft high cocktail stick. At the end of the set, the group climbed aboard a giant lemon that transported them to a B-stage to play an encore. It worked a treat in Vienna but during the tour U2 endured a few Spinal Tap moments when it failed to open and they had to exit the contraption through an escape hatch.

When I went backstage the walls were covered by fly-posters advertising a hastily organised additional gig planned for Kosovo Stadium in Sarajevo on 23 September. After shining the spotlight on the war in the region with their nightly video links during the 'Zooropa' tour, U2 felt it was the right thing to do.

Bono immediately took me aside and said conspiratorially: 'Keep this to yourself – because I've not told management yet – but I'm heading to Sarajevo on my own to see what's really been going on.' A few weeks later they became the first major artistes to perform in the city after the Bosnian War.

We sat down to film the interview at midnight and Bono gave me the inside story of how the most ambitious tour of the band's career so far was conceived.

He told me: 'After *Zooropa* I think we felt it was a bit predictable to cut things down to size. We do this better than anyone else and the reason is we treat it as a different medium. We're not trying to put a small club show on in a stadium where people can't hear or see the band. We're actually saying, there's a chance to do something that hasn't been done before.

'So on PopMart our idea was very simple . . . you know, it was just, eat the monster before it eats you.

'The Beatles gave up touring and playing live because they knew they couldn't get across, they were being drowned out by the crowds. Well I like to think we drown the crowds out . . . it's a real wrestling match.'

But their lavish stage production – focused on the giant lemon – was surely the result of a night on the hard stuff.

'The chicks LOVE the lemon,' said Bono, smiling, 'And yeah, there was some drink involved, that's for sure. It's high as a kite to be out in front of that and I'm NOT touching the stuff. Just to be there is an amazing thing. I can't believe we pulled it off.'

And where did the fixation for supermarkets and 24-hour convenience stores come from?

'I'm not a big shopper. Adam is the Imelda Marcos of the band. He's got the shoes. I don't get out much to be honest with you,' revealed Bono. 'We're just having a laugh, having some fun. If you're gonna step out of a 40ft lemon you either want to be very stupid or have very big balls. You can make your own mind up, Billy.'

At the end of the interview, Adam popped in to say hello.

'Don't tell anyone, but we blew out a couple of big American news channels to slot you in,' he said. 'We just wanted to see a more familiar face. Thanks for coming.'

It was now 1 a.m. and the end of a long day.

'How are you getting back to Vienna?' asked Bono.

To be honest, things had got so hectic, me and my cameraman had still not quite figured that out.

'Come with us. You'll be home in no time,' said the singer.

U2 had a line of chauffeur driven cars and people carriers waiting to go, so we loaded in our equipment and climbed aboard. A team of police motorcycle outriders pulled up alongside us and we were off, speeding through roadblocks all sirens wailing. It was the first time I'd been part of a police convoy. It's the only way to travel . . . I can recommend it.

Another memorable night was when U2 played a free gig at the much-missed Astoria Theatre in London's West End on 7 February 2001. The 1500-capacity crowd was largely made up of radio competition winners lucky enough to get hold of the gold dust tickets. The hysteria surrounding the 'secret show' brought Charing Cross Road to a standstill and I witnessed a ticket tout buy one from a punter for £800. You can bet he had a customer in a pub around the corner willing to fork out double that to get into the gig.

Was I tempted to sell my ticket? Definitely not, for no amount of money could compensate for not seeing U2 perform in such an intimate club setting.

I had a good spot in the Astoria balcony at the VIP area which boasted a veritable Who's Who of rock with Mick Jagger, Thom Yorke, Bob Geldof, Kylie Minogue, Noel Gallagher, Roger Taylor, Dave Stewart, Sharleen Spiteri plus author Salman Rushdie, supermodels Naomi Campbell, Jerry Hall and Helena Christensen and actor John Hurt in attendance.

As U2 powered through an impressive set, Bono mischievously told the audience: 'We are reapplying for the job as best band in the world.'

The quote hit the headlines with the *The Guardian* saying: 'U2 have been parodied, sneered at, mocked and misunderstood. However, when they are on this form they are unstoppable.'

The U2 juggernaut continued to gather momentum with the albums, *How to Dismantle an Atomic Bomb* in 2004 and *No Line*

On The Horizon five years later. I was among the first people to hear the latter when the band staged an exclusive playback for the media at the chic Saatchi Gallery in King's Road in London. The event was another hot ticket.

To promote *No Line On The Horizon* they embarked on the U2 360-degree world tour . . . a string of dates spread over a two-year period in North and South America, Africa, Europe and the UK. It was their biggest live show yet and they performed in the round on a circular four-legged structure nicknamed 'The Claw', at the time the largest stage set ever constructed for a rock event.

When I caught up with the band – for a radio special at Wembley Stadium on 14 and 15 August 2009 – I got a behind-the-scenes look at how the show was conceived.

The Edge was quoted as saying 'There's no point in being the biggest unless you're also the best' so I asked him if the elaborate 360-degree production ticked both boxes.

'I think so. In all honesty there's nothing that comes close in terms of just the combination of the show itself, the actual hardware and the U2 audience being the best in rock and roll,' he told me. 'So just to be there is an experience in itself. I think the songs are good and we know what to do at this point. We've been doing it for a long time. But it's a combination of everything that makes it a really great show.'

Bono also gave me a unique insight into his personal regime before taking the stage each night.

'I try to spend some quiet time in the day just to think about the show, what city I'm in and what relationship the band have had with that city. And if there's anyone there I need to get even with,' he said, laughing. 'Then I lock myself in a steam room for thirty minutes and do vocal warm-ups.

'They're mostly animal noises. It's a very strange thing to hear. Then I'll work up to some hymns, to get into the right place for my voice.

'As a blunt instrument it's okay . . . I can still sing. But I love it when it's sharper and really doing what I want it to do. That makes the show so much better for me.'

Bono also revealed how he reaches the moment in the show when his vocals and performance really connect.

'At what point do you lose yourself and your self-consciousness? That's really what it's all about. When you're not singing the song . . . the song is singing you, so to speak,' he said.

'I feel it's a little bit like a boxing match. You go out and you're not up against the audience, you're up against yourself. You're throwing a few digs. It can get rough.

'There's a moment usually – and it's not the same moment every night – where you look around and think, there's something going on here. So you're always waiting for that little magic feeling and it can be annoying because it's so unreliable.

'You can attach all kinds of emotions to music. I do. People say that U2 is the ultimate band for weddings, funerals and bar mitzvahs. I think that's SO right. At times of great joy and despair – or just the times when you feel alive – that's what it seems to be about.

'We weren't a punk band but we came out of that scene. We went to see The Clash when we were sixteen or seventeen years old and believed we could be a garage band from Garageland . . . just like that line in their song.

'So we stepped out of the audience on to the stage if you like. We were very determined to have the punk ethos that we would not separate ourselves. We tried to keep that distance between us and the audience a short one.

'It's not about the size of the venue, whether you're playing a club or a stadium. In a club you might be right next to the singer but he's a million miles away from you in his head. Just in terms of attitude, he's removed. We've always tried to cut down the distance, whether it was me stage diving at those early gigs or going into the crowd or creating the satellite B-stages.

'So on the 360-degree show we're always trying to break what they call the fourth wall.'

I talked to the band again on the 'Songs of Innocence' tour in 2015 to promote the album of the same name inspired by their childhood and teenage years in Dublin. Bono described it as: 'the most personal album we've written.'

The band played incredible shows at the SSE Hydro in Glasgow on 6 and 7 November. They performed between two stages connected by a 96ft video screen that recreated Cedarwood Road in Dublin where Bono grew up.

The Edge and Adam joined me on my BBC Radio Scotland show. 'Bono and I felt that making an album that centred on Dublin seemed to be a very fertile place to go from a lyrical point of view,' revealed The Edge. 'He felt, and rightly so, that if you talk about what we went through from the ages of fifteen to twenty, not only does that tell you a lot about us as people but also a lot about what formed the band.'

'It's also very colourful. That time – there's so much to write about and explore – turned out to be a very good place to draw ideas from. The album is a very powerful record for that.'

Adam told me: 'In a way it was humbling to realise where we came from, that we thought wasn't worth very much. Yet, we've had amazing success off the back of it. It was much more powerful than we realised at the time.'

U2 also went back to the future two years later when they celebrated the thirtieth anniversary of their classic 1987 album, *The Joshua Tree*.

On 9 July, I was invited to their show at Twickenham Stadium – the home of English rugby – and attended the gig with my son, Paul, now thirty-nine, and a father of two beautiful daughters.

As we relaxed in the hospitality area, U2's publicist grabbed us and said Bono wanted to say a quick hello before going on stage. We were led into the band's private compound where famous friends like Brian Eno, Natalie Imbruglia, Stella McCartney and Jude Law were hanging out. He was in good spirits – and already buzzing – before the gig.

'How's Jimmy Kerr?' he said, inquiring after our mutual friend, father of the Simple Minds' singer. I told Bono he'd recently celebrated his eightieth birthday and we'd had a celebratory fish and chip night with a few friends at Jim's house in Glasgow.

'Shit, I didn't know it was a big birthday. I should've got him a card,' he said.

Bono asked his PA if she could quickly find a piece of blank card, but the best she could come up with was a large white napkin. He grabbed a Sharpie and drew a caricature of himself and birthday cake – with the letter 'J' and a candle on top – and wrote: 'Happy Birthday Jimmy – 80!'

With just thirty minutes to go before show time, Bono must have had a million other things running through his mind, but sending Jimmy Kerr a belated birthday greeting was his number one priority. I got the 'birthday card' framed – with a picture of Bono – and gave it to Jimmy. He was knocked out and it was given pride of place on his living room wall.

I got similar personal treatment when U2 played Manchester Arena on the opening night of the UK leg of their 'eXPERIENCE + iNNOCENCE' tour a year later. Paul and I had planned to drive down from Glasgow to see the show but one of his girls was ill. So he called off at the last minute and a mate came along with me instead.

As U2 took the stage of the 20,000-capacity arena I got a text from Bono's PA asking for my seat number.

'I've got something for you,' said the message.

Twenty minutes later, with the gig in full swing, she arrived and handed me a carrier bag.

Inside, was a handwritten card from Bono apologising for not being around before the show. He had problems with his throat and the band were forced to cancel an earlier date in Berlin. He'd heard about my granddaughter being poorly, so inside the bag were two U2 'eXPERIENCE + iNNOCENCE' tour T-shirts . . . one for each of the girls.

On the front of the card was a self-portrait sketch – complete with top hat and devil horns – and he wrote: 'Billy is in the building!!! I hear your lass a bit ill . . . hope tonight gets your mind off it. Band on form. Could be good. I'm on vocal lock down and can't get out to say hello . . . but Mac Bono says, hello anyway.'

I was bowled over. It was a lovely gesture. And again, on the first night of a major tour I'm willing to bet the singer had other, more important things to be taking care of.

I then received another text saying: 'The Edge would like to invite you back to the Lowry Hotel after the show for a bit of supper.' He was pleased to see us and we spent an hour with the guitarist before jumping in the car and heading back to Scotland in the wee small hours.

I eventually caught up with Bono when he appeared at The Armadillo in Glasgow in November 2022 to launch his autobiography, *Surrender: 40 Songs, One Story*.

The solo show – described as 'an evening of words, music and some mischief' – showed another side of his talents. Bono proved a natural raconteur, delivering spoken word passages and humorous monologues illustrated by some of U2's most famous songs, accompanied by two female musicians playing violin and cello.

He was such an accomplished storyteller the audience quite literally never wanted the show to end. Bono could have talked all night. I'm sure he would have, if given the chance.

I talked to him the following day for my radio show and he was delighted the gig had gone so well. Until now, the singer had told his remarkable story through U2's songs but what was it like to relate it over 557 pages of a book?

He told me: 'It's not a confessional in the sense that some of these memoirs are. You've got to be careful of the cliché a little bit. I think it was John Hurt – the actor – who said: "Got a touch of the memoirs, have we darling?"

'I wanted to explain myself to myself, first off. And then to my family and friends as to what I'd been doing to their lives as well as my own. My family permissioned me to do this . . . whether that was being in a band or being an activist.

'The other thing is that to be around for a few decades and to be in people's face you turn into a bit of a caricature. There's always that danger and I wanted not to be a caricature of myself.

'I wanted to fill in the details and do some shading so people can make up their own minds then on who I actually am. But at least they know through me . . . but not through some other drawing of me.'

The statistics of U2's global success are staggering, and it's not over by a long chalk. They've sold in excess of 170 million albums and written some of the finest songs in music history. The band's recordings have earned twenty-two Grammy awards and they were inducted into the Rock and Roll Hall of Fame.

They've also firmly pinned their colours to the mast for such human rights and social justice causes as Amnesty International, the ONE Campaign and War Child.

U2 were ranked at number twenty-two by *Rolling Stone* magazine on its list of the 100 Greatest Artistes of All Time.

They've achieved all of that led by a singer – who apart from being a little more famous – is still the same down-to-earth guy I first interviewed in a vacant gent's toilet in Strathclyde University in 1981.

Yes, he can be a polarising figure. And he knows that. That's the price you sometimes pay for raw passion. But more than forty-two years on, Bono's heart is STILL in the right place. I won't hear a word said against him.

Chapter 30
Tales of the Unexpected

PAOLO NUTINI AND I are looking straight ahead. He's standing at the first urinal . . . and I'm positioned at a porcelain bowl further along the wall. I break the silence when I say: 'Paolo, people will never believe this. We're having a piss in The White House!'

If this often-crazy job has taught me anything, it's that you never know what's going to happen next. Always expect the unexpected.

I'd gone to Washington D.C. to write an on-the-road feature on Paolo for the cover of the *Sunday Mail* magazine. He was playing a sell-out show at the 9:30 Club, a 1,200-capacity venue reminiscent of our own Barrowland Ballroom. It was a key date on his first headline tour in the States and he was attracting encouraging interest from the US media.

On the afternoon of the gig, I'd interviewed the singer on his tour bus focusing on his love of the music and pop culture of America. The chat had gone well, but in terms of content it wasn't earth shattering. Paolo had seemed a little distracted. I needed a strong line to lead the article. A few minutes later, one landed in my lap. Paolo took me aside and said: 'Do you fancy going down to check out The White House?'

While we'd been talking, the tour manager received a phone call from a girl who claimed to be one of his biggest fans. It was the usual blag. 'I love the album. I didn't realise the show was tonight. I tried to buy a ticket but they've all gone. Can you get me in?'

She was just about to get a polite refusal when she said the magic words: 'I'm a member of President Obama's staff at The White House.' That changed the complexion of the conversation rather sharply. Her name would be added to the guest list. Could she return the favour? 'I don't think that will be a problem,' she said.

There was no time to waste . . . we made our way to 1600 Pennsylvania Avenue NW, Washington D.C. 20500. The paper had hired a photographer from a local news agency to do our cover shoot. He had vast experience of working in The White House and as a member of the official press corps was given security clearance to enter the building.

On the drive downtown, he regaled us with stories about snapping every US President from Jimmy Carter to Barack Obama. We arrived at the South Gate of The White House full of nervous expectation. But the photographer issued a warning, saying: 'This is THE most fortified building in America. There is a ring of steel around the whole area. You can't just turn up and walk in. I'll wait inside for twenty minutes and if you don't show up I'll know entry has been refused.'

At the gate, we surrendered our passports and passed through airport-style security scanners. I could see the armed guard making a series of phone calls and scrolling through information on his computer. The female staffer appeared and they checked all the relevant information. The guard thanked us for our patience and a few minutes later we were walking in the grounds of The White House.

After Paolo and I made a quick pit-stop in the rest room, she gave us a private fifty-minute guided tour of the building. Unfortunately, President Obama was not at home. He was out of town on official business. But we visited the Oval Office in the East Wing, used by his wife, Michelle, the First Lady. When I looked out of the window the area looked familiar . . . it was the lawn where *Marine One*, the Presidential helicopter, touched down.

As you'd expect, the Presidential Library was stacked floor to ceiling with historical books. There were weighty bound volumes on subjects like the civil war and the history of the Native American Indian, alongside biographies of figures such as William Frederick Cody, known as Buffalo Bill, and Martin Luther King, Jr.

But one book caught my eye, Bob Dylan's *Lyrics 1962–2001*. I could imagine Bill Clinton – a real rock music lover – poring over that of a quiet evening.

On the walls of every corridor, there were informal photographs of presidents through the years. I loved the shot of George W. Bush surrounded by a class of schoolchildren all waving and high-fiving to the camera. Another brilliant snap showed Barack and Michelle Obama, embracing in a service elevator, with his team of aides and Secret Service agents averting their gaze so as not to intrude on their private moment.

But the most moving picture was the official Presidential portrait of John F. Kennedy, painted posthumously by artist, Aaron Shikler, seven years after his assassination. The striking character study showed Kennedy looking pensive, with eyes downcast, and his arms folded.

Next, she led us to another instantly recognisable location . . . the famous double doors with twin flags and the official Presidential crest overhead. Now, every time I see Joe Biden walking down the red carpet to meet world leaders, I think of Paolo and I standing proudly on that exact spot . . . saluting for the camera.

From first to last, it was an amazing experience. We were even given a goody bag as a keepsake, full of items such as a ceramic Easter egg 'autographed' by the Obamas and a pad of official White House headed notepaper.

Later, I called the picture editor back in Glasgow to give him an update. He asked if we had good shots of Paolo posing outside the frontage of the building. We'd taken a few but they hadn't quite worked out. When I told him he went potty. But I said: 'Hang on, I've not got any decent shots of Paolo outside The White House . . . but I've got dozens of great snaps of Paolo INSIDE The White House.'

There was silence on the line. I thought we'd been cut off. Then he said: 'How the fuck did you get into The White House?'

'It's a long story,' I told him. 'You won't believe it.'

When an interview takes a sudden U-turn you don't know what is going to happen next or how the job is going to turn out. You've just got to go with the flow.

I've spent a lot of time talking to Tom Jones over the years. He's now eighty-two years old and his work rate is phenomenal. Tom joined me on my radio show to play tracks from his 2021 album, *Surrounded by Time*.

During our chat, he looked back with real nostalgia to his Las Vegas years in the late 1960s when he became one of the first artistes to play a residency at Caesars Palace on the famous Strip, paving the way for acts like Elton John, Celine Dion, Rod Stewart and Adele.

But his punishing schedule took its toll, even when he was a young man. Especially when his close friend, Elvis Presley, was in town, playing a residency of his own at the Las Vegas Hilton.

'Elvis was a very musical person. He loved music as much as I do. And every chance he would get to sing, he would,' revealed Tom. 'So when I used to hang out with him in Las Vegas he would be singing all night. We used to do a month straight, two shows a night.

'Sometimes we'd overlap. He'd finish his shows before I would finish mine. He would come over to see me a lot. My son Mark would say: 'Oh my God, Elvis is coming again tonight.' He knew it would be an all-night session.

'We would go back to the Hilton and hang out in his suite. To the point I would say: "Elvis, I've still got two shows to do, tonight." He would say: "Yeah, I got it Tom."

'And I'd say: "Well, do you mind if I leave now?"

'I thought, my God, if somebody had told me when I was in Wales that I would be asking Elvis Presley could I leave, I wouldn't have believed them.'

Then midway through our chat, Tom claimed he was going to share a secret about Elvis, he'd never told a single person until now. I had no idea what was coming next. Seconds later, he revealed that the King of Rock and Roll had a plan to form THE greatest supergroup in music history.

'I'll tell you a story that I don't think I've said before. Which is, and this is the truth, in 1970 Elvis said to me: "I hear The Beatles have broken up,"' recalled Tom.

'I said: "Well, yeah. I think Lennon and McCartney are still writing together but they're not going to do live shows any more."

'Elvis said, and this is a fact: "What a shame, because wouldn't it be great if we could use The Beatles as a backing band? We could go on stage and you could sing some of your songs and I could sing some of my songs . . . and we could have The Beatles to play."

'On my life. That's exactly what he said.

'And I told him: "Well it sounds like a great idea but it's not going to happen." But that was an idea he had and he would've loved to have done it.'

Maybe it was just as well Elvis didn't pull it off. You'd have needed a lottery win to buy a ticket.

I've also always enjoyed crossing paths with Roger Davies, the Australian manager who is credited as the man who revitalised the music career of Tina Turner and steered her to superstardom. Alongside Tina on his A-list artiste roster were Olivia Newton-John, Janet Jackson, Sade, Joe Cocker, Pink and Cher.

We first met when I went to Paris in 1987 to interview Tina who was appearing at the Bercy arena. Her show was sensational and it was a thrill to sit backstage with the voice of classic hits like 'River Deep – Mountain High', 'Nutbush City Limits' and 'Proud Mary'. At the end of our chat Tina took me by surprise when she said: 'Would you like to go to a party?'

Roger revealed that EMI Records in France were throwing a lavish after-show bash to celebrate the success of *Private Dancer* and *Break Every Rule*, the albums that had turned her career around. And the venue was a bit special . . . the restaurant on the first level of the Eiffel Tower.

'Billy, you're coming with us,' he said.

A few moments later, I was sitting in the back of a limousine with Tina and Roger, speeding through the streets of the French capital at midnight. We arrived at the Eiffel Tower to be met by a posse of paparazzi waiting to photograph her. When Tina and I stepped out of the car we were hit by a barrage of camera flashes.

The photographers knew Roger, but they didn't have a clue who I was. So they quickly put deux + deux together and got cinq. They presumed I was Tina's new boyfriend. It was hilarious. They began asking my name and how long we'd been dating. I told Tina I was more than happy to be her 'toy boy' for the night. She laughed her head off.

We stepped out again three years later, this time much closer to home.

One of my best friends is Bernard Doherty, a top UK music publicist who represents Tina and The Rolling Stones. He is a highly respected figure in the music industry.

His partner, Anne Docherty, a fashion designer from Glasgow, made some of Tina's early stage costumes including her trademark red leather dress. When Bernard and Anne got married in 1989, Tina and Roger were guests at the wedding. They joined us for the ceremony at Eastwood Registry Office on the south side of the city.

The reception was held in the nearby MacDonald Hotel. The staff did a double take when we walked in with Tina Turner in tow. Both Tina and Roger had never experienced a typical Scots wedding. When she was called on to 'give us a song' – as is the tradition – she jumped to her feet and performed great versions of 'Help' by The Beatles and 'The Way We Were' by Barbra Streisand. It was quite a night.

On 15 April 1998, Roger invited me to interview Janet Jackson at The Ahoy Arena in Rotterdam, Holland. The US superstar planned to kick-start her massive 125-date 'Velvet Rope' world tour – which included a show at the SECC in Glasgow – with a concert at the venue the following day. But no sooner had I arrived, than he faced a major problem.

Janet had spent three hours getting her hair and make-up done by a stylist she'd never previously worked with. But she hated the end result and wanted to cancel all TV interviews. Roger took me aside and told me the situation.

It was a disaster. We'd flown in from all over Europe and it now looked like we'd go home empty handed. All was not lost, however. I suggested that he take all the TV crews to catering and let them have dinner. 'By the time they've had something nice to eat – then come back and rechecked their camera equipment – that will kill a couple of hours,' I said. 'During that time, Janet can get her hair and make-up done again, to her satisfaction.'

Roger swung into action. We enjoyed a leisurely meal backstage and the problem was solved.

When Janet finally appeared, she looked a million dollars. The superstar singer then went down the 'rabbit run' of TV presenters – talking to every one – and made sure we all got the footage we needed. It was great to talk to her.

The next time I heard from Roger was in 2004. He contacted me out of the blue on behalf of another of his artistes, Cher. This time, it was for a much more serious matter.

He left me a message on my office number that said: 'Billy, call me right away. I need your help with something.'

Cher was in Glasgow to play a show at the SECC and saw something on TV that made her blood boil. She watched a report on the lunchtime news saying that the Glasgow Homeopathic Hospital – located at Gartnavel in the West End of the city – was in trouble. The news item revealed that the government were slashing the health budget by £58 million and the shock announcement meant the unit would have to close. The singer was furious.

When I called Roger he was with Cher at her hotel. She came on the line and said: 'We can't let this happen . . . we've got to do something.'

Then, without hesitation, she told me she wanted to donate 25,000 euros – then around £13,000 – to help staff and encourage others campaigning to keep the hospital open. It was an incredible gesture. Roger promised me a full interview with Cher once he'd calmed her down. She was seething.

Later that night, I met the singer in her dressing room just minutes before she went on stage. She wore an incredible figure-hugging costume and looked stunning.

'We need a picture of you two together,' said Roger, so my photographer took a snap. He knew it would fly straight into the paper.

Cher was heading back to London after the gig, so Roger promised me he'd hook us up the following day so I could get the full story. She had calmed down considerably by that time and put forward a very measured argument. And as it turned out, she was speaking from experience.

Cher revealed that in 1987 she had been struck by a debilitating viral illness that caused chronic fatigue and bouts of pneumonia.

I was completely taken aback that she was prepared to share such personal information with me. 'I could barely get out of bed in the morning . . . I was so weak,' she told me.

'I didn't know what was wrong with me. I'd never felt like this before. I went to doctor after doctor and they all said there was nothing wrong with me. I tried regular medicine and it just didn't work. They said any illness was all in my head. People thought I was crazy.'

The condition got so severe she was disabled from working for two years. The singer was at her wits' end. Cher told me that she decided to try something different. 'I turned to a Sikh homeopathic doctor, almost in desperation,' she said. 'He started doing homeopathic stuff with herbs and vitamin therapy. Many doctors didn't believe in all that back then. Within four months, he'd got me up and back on the road again.'

So the singer was adamant that the Glasgow unit – which treated 500 patients per year – HAD to be saved.

'We should be opening more hospitals not closing them,' she said firmly. 'I'm prepared to do anything I can to help.' Her efforts paid off and after a high-profile campaign, the homeopathic unit was saved a few months later.

One of the most unexpected stories of my career was when I tracked down the 'secret wife' of my old mate, Billy Mackenzie of The Associates. Looking back now, I don't even remember how I landed the exclusive interview. It seemed to come out of nowhere.

I succeeded in persuading Chloe Dummar to break her thirty-year-long silence to talk about her bizarre marriage to the Scots music icon. She wed Billy in Las Vegas in 1976 but after just three months of marriage he walked out on her and she never spoke to him again.

In 2007, ten years after he died tragically – aged just thirty-nine – I was stunned when Chloe opened her heart about the man she called 'the one big love of my life'. When I called her home in Lava Hot Springs, Idaho, USA, she got very emotional and said:

'If Billy was alive today I'd tell him that I still loved him. I can't explain why I still feel like that after more than thirty years . . . you can't tell your heart what to do.

'I never stopped loving him. I didn't fall in love again and never remarried. The man I loved vanished off the face of the earth.

'It was pretty devastating. It took a long time to get over Billy. To be honest, I don't know if I ever did. He was special.'

Billy's life and music career were surrounded by some colourful myths. It was claimed his relationship with Chloe was simply a marriage of convenience to extend his visa so he could continue living in the US. One report quoted him as saying: 'I wanted to sing with the New Orleans Gospel Choir so I married my Aunt Veronica's sister-in-law. She was a Dolly Parton clone. It was purely a business deal.'

Another was that, through marriage, the Dundee-born singer was now connected to Howard Hughes. Chloe was a cousin of Melvin E. Dummar, a Utah man who rescued the eccentric billionaire recluse after he'd had a motorcycle accident in the Nevada desert in 1967.

The real-life story – recreated in Jonathan Demme's 1980 movie, *Melvin and Howard* – claimed that in a handwritten last will and testament he'd been named as a one-sixteenth beneficiary of the Hughes' estate with a share worth an estimated $156 million. But a judge dismissed the case in a US court in 1978.

The longer my chat with Chloe went on the more adamant she was that she and Billy had enjoyed a proper – if whirlwind – romance. They married in a $30 ceremony at the Wee Kirk o' the Heather – the oldest wedding chapel on the Las Vegas Strip – which opened in 1940.

'At seventeen, Billy was a real sweetheart. He was gorgeous,' Chloe recalled. 'He proposed in Vegas. I had no idea he was going to ask me to marry him. So we just got married right there and then. I wore a white, Western-style outfit and Billy wore a smart jacket. He paid the $30.'

But after just three months, Billy returned to his native Dundee. Chloe never saw him again.

'The story Billy got married just to stay in the US is not true. We had a romance and officially were married for four years,' she insisted. 'We did all the things other married couples do. We'd go shopping or sightseeing. We had a very normal life together. But he really wanted to make it as a singer and felt he couldn't do that in America. It was a little bit strange when my new husband disappeared but I didn't worry about it because I thought he'd come home again.

'Billy just left. He didn't keep in touch by letter or telephone.'

Chloe decided not to follow her husband to try to bring him back.

'I couldn't afford to leave home, jump on a plane to Scotland and start looking for him,' she said, ruefully.

'I didn't know how to contact Billy. I tried to reach him through Veronica but I guess he was too busy. I never spoke to him again. It was a strange situation.'

The marriage was officially dissolved in 1980.

Sadly, Billy took his own life on 22 January 1997, at his family home in Auchterhouse, near Dundee, while suffering from depression after the death of his mother Lily from cancer the previous year.

I met the singer backstage at T in the Park on 13 July 1996 and he was on top of the world. He looked so healthy, he positively glowed. When we talked, he revealed a plethora of exciting new music projects he had planned for the coming months. But our chat was cut short when Billy received an urgent message to call his father.

His mother's health was deteriorating and he immediately left the site to drive home. But when he arrived at the house she had already passed away. Billy never recovered from the trauma.

Three years after Billy's death, his father James agreed to speak to me about the tragic loss of his son. His story was heartbreaking. James recalled how, one day, he returned to the house and couldn't find Billy. He later discovered him lying dead on the floor of the garden shed. The singer had taken an overdose of prescription drugs and left a suicide note that simply said: 'Sorry'.

'I put my hand into the shed and felt something cold. It was Billy's hand. I knew immediately he was dead,' recalled James, just yards from the spot from where the tragedy occurred. 'He'd been very depressed. He couldn't think straight, write songs and he didn't want to face anybody. He was very, very confused. Things just seemed to get on top of him.'

I attended Billy's funeral and friends from the Scottish music industry turned up in numbers to pay their respects to one of our most innovative and inspiring talents.

Chloe was devastated when she heard about his death. She claims it is too painful to listen to him sing, so she doesn't own any of his records and refuses to watch video footage of her former husband performing.

'Billy had an incredible voice. He used to sing to me at home. His favourite song was "Summertime" by George Gershwin,' she told me. 'I only realised he'd become a pop star through Veronica. I was happy for him that he got what he wanted – but very sad that I didn't.'

I'll close this chapter on a lighter note detailing my encounters with two of the biggest names in American music history that didn't quite go to plan.

I once camped out in the foyer of The Holiday Inn in Glasgow, hoping to get a few words with the legendary Bob Dylan for the *Daily Record*. The superstar was appearing at the SECC, his first concert in the city for many years.

But I had company. There were reporters and photographers from several other papers also staking him out. Dylan never speaks to the media. He doesn't need to. Or more importantly, he doesn't want to.

I wasn't optimistic that we'd get anything for the next day's edition. Then I got a break. The concierge tipped me the wink that Dylan was planning to evade the media in the most unusual fashion. I thought he was at the wind-up when he discreetly told me: 'Dylan is leaving by a service entrance around the back of the hotel . . . he's going to CYCLE down to the SECC.'

It had to be a joke, surely. But no, his information was one hundred per cent accurate. Dylan was heading to the venue on pedal power alone.

My photographer and I slipped out of the foyer unnoticed and positioned ourselves behind a wall at the rear loading bay. We didn't have to wait long. A door opened, and a hunched figure wheeled a mountain bike out on to the pathway. It was Bob Dylan. At least, I think it was. The guy was dressed in a cagoule, with the hood pulled tightly around his face. His nose, mouth and chin were covered in a ski-mask and he wore large black wrap-around shades. The only bit of him that was visible was a tiny strip of his forehead. It could have been anyone.

My snapper fired off a few frames. But we were spotted by two minders, who tried to obstruct our view. They grabbed Dylan and virtually threw him into a minibus.

Had we known of Dylan's plan in advance we could have positioned ourselves along the route and snatched a picture with ease. In fact, he'd have ridden past the front door of the *Daily Record* office. What an exclusive snap that would have been.

I discovered the minders had driven the minibus not to the venue, but to Carlton Place – an area alongside the River Clyde – across the suspension bridge in the city centre. Dylan happily rode his bike up and down for the next thirty minutes and nobody realised it was him.

Later that day, Dylan announced his arrival at the SECC in the most bizarre fashion. A mate, who worked for the concert promoter, was sitting in the production office when he received a message from one of his security staff.

The voice on his radio said: 'I'm at the back gate and a guy has just turned up on a bike . . . he says he's Bob Dylan.'

My mate responded: 'Well, does he have a laminate pass for the gig?'

But he didn't have anything. No ID. Nothing, that backed up his claim.

'Well, does he look like Bob Dylan?' he asked.

The security guard replied: 'It's hard to tell.'

He walked down to the back gate to be confronted by a guy in a hoodie, ski-mask and shades, who looked like he'd just robbed a bank. It was only when the mystery cyclist pulled his mask down a little that he convinced them he really was the man who'd written songs such as 'Subterranean Homesick Blues' and 'Like a Rolling Stone'.

I fared a little better with Tony Bennett, another of the greatest American artistes of all time. I'd spent months setting up an interview for Scottish Television and when the big day came to meet the maestro all my best-laid plans went out of the window . . . leaving me gripped by a combination of excitement and fear.

The opportunity to talk to Mr Bennett for the first time was a mouth-watering prospect.

He was flying into Glasgow after a concert appearance in Rome and his journey had gone very badly wrong. His plane had been delayed for four hours and, to rub salt into the wound, the airline lost his luggage. He eventually arrived in the city to be informed that his suitcases were revolving on a baggage carousel, who knew where. Sitting down to talk to me after such a trying day would surely be the last thing he wanted to do.

I was back at The Holiday Inn. I'd got there early – with my cameraman – so we could get set up for the interview. The hotel manager very kindly gave us the use of a vacant room so we could conduct our chat without any distractions. But we had some work to do. The place was tiny, so we tried to rearrange the furniture to make it look a little more pleasing to the eye.

We drew the curtains and cleared a small area between the bed and the window, placing two chairs facing each other . . . one for me, the other for Mr Bennett. By the time we'd set up our camera gear and lights, you couldn't swing a cat in the place. It was far from perfect, but in such a confined space it was our only option. Then, we waited. And waited.

I was nervous. I defy anyone not to get the jitters while anticipating the arrival of a star of such stature. There was also the real fear that he'd be in such a foul mood after his travel ordeal, that when he set eyes on the chaotic clutter of our 'studio set' it might just tip him over the edge.

I could not have been more wrong.

There was a knock on the door and when I answered, there stood the one and only Tony Bennett. No aides or minders. He was on his own.

'You must be Billy,' he said, as he shook my hand. He was the epitome of cool, dressed in a casual Italian-style jacket, open-neck shirt and silk cravat.

We squeezed into the room and I shut the door. He looked at the chair in the corner – wedged in between the window and the bed – and said: 'I guess you want me over there?'

I nodded in embarrassment. Then, without hesitation, the super-star hailed by Frank Sinatra as 'the best singer in the business' climbed over the bed to get to his seat.

'Right, I'm good to go,' he said. 'What would you like to know? Shoot.'

What happened over the next twenty minutes was one of THE most enjoyable interviews of my career.

Tony Bennett was a class act. One of the true greats.

Chapter 31
And in The End

IF YOU'VE GOT THIS far, I commend you. I hope you've found my rather offbeat adventures entertaining and maybe even a little illuminating.

To revisit some of my favourite moments as a music journalist has been a rewarding, if jarring, experience. Your memory can often play tricks, particularly when it comes to recalling names, dates, times and places accurately. I've strived to be as careful as I can to match them up correctly and in the right sequence.

There have been so many instances where I've had to pinch myself to ensure I wasn't imagining some situations. Was I really locked in conversation with that famous musician? Or did I actually walk in the footsteps of an artiste who made rock history? The answer is in the affirmative. So it's a wonder I'm not permanently black and blue.

One such occasion, which leapt to the forefront of my memory as I put the finishing touches to this book, occurred in 2006. My thoughts rewound to an afternoon I spent sitting in Studio 2 at Abbey Road in London listening to an exclusive first playback of *Love* by The Beatles. The album featured the group's songs compiled and remixed as a contemporary 'mash-up' by their legendary producer George Martin with his son, Giles.

It was the soundtrack for a project of the same name by the Canadian circus troupe, Cirque du Soleil, who reimagined their music in a spectacular show that has since broken box-office records at The Mirage hotel in Las Vegas.

To hear The Beatles' songs played in the same room where they were conceived was a thrill that almost defies description. I interviewed George Martin sitting on the exact spot where he had recorded their debut album, *Please Please Me* for Parlophone Records in 1963.

Who could have predicted what would happen next?

As I glanced over his shoulder, I could see the staircase leading up to the control room where he looked down on 'the boys' as they made their magic over twelve fabulous LP records. The studio is exactly as it was when they put 'Love Me Do' down on tape for the very first time.

When we finished our chat, I couldn't resist it. I climbed the stairs and looked down through the glass as George stood on the floor of Studio 2 – just as he had done on so many occasions, as the creative brilliance of John Lennon, Paul McCartney, George Harrison and Ringo Starr was realised. It was THE ultimate goosebumps moment.

I've enjoyed similar experiences visiting locations such as Sun Studios in Memphis – where Elvis recorded 'That's All Right' in 1954 – and Hitsville U.S.A. in Detroit – where Barrett Strong laid down 'Money (That's What I Want)', the first hit on Motown Records, five years later.

My chosen profession has given me the ultimate Access All Areas backstage pass. Such good fortune is something I've never taken for granted. I'm very appreciative, even if I still can't quite believe my luck.

So, let's go out where we came in.

At the start of this book, I boldly claimed I was once the lead singer of Coldplay for a twenty-four-hour period. If nothing else, it's not a bad line to casually drop into a conversation down the local pub.

On 24 April 2001, singer Chris Martin, guitarist Jonny Buckland, bass player Guy Berryman and drummer Will Champion were on the cusp of greatness. The band had scored their first two hit singles – 'Yellow' and 'Trouble' – with both songs taken from their Grammy-award-winning debut album, *Parachutes*. The sky really was the limit.

I travelled to Edinburgh on that day to interview Guy – a proud Scot who was born in Kirkcaldy in Fife – for the *Daily Record*. We met in the lounge of a hotel in Edinburgh before their show at The Corn Exchange across the city for 2,000 fans. Within the next eighteen months, Coldplay would graduate to performing in massive arenas and sports stadiums all over the world.

At the end of the interview, I got the four band members together for a photograph to accompany the feature. I asked if they'd be willing to step outside the hotel so we could shoot them with the historic Royal Mile as a backdrop. At the end of the session, I asked – as a fan – if I could have a quick picture taken with the band. They were more than happy to oblige. It was another great snap for my collection.

But just four weeks later, that photo would resurface in the most unlikely of circumstances. A story broke in the UK press that a number of artistes had been signed up by Michael Eavis, the organiser of the Glastonbury Festival, for a special charity event. He planned to stage the inaugural UK Farm Aid benefit concert – set for 27 October at the 50,000-capacity Millennium Stadium in Cardiff – to help farmers whose livelihoods had been affected by an outbreak of 'mad cow' and foot-and-mouth disease.

Coldplay were one of the first acts to pledge their support when they agreed to play at the event. The bill also included Ash, Toploader and Reef, with a promise of many more names to be added. It was big news. The *Independent* thought so, and splashed the story prominently across a full page with a huge photo of Coldplay . . . standing on the Royal Mile. But the band appeared to have FIVE members, Chris, Johnny, Guy and Will, plus yours truly.

It appeared that some well-meaning sub-editor on the paper had gone into the picture database – shared by several publications including the *Daily Record* – and selected the most up-to-date shot of Coldplay that was available. It showed me standing up front like the lead singer, with Chris at the back, almost as if he'd photobombed his way into the shot.

No sooner had the *Independent* hit the streets when Coldplay's publicist, Murray Chalmers, received a panic phone call from the band's management.

'They said: "Who on earth is this guy, Murray? We've never seen him before,"' he recalled. 'They were completely bewildered, and didn't have a clue who he was. When I told them the real identity of the new 'band member' they had a good laugh about it.'

But it's no laughing matter. It's there in black and white in the pages of the *Independent*. So it must be true.

Don't split hairs. Indulge me for a brief moment. I WAS the lead singer of Coldplay for a twenty-four-hour period. It was yet another 'what if' yearning where I wondered how better life would be, centre stage, bathed in a white spotlight.

I guess I'll never know.

Thanks to . . .

MY LOVING FAMILY – for their support and encouragement.

Kevin Pocklington – for all his efforts on my behalf and for having total faith in this project.

Jim Kerr, Charlie Burchill and Jimmy Kerr – for some unforgettable on-the-road adventures.

Tim Barr and Ronnie Gurr – for their valuable friendship and support.

And . . .

Janice Hamilton.

Isla Cruickshanks, Billy McKendrick and Alan Philip at Radio Clyde.

Mark Mackie and all at Regular Music.

Francesca Piilberg and Greg McCarron at Scottish Television.

Debbie McWilliams and Julie Carson at the SEC Scottish Event Campus.

Nick Low at Demus Productions.

Jools Gizzi and Paul McManus of GUN.

Clare Grogan.

Many thanks to: *The Daily Record*, *The Sunday Mail*, U2/RTE Television, Mark Mackie at Regular Music, Dougie Souness at No Half Measures Management, the SECC, George Mahoney Photography and *The Independent* for kind permission to reproduce their images in the picture sections of this book.

I also dedicate this book to . . .

My mother Peggy, father Bill and brother Alan – I hope they were proud of me.

My wee pal, Maisie Hamilton – who spurred me on.

Gary Lovatt – a lovely man I was proud to call my friend.

Green's Playhouse and the Glasgow Apollo – where my incredible journey began.

BILLY SLOAN is a journalist and broadcaster who has written about music for forty-five years . . . and counting. Much of that period was spent working for Scotland's two biggest newspapers, the *Daily Record* and the *Sunday Mail*. He has also contributed to publications such as the *Glasgow Herald*, the *Sunday Post*, the *Daily Express*, the *Sunday Times* and *Record Mirror*.

As a music biographer, he has worked on successful album projects with **Simple Minds, Cliff Richard, Wet Wet Wet, Hue and Cry** and **The Associates**.

His broadcasting career began in 1979 when he presented a groundbreaking alternative music show on Radio Clyde that championed new bands from Scotland and beyond – giving many their all-important first plays on air.

He was the music correspondent and a producer for Scottish Television, working on programmes like *Scotland Today* and *T in the Park*.

Billy was awarded a Tartan Clef by the charity Nordoff Robbins (Scotland) in recognition of his contribution to music. He is also the first member of the media to be inducted into the Glasgow Barrowland Hall of Fame.

Billy currently hosts a weekend music and chat show on BBC Radio Scotland. His favourite single is 'State of Independence' by Donna Summer. And his favourite album is *Station to Station* by David Bowie.